RICHARD CLEROUX

# Official Secrets

The Inside Story Of
The Canadian Security
Intelligence Service

**M&S**

An M&S Paperback from
McClelland & Stewart Inc.
*The Canadian Publishers*

An M&S Paperback from McClelland & Stewart Inc.

First printing June 1991

Cloth edition published by McGraw-Hill Ryerson Limited 1990

**Canadian Cataloguing in Publication Data**

Cleroux, Richard
Official secrets: the story behind the
Canadian Security Intelligence Service

"An M&S paperback."

Includes bibliographical references.
ISBN 0-7710-2160-7

1. Canadian Security Intelligence Service.
2. Internal security - Canada - History.
3. Intelligence service - Canada - History - 20th
century. I. Title.

HV8157.C54 1991    327.12'06'071    C91-093503-3

Cover design by K.T. Njo
Cover photograph by Hal Roth

Printed and bound in Canada

McClelland & Stewart Inc.
*The Canadian Publishers*
481 University Avenue
Toronto, Ontario
M5G 2E9

# Contents

*To the men and women*
*of CSIS*

# ACKNOWLEDGEMENTS

A book of this size, especially a first one, is the result of a great deal of hard work by a number of people, and inspiration and encouragement from many others, including friends, acquaintances and even at times total strangers, on whom I have had to rely for kindness and interviews.

The problem is trying to remember the name of every person who helped, who encouraged, and who inspired along the way. Authors are more likely to remember the subjects and the substance of interviews than they are to recall who suggested the interview in the first place. Yet without the suggestions there would not have been the other.

Much of the material in these pages has been obtained from men and women who work or who used to work — for the Canadian Security and Intelligence Service, the Royal Canadian Mounted Police or the federal public service. I am deeply grateful to all of them, but alas, because of the nature of the work they do or did, I cannot name them here. They know who they are and they should know I am thankful. Without them this book would not be possible.

I am grateful to CSIS Director Reid Morden and to his able director of communications, Gerry Cummings, for answers to some questions. I owe even more thanks to former CSIS Director Ted Finn and his deputy director Archie Barr, who both agreed to talk about certain things, the memories of which are still painful. To the many people who gave me material anonymously and who will not find it in the book, I must apologize. Unless I could verify what I was told through an independent source, I could not use it, even though I knew in my heart that it was accurate.

The idea for this book came from Helen Heller, my literary agent, who is undoubtedly the best agent any author in this country could have — and the only "agent" in this book whom anyone should trust. At every step, she has shown patience, understanding, enthusiasm and concern.

My everlasting thanks must also go to my editor, David Kilgour, a consummate craftsman who showed patience and tolerance and, by the end of the book, came to know my mind better than I did.

I am deeply indebted to my research co-ordinator, Kathleen Leccese, who kept an unceasing flow of well-organized material heading my way, as well as providing devoted support when it was most needed. There are some people whose contribution was especially important to me: Anthony Westell, director of the School of Journalism at Carleton University, who generously offered the school's extensive facilities at a time when I most needed them. Erik Spicer, the Parliamentary Librarian in Ottawa, was helpful and generous right from the start and facilitated much of the research for this project.

I am also thankful to my former colleagues at the *Globe and Mail* who were supportive, particularly Graham Fraser, the Ottawa bureau chief, and Mau Harrison, the office manager, and, in Toronto, Christopher Waddell, all of whom helped and encouraged me.

I am especially grateful to my spouse and constant support, Arlene Wortsman, who so graciously put up with a great deal of turmoil on the home front, to say nothing of my frequent and long absences, and did more than my share of the work in our home during this time. And thanks to Joel, my three-year-old son, who thinks I am writing this book for him and wants to see the pictures and have it read to him at night. And to our nanny, Stephanie McColm, thank you, for the extra burden you carried.

Thanks too to Denise Schon, and to the kind and patient people at McGraw-Hill Ryerson.

There are some people to whom I owe a particular debt: Joan Bryden, Jim Brown, Dan Donovan, Marlys Edwardh, Rick Gibbons, Stuart Farson, Andrew Kavchak, Normand Lester, Victor Malarek, Richard McNeely, John Sawatsky and Lorne Waldman.

Last, in strictly alphabetical order, some of the people who agreed to talk to me, or helped in other ways: Warren Allmand, Susan Angus, Maurice Archdeacon, George Baker, Stephen Beatty, Bruce McDougall, Monique Bertrand, Stephen Bindman, Richard Boraks, John Brewin, Pierre-H. Cadieux, Stevie Cameron, Robert Corbett, Howard Crosby, Marshall Crowe, Gordon Cullingham, Annie Demirjian, Richard Doyon, Mike Duffy, Paule Gauthier, Brian Gorlick, André Henrie, Gary Ho, Sandy Hunter, Terry Jabour, Barbara Jackman, Ernie Jacubo, William Johnson, Blair Johnston, Robert Kaplan, Greg Kealey, Evgeni Kussinikov, Jean Keable, Bhupinder Liddar, Jim Littleton, Igor Lobanov, Gaetan Lussier, Heath Macquarrie, Sergio Marchi, Lawrence Martin, Don McCleery, Vivian Bercovici, Mahmoud Mohammad Issa Mohammad, Rae Murphy, Bogdan Miros, Jean Morin, Ahmed Mousani, Ahmed Murad, Jacek Niedzielski, Gordon Osbaldeston, Ryszard Paszkowski, Zygmunt Paszkowski, Stanislaw Pisarski, Don Reid, Svend Robinson, Philip Rosen, Clayton Ruby, Rashad Saleh, Jeff Sallot, Robert Samson, Marshall Shapiro, Mark Starowicz, John Starnes, Courtney Tower, Carole Vincent, Reg Whitaker, Gilbert Zamonsky. I hope you all enjoy the book!

R. C.

# PREFACE

One of the responses I most frequently encountered while writing this book was, "Why are you writing a book about spies? There aren't any spies in Canada." We tend to be complacent about security and intelligence matters here. We like to think of Canada as a big, bland, beautiful country, where nothing "interesting" ever happens to trouble our landscape. We have other issues that occupy us. Few countries spend as much time as we do talking about their constitution, or which languages they should speak.

Our reticence and self-deprecation do us a great disservice. Although we may not know this, Canada is important strategically and economically and other countries are well aware of it. We are not as isolated from the world as we like to think; nor, perhaps, are our citizens and visitors as safe as they should be. Canadians were shocked by the June 23, 1985 bombing of Air India Flight 182 in which 329 people died. It was a brutal reminder that our country is not immune to terrorism and covert activity.

Any nation's safety depends a great deal on the ability and efficiency of its counter-terrorism and counter-espionage agency. In Canada, this responsibility is held by the Canadian Security Intelligence Service — a little-known agency that is only six years old. It is our FBI and CIA rolled into one, minus the foreign spying responsibility of the CIA.

CSIS has more power to intrude on our lives and activities than any other Canadian government agency has ever had, and yet, so far, the Canadian people have paid it but little attention. During the past six years, CSIS has investigated extensively the activities of Natives, trade unions, peace groups, immigrants, and diplomats and foreign visitors. The agency must concern itself with any possible threat to the security of Canada — and it decides who is a threat and who isn't. Action or inaction by CSIS can save or cost lives, and that makes our relative lack of interest in the agency all the harder to understand.

Perhaps our complacency about spies extends to a complacency about spycatchers, and that's not necessarily a healthy attitude. We should not be asking, "Are there spies in Canada?" but, "What is being done about the spies in Canada?" And, "Who and what are the people who are responsible for doing it?"

This book does not presume to have all the answers to those questions, but I hope it will answer them in some part and offer the reader insights into the workings of a brand-new intelligence agency, from the daily routines of intelligence officers and surveillants to the bureaucratic manoeuvrings of senior officials. For the people who are and have been inside CSIS — and for those of us who are interested bystanders — it's been an interesting, frustrating, occasionally frightening six years. There have been triumphs as well as disasters, and I have attempted to document both fairly.

I must make the point that this is not meant to be an exhaustive study of espionage and terrorism in Canada. I haven't, for instance, spent much time covering those famous cases that have already been dealt with at length by the media. Nor have I tried to write a standard, chronological "history" of CSIS; the agency is too young for that. What I have attempted to do is take a series of snapshots – a collage, if you will – that presents the reader with an understanding of the realities of life in the service.

Some members of CSIS may object strongly to having their operations made public. And they have good reason to fear exposure: an effective security and intelligence service has to function in secret much of the time. And yet, CSIS, like any other government agency, must be accountable to Canadians. Perhaps now, entering a decade of unprecedented global political and social change, it is particularly vital that we keep an eye on the service that keeps an eye on us.

Richard Cleroux
Ottawa
June 1990

# ROUND TRIP

**5:30 P.M. MONDAY, FEBRUARY 22, 1988**
Lester B. Pearson International Airport, Toronto

In the international area on the departures level of Terminal Two, passengers were already waiting to check in for Air Canada's Flight 856 to London, England. Apart from the usual mix of families, students and young people, the line-up reflected the popularity of the overnight flight with business people. It was not a typical Canadian winter day. In fact it had been relatively warm — seven degrees Celsius — three degrees above the average; warm enough for some passengers to wear windbreakers or trench coats instead of the thick jackets and scarves they would normally sport in February. The travellers queued up politely in a typically Canadian way, without having to be asked, and chatted with each other or with friends who had come to see them off. There was still a full two and a half hours before take-off.

One floor below, in a tiny, windowless room in the basement of the poorly designed airport terminal, three nervous Royal Canadian Mounted Police officers gazed thoughtfully at a frightened-looking, slightly overweight, grey-haired man: Mahmoud Mohammad Issa Mohammad, a forty-six-year-old, Palestinian-Canadian businessman from Brantford, Ontario who had once been a terrorist.

Two decades earlier, on December 26, 1968, Mohammad had attacked a New York-bound El Al Boeing 707 jetliner at Athens airport and shot to death one of the passengers. It was a mistake to have let Mohammad into the country at all. But the Canadian Security Intelligence Service had admitted him in a bungled attempt to recruit him as a CSIS informer spying on Canada's Palestinian community. And now the Mounties, with the discreet blessing of the highest levels of government, including the minister of immigration, the federal cabinet and the prime minister's office, were doing their best to extricate Canada from the mess. They were trying to sneak the former Palestinian terrorist out through the nation's busiest airport — without CSIS knowing — past the dreaded Israeli Mossad agents who wanted to get their hands on Mohammad the moment he was out of the country. Timing was essential, secrecy was paramount. Everything was planned down to the minute. A single small mistake and the elaborate plan worked out by the RCMP would collapse and come crashing down, covering them all in ridicule.

Mohammad, his wife Fadia and their three children had been living quietly in a semi-detached bungalow in Brantford, until Mohammad's presence had been discovered by the news media a month earlier. Now the Palestinian was a public embarrassment and he was on his way out. If necessary, the Mounties would send an armed escort with him to London, to make sure he got there safely. Once there, the secrecy would continue. Even British intelligence officials would not be told. Using nothing more than a temporary Canadian government identity document, good for one week, Mohammad, a stateless Palestinian with neither visa nor passport, would be passed through Heathrow airport security and put on a connecting Air Algérie flight to Algiers. There a plane would be waiting to take him to a black African country which was willing to accept him temporarily.

The purpose of this strange, complicated exercise was to save the Canadian government the political embarrassment, the considerable financial expense and the inordinate amount of time required if Mohammad was to be formally deported. He had been admitted to Canada as a *bona fide* landed immigrant and as such could not be removed summarily. He had a right to a full deportation hearing which could take anywhere from two to four years. And the government did not want to risk the political embarrassment of taking him to court and losing the case. Imagine the headlines: "Terrorist Let in by Mistake Can Stay, Says Court" or worse still "Government Lets in Terrorist; Can't Boot Him Out."

CSIS was deliberately excluded from the plan to spirit the unfortunate would-be Canadian out of the country. Simply put, the federal government did not trust the little intelligence agency it had created four years earlier. They thought CSIS had done quite enough for Mohammad already. And they knew that if the agency were brought in on the plan they would have to tip off the American Central Intelligence Agency, or worse Mossad, both of which had made reciprocal intelligence agreements with CSIS. The agency that decides who is a security risk in Canada had itself become a security risk in the eyes of the government.

Canada Immigration negotiated a deal directly with Mohammad's lawyers. If he left voluntarily, his family could stay behind in Canada and apply legally for citizenship in two years' time. Once they had become citizens, he would be allowed to come back to Canada to visit them. The Mounties would look after the logistics of spiriting him out of the country and getting him as far as Britain. External Affairs would provide him with a temporary certificate of identity which would be valid for one week — enough time to get him safely to Algeria. He would be on his own after that. They made one concession: if anything went wrong anywhere along the way to Algeria, he could come back to Brantford no questions asked and submit to a regular immigration hearing.

The Mounties were laughing. The plan seemed foolproof. For them it would be another victory in their continuing turf war against CSIS, the organization that had eaten into their responsibility for all matters of national security, and they were delighted with the challenge posed by Operation Mohammad. But for the government there was no joy. Prime Minister Brian Mulroney's Conservative administration regarded Mohammad as a major embarrassment at a time when it was trying to get Parliament to pass a harsh new immigration law cracking down on bogus refugees trying to get into Canada. The contradiction had been highlighted in a major way when *Globe and Mail* reporter Victor Malarek broke the story of Mohammad's presence in Canada. In a story splashed all over the *Globe*'s front page, he wrote that a former convicted Palestinian terrorist had entered Canada illegally with his family a year earlier and that the government, which had known about it all along, had not done anything. It was the stuff that political scandals are made of, the sort of story that costs cabinet ministers their jobs. Was somebody in the government protecting Mohammad? Was Canada doing a favour for some foreign country by providing a safe haven for a superannuated terrorist? The sooner Mohammad left, the better.

Twenty years earlier on another winter's day as grey and almost as cold as this one, a young and fiercely committed Mohammad had spent anxious moments waiting in the Athens airport transit lounge. He had travelled from Beirut with another terrorist — a twenty-two-year-old student from Tripoli, Maheb H. Sleiman — aboard Air France's morning flight to Paris. The two men concealed Kalashnikovs under their windbreakers and carried a small arsenal of assorted hand grenades, incendiary bombs and other terrorist goodies in their hand luggage. Airport security was not what it is today. When the flight landed in Athens at 10:34 a.m. they got off and headed straight for Air France's in-transit lounge. Their absence on board was noticed and they were paged before their aircraft took off again. They ignored the calls and their plane took off for Paris without them at 11:22 a.m. Twenty-eight minutes later they sneaked out to the tarmac and attacked an El Al jetliner as it was preparing to take off.

They rushed at the plane and opened fire with their automatic weapons, shouting at the passengers to get off the aircraft. The forty-three passengers and crew of ten fled immediately. Some went down emergency chutes as best they could. Mohammad destroyed the left front engine by tossing an incendiary grenade into it. Both terrorists stood there on the tarmac in full view of everybody shooting away and scattering handbills in the air. The leaflets, written in English for the benefit of the foreign press, identified them as members of George Habash's Syrian-based Popular Front for the Liberation of Palestine. From its base in Beirut, the PFLP immediately claimed credit, announcing in a press release also written in English that Mohammad and his pal had been sent on a mission to Athens "to damage Israeli aircraft and kill Jews." The PFLP also issued a helpful photograph of Mohammad and Sleiman for the benefit of the media. Meanwhile, back at Athens airport, Mohammad was brought down with a well-placed club to the back of the head by a Greek policeman who had rushed up to him as he stood near the empty aircraft, still bravely shooting away and heaving his leaflets into the air. His accomplice, Sleiman, was caught trying to escape. When Greek police boarded the plane, they discovered that a passenger, Leon Shirdan, a maritime engineer and former Israeli naval officer, had been killed in the first hail of bullets that ripped through the fuselage.

The Athens airport attack was big news. Mohammad's photo was flashed around the world and ran the next day on the front pages of the world's newspapers. He became instantly famous. His photo and the news account of his terrorist act went into the files of every intelligence agency in the world with a pair of scissors and a subscription to the *New York Times*.

Mohammad sat in a Greek jail without bail for almost a year until he was convicted on March 26, 1970 and sentenced to seventeen years and five months for willful negligence causing manslaughter, illegal possession and use of weapons and explosives, arson and obstructing air navigation. But a few months later the supposedly tough, right-wing military regime known as "the Colonels" that controlled the Greek government at the time suddenly granted a full pardon to Mohammad and released him along with six other Palestinian terrorists in a hostage exchange. He had spent a total of twenty-two months and nineteen days in Greek jails.

He made his way back to Lebanon, after a brief but unpleasant stay in Jordan — where he was questioned about another aircraft attack — and opened a variety store. He sold insurance, bought real estate and made lots of money. He got married, had three kids and managed to stay out of the papers. In 1984 he moved his family to Barcelona, Spain and set up a prosperous textile business selling Spanish fabrics to Saudi Arabia and the United Arab Emirates while he waited for the Canada Immigration application he had filed a year earlier in Beirut to be processed.

Mohammad was already familiar with the country. He had been there twice before, using his real name, date and place of birth. On neither occasion had he had even the slightest problem getting in. In 1983, he had come as a visitor to see a cousin in Brantford, staying twenty-five days and scouting out the possibility of immigrating and opening a fast food restaurant there. In 1985 he came again as a visitor to scout out the possibility of opening a textile business in Montreal. On the first two visits, immigration officials never asked about his political beliefs or his terrorist past or the attack at the Athens airport.

When he applied to immigrate in November 1986, Immigration Canada officials reviewed his medical papers, looked over his business prospects and told him he would be welcome in Canada as a business-class immigrant. But less than a month later, in mid-December, he received a letter marked URGENT telling him to show up the very next day for an interview at the Canada immigration offices in Madrid. This was unexpected, but Mohammad gladly complied.

When he arrived at the immigration offices, he was whisked into a small room and met a man he would later learn was a CSIS official using the pseudonym George Smith. Mohammad quickly realized that Smith was no immigration official. This was an intelligence officer conducting a security check! Smith probed Mohammad's political beliefs, asking him if he had any connection or relation to the PLO. Mohammad replied that he did. His answer didn't seem to frighten Smith. He asked Mohammad if he had a rank in the PLO or had had any special training. The

Palestinian lied and answered "no" to all such questions.

Smith was particularly interested in previous trips that Mohammad had made to Cyprus, Syria, Egypt, Morocco and elsewhere in Africa. He seemed to know just about everywhere Mohammad had been. But he didn't mention Athens, and Mohammad wasn't about to volunteer information about his brief sojourn in the Greek prison system. Apart from not asking the one crucial question that would have put Mohammad on the spot, Smith seemed very well informed, thorough and fair. He questioned the would-be immigrant about Beirut. He even seemed to have a first-hand knowledge of the city. Mohammad was pleased with his security interview. Smith never suggested that CSIS would prepare a favourable security report in return for spying on the Palestinian community in Canada.

Smith did ask one compromising question, however: did Mohammad have any prior criminal convictions? Mohammad replied no, although he was lying and he knew it. He would later justify this by saying he had felt at the time that he had no criminal conviction since the Greek government had given him a full pardon when it let him out of jail. The real reason he lied, however, was much less complicated. He wanted to get into Canada and he knew that if he told Smith about Athens, neither he nor his family would ever see Brantford.

Smith had in front of him a man who identified himself as Mahmoud Mohammad Issa Mohammad, the same name, with the same date of birth and the same place of birth (Umm al-Farraj, Palestine) as the terrorist who had made all the newspapers twenty years earlier, and who had been released and set free in 1970 along with six other terrorists in a much publicized hostage swap that also made the newspapers and went into the clipping files of intelligence agencies. As well, Smith had before him a file that had been examined by officials at the Canadian embassy in Damascus, Syria, and by CSIS security officers in Amman, Jordan before it was transferred to him in Madrid. Even if Smith had had no knowledge whatsoever of Middle East terrorism, somebody else along the line might have made a note

of the incredible coincidence in identities. Only Mohammad's
eagerness to immigrate could lead him to believe that Smith
hadn't put two and two together. Mohammad was sure no mistakes were made. Smith knew full well who he was; the apparent
oversight was deliberate — part of an elaborate plan by CSIS to
let him into the country. Once in Canada, they would tell him
they knew who he was and pressure him into turning informer
on the Palestinian community in return for being allowed to stay
in the country. "They wanted to put me 'under control,'" recalls
Mohammad, who had begun to master the vocabulary of the
intelligence community.

There was an added feature to the CSIS security check in
Madrid. The majority of landed immigrants who come to Canada
are given visas good for a period of several months during which
they can enter Canada, and after which the visa is no longer valid.
This was what Mohammad had been given on his two previous
visits to Canada. On this third occasion, however, he was given
very specific instructions by Smith which he found strange, but
did not question at the time.

Smith told him, he recalls, "The visa is on the table but you
have to give us some information. You have to give us the
departure, the airline, the number of the flight, and if you have
any change, you have to tell us."

Mohammad and his family flew as he had promised CSIS, via
Iberia to Amsterdam and then on KLM on to Toronto on
February 25, 1987. It was only later that he realized why CSIS had
wanted to know exactly when he would arrive in Toronto. They
wanted to be ready to greet him. In fact, Mohammad and his
family had been in the country barely twenty-four hours when
Roger Payne and Rick Fluke, two Palestinian specialists at the
CSIS division in Toronto, showed up on his cousin's doorstep in
Brantford. Payne told the Palestinian they had waited a day to
make sure he liked being in Canada before they moved in.

The men told Mohammad they knew who he was. Mohammad,
who wanted to stay in Canada, replied: "No, you're mistaken.
That's my cousin with the same name back in Lebanon." They

stuck to their charge, and he stuck to his lie. Two RCMP men came in and took fingerprints and photos of him but he had no further contact with the Mounties at that point.

So began a strange cat-and-mouse game between CSIS and the former terrorist that would last a full year and would be the cause of much government embarrassment later on. Everyone wanted to know why they didn't move against Mohammad right away, as soon as they knew his real identity. One of the stories CSIS put out on the street later to try to explain this was that while in jail in Greece in 1970, Mohammad had shared a cell with George Mangakis, a Greek lawyer who had run afoul of the Colonels' regime. The two became friends. Later when Andreas Papandreou took over the government in Greece, Mangakis became his justice minister and it was he who deliberately slowed up the identification process of his old cell-mate Mohammad.

Now this is a great story, and it reads well in the files at CSIS headquarters, but the trouble is it never happened. The two men never shared a cell. The closest they got was the same cell block, along with several hundred other political prisoners. And by the time Mohammad was jousting with CSIS in his living room in Brantford twenty years later, Mangakis had retired as justice minister. Meanwhile Payne and Fluke became regular visitors to Mohammad's home. They returned night after night, making his life miserable. He kept lying to them about who he was. They kept trying to break him. He hoped they would tire and go away. They didn't. Mohammad believes now they wanted to play with him a while, to see what he would do. Had he admitted who he was, they would have told him that he had to co-operate by becoming an informer or else be deported.

They grilled him a total of ten times in three months. But if they hoped to recruit him as an informer they certainly got off on the wrong foot. "They said, 'We are the people who can help you. We know who you are but we can give you a new identity. We can move you to Toronto. You can be in security there. The British, the Americans and the Israelis are after you but we can help you.' " Mohammad believed the stuff about the Americans and the Israelis, but he couldn't figure out what the British could possibly want with him. Even stranger, the Mounties appeared to go along with what was happening. Solicitor General James Kelleher later told the Commons that three days after he arrived the RCMP interviewed Mohammad but did not arrest him. Kelleher never said why.

After three months the CSIS agents stopped coming. But they hadn't quite finished yet. Palestinian-Canadians he knew began coming to him and saying that CSIS agents had been making inquiries about him. It appeared an extensive surveillance system had been established. But at least their nocturnal visits had ceased, and he was able to try to build his life in Canada. He found work hauling concrete blocks on a construction site, but the job proved too strenuous for him. He took a marketing course at Sir Wilfrid Laurier University, and a course in small business at Mohawk College that included a two-week adult-training course at the Keep-Rite air conditioning plant. His wife took English classes. The children went to school.

He had brought about $120,000 with him when he arrived and the money was quickly disappearing. More than $20,000 of it had gone into a downpayment on a modest semi-detached home. Immigration Canada officials who had allowed him into Canada on the promise that he would open a business never bothered him. Nobody showed up to ask him where the textile business was he had promised to open. He was a businessman without a business.

But behind the scenes in Ottawa, Mohammad was the subject of top-level meetings. And at this point CSIS was very much involved. A positive identification of Mohammad had been made through fingerprints in May 1987. The government could easily have moved against him at that time, but the information was merely turned over to Immigration Canada, which sat on the file for another eight months. Later the minister of state for immigration, Gerry Weiner, would try to explain that the delay in deporting Mohammad was a question of trying to build a better case, even though documentary evidence in immigration files shows that as of June 1987 Immigration Canada had all the evidence it needed proving their man in Brantford was a former terrorist who had lied to get into the country.

Meanwhile Mossad — through its reciprocal information exchange agreement with CSIS — began feeding CSIS information that Mohammad had been "an important figure" in the PLO in Beirut after he had quit the PFLP in 1972. Mossad reports, which later found their way into immigration department files, described Mohammad as "an organizer of terrorist activities."

On June 19, 1987 senior CSIS officials met in Ottawa with senior officials from the departments of external affairs, immigration and the solicitor general to try to decide what to do about Mohammad. CSIS warned that "The Israelis could try in some manner to embarrass Canada if we appear to move too slowly on Mr. Mohammad's case. Or they may even attempt to seize or eliminate him in Canada if we try to move him to another Arab country." Meanwhile, CSIS tightened its watch on Mohammad in Brantford. If he was the dangerous terrorist organizer that CSIS claimed, he certainly had a peaceful way of showing it. The most violent thing he did that summer was cut his lawn.

On July 18, 1987, Deputy Minister of Immigration Gaétan Lussier issued a memo saying that Mohammad was now only a "potential" security threat and that CSIS did not consider him an immediate threat to the safety of Canadians. But still they watched and waited, until finally, on October 27, 1987, Immigration Minister Benoît Bouchard advised his officials to begin deportation proceedings.

Again the immigration people stalled. They waited until December 29 to call Mohammad in for a meeting, and it was then that an Immigration Canada official, Carl Fiamelli, told the Palestinian politely that they knew who he was, that he had broken Canadian immigration laws and that he would have to leave the country. But he was told he might be able to get back in at a later date. "He told me you have to apply from outside the country and tell the truth about yourself and then maybe they'll give you a visa to visit your family. If you leave voluntarily, [your wife and family] can stay here. We have nothing against them."

A January 15 meeting was arranged between Mohammad's lawyer, Brian Pennell, and immigration officials, and arrangements were made for him to leave the following week and apply from outside the country. But Mohammad's exit plans were quashed when somebody leaked the whole story to the media.

Mohammad's life collapsed around him as he became the biggest news in Canada that day. Journalists descended on his home, camped on his doorstep and chased after his friends and neighbours for comments and opinions. Mohammad was desperate and he turned to the one man he felt he could trust, Rashad Saleh. As well as owning and operating a family restaurant on Spears Road in Oakville, Saleh had been a president of the Canadian Arab Federation. He was a long-time supporter of the Palestinian cause, an expert on CSIS, and the trusted confidant of many Palestinian-Canadians.

Saleh was on Mohammad's side, but no one else appeared to be, and the aftermath of the press coverage was frightening. His car insurance soared from $900 to $2,200 a year; the insurance company promptly cancelled the coverage on his home; his nine-year-old son Khaled came home in tears. The boys he tobogganed with in the ravine had called his father a murderer. Mohammad put everything in his wife's name and made plans to leave. And then, worst of all, Payne and Fluke showed up on his doorstep again after an absence of eight months and told him that he should go with them because who knew who might be lurking among the reporters on his front lawn.

A strange, late-night meeting was arranged with CSIS at Brian Pennell's office in Hamilton. At 3:00 a.m., after grilling him for a while without his lawyer being present, a CSIS team took Mohammad away to a room in the Sheraton Hotel in Mississauga, near Toronto. Over the next three days, they kept him moving from one hotel to another every few hours, allowing him no food and little sleep. He recalls a couple of Holiday Inns and a Howard Johnson hotel in Burlington, Mississauga and Oakville, and at least one or two other hotels the names of which he can't remember. It was not clear what the CSIS agents were after. They appeared simply to be giving him a hard time. They kept threatening him with all kinds of dire consequences should he not finally decide to "co-operate."

Meanwhile, Saleh, who had read the newspapers and suspected what might be happening, found out from Mohammad's wife that her husband had been taken away by Payne and Fluke. Saleh quickly located a good Toronto lawyer, Marlys Edwardh, and hired her to represent Mohammad. She was to find out where CSIS was holding the Palestinian and to try to free him. Edwardh says she brought her partner Clayton Ruby into the case as "a witness."

Edwardh and Ruby demanded to see their client and finally CSIS relented; a meeting was arranged at one of the hotels. They found Mohammad almost mad with fear. Apparently he had been told that if he didn't do what CSIS wanted he would be turned over to Mossad — a suggestion that Ruby found utterly offensive. "They had him in this hotel room when we arrived and they had been questioning him," recalls Ruby. "There were about twenty guys in all, some in cars outside, some in the hotel, maybe ten or fifteen in a room next door, and four guys in the room with him. They had no warrant and he had done nothing illegal. He had not been charged with any crime."

Ruby ripped into the CSIS men for holding his client for so long without food or drink, and as he did so, Edwardh made a startling discovery. "CSIS was with him," she says. "But the RCMP was surrounding the joint. CSIS was inside the room, but the RCMP had the room next door." She made a point of asking the names of the people who were there and writing them down at the time. Later on she checked them out. She is also sure the CSIS agents knew the Mounties were next door. "I don't know why they were there. I've always viewed that as very strange. I guess they were the guards guarding the guards."

Mohammad had noticed that when they moved from one hotel to another at night there were men in cars with the lights off and the motors running in the hotel parking lots. He assumed they were CSIS men, but Edwardh later found out from reliable informants that the unmarked cars idling in the hotel parking lot belonged to the Mounties, not to CSIS, and didn't know what to make of it.

Mohammad left with his lawyers but during the next twenty-four hours a "very bizarre event" took place, says Edwardh. CSIS kept calling up and asking if Mohammad would please speak to them, because they had orders to ask him questions and if they didn't get answers they would be in trouble. The lawyers told Mohammad he didn't have to answer, but he said he was interested in what they wanted to know.

"The questions they put to him had nothing to do with immigration or his status in Canada," Edwardh recalls. "They were of a general intelligence nature. After two days I telephoned the head of CSIS and said to lay off. Then they quit phoning."

She has only one explanation why CSIS would be interested in asking questions of such little interest to Canada. "There is an intelligence community out there that doesn't distinguish nationality," she says.

Solicitor General Kelleher carefully hid from the Commons the next day the fact that CSIS had abducted Mohammad and run him through a three-day hotel room odyssey in the suburbs of Toronto. The public knew through the media that Mohammad was no longer at his home in Brantford and it feared the worst. "Terrorist Disappears" and "Terrorist on the Loose," screamed the headlines.

In the House of Commons the following day, the Opposition, which was equally kept in ignorance, suspected Mohammad had given CSIS the slip and was on the run somewhere in Canada. Opposition members kept asking, "Where is Mohammad?" The solicitor general, who knew CSIS had sequestered Mohammad, could hardly have answered, "We have been holding him illegally in hotel rooms in the Toronto area over part of the past three days and moving him around from hotel to hotel so that you don't know where he is while we are trying to pump information out of him, but two slick lawyers from Toronto found out where he was and now we have to try to be nice to him." In fact, the solicitor general said as little as possible — simply that he couldn't say exactly where Mohammad was, which was true, and that he was sure the Palestinian was under "close surveillance," which was also true. Mohammad knew the time had come for him to leave this weird country.

CSIS had done their best to turn Mohammad into a spy but they hadn't succeeded — and their failure was apparent to spy-watchers everywhere. To add insult to injury, it was decided that the RCMP would be responsible for slipping him quietly out of the country. RCMP planning for Operation Mohammad was meticulous: the day and hour of departure were kept secret even from Mohammad's wife until the last minute. His children were not told. Earlier that afternoon, less than four hours before departure, a phalanx of unmarked RCMP cars had arrived at Mohammad's home on Ash Grove Avenue in Brantford and whisked him at top speed to Lester B. Pearson International Airport outside Toronto. To avoid recognition the Mounties brought Mohammad into the airport through an underground entrance and stopped their cars in front of a door leading to the RCMP's basement security room. Mohammad was out of the police car and into the room in less than five seconds. There was little chance anyone had seen him. The Mounties had assigned to the case their top immigration officer, the director of the RCMP's immigration section in Ottawa, Inspector Giuliano Zaccardelli. "Zacc," as he is known to colleagues, is a slight, fortyish, easygoing man who doesn't panic easily; a quality that would be particularly valuable before the evening was over.

The Mounties took elaborate precautions with the ticketing. They did not want anyone to discover their plan simply by looking into the Air Canada computer. First, they reserved two seats under false names on Flight 856 to London. Then, separately, they reserved a single ticket under the name "M. Mohammad" for the Air Algérie flight from London to Algiers the following day, connecting with an evening flight from Algiers to Tunis.They did not mind using Mohammad's real name on the second leg of the journey because they figured "M. Mohammad" is such a common name on flights between London and North Africa that it would not attract attention. Nor would anyone link it to the false name in the Air Canada computer. The third and most important security precaution of all was listing Tunis on the ticket as the final destination. Mohammad never intended to go to Tunis. The destination was slipped in on the ticket to throw off anyone who might have a look at the Air Canada computer after Mohammad had left Canada.

Tunisia was picked as a credible cover because Yasser Arafat, the PLO leader, had his headquarters there. It also happens that Tunis is not far from Algiers, so that the added cost of paying for an unused portion of the ticket would not be considerable. This was important, because the federal immigration department, foreseeing the questions that might be asked of it in the Commons afterwards, had insisted that Mohammad pay his own way out of the country.

All involved agreed to meet at 5:30 p.m. in the basement room. The plan was that they would wait until all of the passengers on Flight 856 had boarded the aircraft. Then Air Canada's director of security would come downstairs to the room to fetch Mohammad and escort him upstairs across the airport lobby and through a door behind the Air Canada check-in counter, correct the false names, issue proper tickets for Inspector Zaccardelli and Mohammad, check Mohammad's baggage, and escort the two men to the aircraft, which would be held a couple of extra minutes to give them time to board. As an added security precaution Mohammad had been told to remove the name tags from his two bags. Although the RCMP men at the airport had been told of some parts of the operation, no one among them except Zaccardelli knew the entire plan.

Back in Ottawa, RCMP Commissioner Norman Inkster knew, as so did then Deputy Commissioner Henry Jensen, who would play a vital role at a crucial moment that evening. Immigration Minister Benoît Bouchard, whose policies had been under fire from the Opposition for months, was the senior minister who

stood to lose the most if the plan failed. Gaétan Lussier, Bouchard's trusted deputy minister, was the senior bureaucrat involved. Joe Bissett, Immigration's executive director, was told, as
was Gerry Weiner, the minister of state for immigration at the
time. Solicitor General James Kelleher was in on the plan, as were
some trusted people at External Affairs, including the minister
himself, Joe Clark.

J. Blair Seaborn, who was then co-ordinator of security and
intelligence for the Privy Council, was responsible for keeping
Prime Minister Mulroney informed. Negotiating on behalf of
Mohammad were his two lawyers at the time, Marlys Edwardh
and Lorne Waldman. Abdullah Abdullah, the PLO representative in Canada, had helped Mohammad negotiate the Algerian
end of the trip, and some senior PLO people in Tunis knew what
was going on.

Everyone came to the airport from different directions. The
lawyers took a taxi from downtown Toronto, Mohammad arrived
by unmarked RCMP car from Brantford, Zaccardelli by air from
Ottawa, and Saleh drove his own car from Oakville. Lorne
Waldman and Marlys Edwardh arrived a bit early. There was no
one in the basement security room so the two lawyers went up to
the airport bookstore. As they headed back to the stairs, they met
Saleh and all three went down together. They had barely set foot
on the floor below when they froze in horror. Less than ten
metres away, standing almost next to the RCMP's security room,
were CSIS officers Roger Payne and Rick Fluke, making no effort
to hide themselves. Edwardh and Saleh recognized Payne immediately. Fluke they identified only later.

Saleh recalls the feeling of horror he had in the pit of his
stomach. CSIS knew! And if CSIS knew, Mossad — who had
sworn to get Mohammad — knew as well. But CSIS was not
supposed to be involved; the RCMP had given their word. So
what were Payne and Fluke doing here standing around outside
the Mounties' security room? Saleh was sure they had been
double-crossed. Edwardh recalls thinking that her client's life
was in danger. Payne and Fluke did not run after they were

spotted, but continued to stand there, staring. The two lawyers and Saleh burst into the RCMP office yelling, "What the fuck is going on here?" The other two RCMP officers from the Hamilton detachment who had been acting as Mohammad's bodyguards charged out of the room. A shouting match ensued between the RCMP men and the CSIS guys in the hallway outside. The two CSIS officers fled.

Pandemonium broke out in the little security room and the lawyers decided to call the whole thing off. Zaccardelli refused to panic and immediately called his boss in Ottawa, Henry Jensen, who was then deputy commissioner, to tell him their elaborate plan was already coming apart. Mohammad, frightened enough as it was, panicked and refused to leave the RCMP office under any circumstances, much less board a commercial flight to London. He was convinced that he was being set up to be killed by Mossad agents either at the airport, or in London, or on his way to North Africa. How else could he explain the fact that CSIS had penetrated the carefully laid plan of the RCMP? "I was on the telephone to Gaétan Lussier in two seconds," says Edwardh. "I had Lussier on one phone and the deputy commissioner on the other." Lussier had called Jensen, who had called CSIS director Reid Morden and extracted a promise that his people would "not intervene." Jensen relayed over the telephone to the lawyers the news that CSIS had not been "formally involved," recalls Edwardh. "He said: 'Maybe it was just an accident.' "

Only later did she realize how unlikely it would be for Payne and Fluke, who did not regularly work at the airport, to arrive by coincidence at the same airport on the same day in front of the same RCMP basement office at the same time as the individual they had had under surveillance night and day in Brantford for the past year. CSIS, obviously unhappy about being excluded from this caper, and worse supplanted by the Horsemen, was taking a very close interest in what was going on. The fledgling agency had been responsible for bringing Mohammad into Canada in the first place. And they'd spent time and trouble trying unsuccessfully to get him to spy on his fellow Palestinians. Now he was being smuggled out of the country and no one had made any attempt to contact *them*. In this round of the RCMP vs CSIS Games it looked like the Mounties were ahead on points. But the match wasn't over yet.

In the crowded little basement room with two and three lines to Ottawa going at once, there was a noisy debate about what should be done. At first the lawyers and Saleh were adamant that Mohammad should not leave the country. Then, little by little, they allowed themselves to be convinced that maybe he *could* go, and finally everyone decided that the Palestinian would probably make it safely to London at least, and maybe on to his final destination, if he was accompanied all the way by an armed guard. Saleh said he'd go if someone gave him a gun. This seemed to reassure Mohammad but no one else thought it was a good idea. The politicians in Ottawa were not interested in seeing screaming headlines about a civilian being nabbed by a metal detector when he tried to board an aircraft with a gun given him by the RCMP. Especially since he was travelling with a Palestinian ex-terrorist. "So 'Zacc' had to go," says Edwardh, "because he was the only one who could get on board an Air Canada plane with a gun."

Zaccardelli had already been cleared by his boss Jensen to go as far as London, with or without a weapon, but now Waldman, Edwardh and Saleh were asking that the Mountie officer go armed all the way to Algiers as well. He didn't have any kind of visa, and the lawyers smiled at the thought of the Mountie being immediately deported back to Canada.

Finally Mohammad made the decision. He felt he had to go through with it because he'd already committed himself. Then there was the question of who apart from Zaccardelli would go with him. Saleh wanted Edwardh to go since she was Mohammad's lawyer, but she had no burning desire to visit Algeria. Finally they agreed that Rashad Saleh would go — but he had no passport with him. Saleh and the Mounties tore out of the airport and drove to his home in Mississauga where he packed his bag, picked up his passport and explained to his wife he was going out of town for a couple of days but she shouldn't worry. He'd explain it all when he came back. The trip to his home and back took less than forty-five minutes. To ensure the three men could all sit together, they would have to fly first class.

The director of security for Air Canada arrived and the seven of them — Mohammad, Saleh, Zaccardelli, Edwardh, Waldman and the two RCMP bodyguards — headed up the stairs. They kept an eye out for the two CSIS men, but they were nowhere to be seen. Still, that didn't mean that CSIS had given up. The two officers had been replaced by a surveillance team — Reid Morden, the agency's boss, had promised that his people wouldn't intervene, but he hadn't said he'd pull them off the case. In fact, CSIS agents were to gleefully report back to Ottawa later that Mohammad came out of the room wearing a fedora hat and dark glasses. He could not have attracted more attention, they said, if he'd borrowed Igor Gouzenko's paper bag with the holes in it.

Everyone rushed upstairs and across the foyer and into a back room behind the Air Canada ticket counter. They were only in public view for about fifteen seconds. However, in CSIS files this would be noted as a major tactical blunder by the RCMP. A lot of conservatively dressed men hurrying through an airport lobby at rush hour, huddled around another man in a large hat and dark glasses, was not the best way to avoid attention. In the room behind the ticket counter, their bags were searched by a security guard. Zaccardelli flashed his RCMP identity to get past the guard without having to go through the metal detector with his weapon. The Air Canada security chief had someone change the names in the airline's computer and print the proper tickets. They ran and caught the flight before it left for London. "He's on at last," sighed Edwardh.

Mohammad did not say much on the plane. The real danger lay now in the next flight, from London to Algiers. Saleh feared an Israeli agent might hijack the plane somewhere over the Mediterranean and divert it to an American air base in Italy where Mohammad would be taken off and turned over to waiting Israelis. Meanwhile, back in Toronto, unaware that the real drama was just beginning, Edwardh headed downtown to meet Clayton Ruby at a Toronto restaurant, to brief him on the harrowing episode with CSIS at the airport. They had barely begun their soup when there was a call from a reporter for Ruby, who had left with his children's nanny the name of the restaurant where he could be reached. Less than an hour after the flight had taken off, two men in Toronto had found out what had happened and were systematically calling up radio and television stations, newspapers and news agencies and telling them Mohammad the "convicted terrorist" had fled the country to avoid deportation and was on his way to Algeria. Calls from journalists were piling up on Edwardh's answering machine at home and at her office. Suddenly it seemed the whole city knew that Mohammad was on his way to Algeria and soon the world would know. Once again Edwardh had that sinking feeling that Mohammad had been double-crossed.

In the newsroom at Toronto's CTV network affiliate, CFTO, newsman Ken Sherman got an anonymous telephone call from a man shortly before 9:30 p.m. The man said his friend had spotted Mohammad boarding a plane at the airport earlier that evening. Sherman remembers the call vividly. He says it was one of those occasions when his instinct as a journalist told him that as weird as the story sounded, it was probably true. But he couldn't put hearsay on the air. He had to get it confirmed. "I was tearing my hair out," recalls Sherman. "We went full bore on this one." He and other reporters were calling all around the city, thus destroying any hope Mohammad had of arriving in London unnoticed.

Shortly after 10:00 p.m., the anonymous man telephoned CFTO again. This time he identified himself as Marshall Shapiro, a Toronto businessman, and asked if the story had been used on the air. Shapiro said a friend, Gilbert Zamonsky, who had been at the airport that night to board a flight to Tennessee, had called to say goodbye from the airport and told him about seeing

Mohammad leaving Toronto. Shapiro, who spoke this time to news editor Ken Shaw, said that Zamonsky had recognized Mohammad because he followed Middle East affairs closely. But Shapiro offered no explanation as to how Zamonsky, who was supposedly boarding a flight at the time, was able to find out Mohammad was bound for Algiers.

Shaw, a veteran newsman, had a funny feeling about Zamonsky. Shapiro said he worked at Parcel Air, a small parcel delivery firm with an office in the basement of the Royal York Hotel in Toronto, but the following day Shaw called Parcel Air and discovered that not only had Zamonsky not flown to Tennessee the night before, as Shapiro had claimed, but he had not even been at the airport. Zamonsky told Shaw that it was not him, but yet another friend, whom he did not want to name, who had seen Mohammad at the airport and told him about it. The story was becoming more complicated by the minute.

Zamonsky said his friend had called him from the airport and told him that he had seen Mohammad and "heavy cops," and then had been informed later that Mohammad was flying to Algiers. But four days later in another interview Zamonsky altered his story. His unnamed "buddy" had not seen Mohammad. He had merely overheard "an airport ground hostess" tell a group of people, "Would you believe we just boarded that terrorist from Brantford?" and then explain to them that Mohammad was headed for Algeria. But the friend had not called him from the airport with this conversation, said Zamonsky. Instead he had driven into downtown Toronto to the Wheat Sheaf Tavern on Bathurst Street and called Zamonsky from there. Zamonsky got in touch with Shapiro, and together they began calling up various news media. However, even a cursory examination of this story shows that it doesn't make sense.

If the airport ground hostess knew Mohammad was leaving because she had seen him boarding the aircraft, she should have shouted that Mohammad was on his way to London. It was a flight to London, not Algiers, that Mohammad took from Toronto. If she had been nosy enough to look up his itinerary in the airline computer, she might have discovered that he was flying first to London, then on to Algiers and then Tunis. So she would have shouted, "We've boarded that terrorist from Brantford, and he's on his way to Tunis." Why focus on a No. 2 stop on a three-stop ticket?

Only someone with inside information on the whole operation would know that Mohammad was going to Algeria and not Tunisia, even though Tunis appeared as the final destination on his itinerary. Someone with inside information and a vested interested in blowing the whole story wide open. Someone with a grudge against Mohammad, or maybe with a grudge against the RCMP. A British Airways flight which left a few minutes after the Air Canada flight did list a "Mr. Payne" as being on board, so CSIS may have still been keeping an eye on the situation, but there were so many plots and counterplots going down at Lester B. Pearson airport that night, "Mr. Payne" could have been anybody or nobody at all.

Meanwhile, Zaccardelli and Saleh, completely oblivious to what was happening in Toronto, were comfortably ensconced in their seats sampling Air Canada's first-class hospitality and trying to convince Mohammad this would not be his last meal. (Zaccardelli was also trying to figure out a story to tell the Algerians when they asked him what he was doing in Algiers with a gun and no visa.) It was only when the plane landed in London that the three men realized how terribly wrong things had gone back home. They were greeted by two RCMP officers . . . and every spy and secret agent in London, hiding behind the potted plants and luggage racks, watching the famous "terrorist" arriving in town without being seen. It was like a convention for the London chapter of Secret Agents Anonymous, and there may have been more people there for Mohammad than for all the rest of the passengers on the flight put together. Saleh called Marlys Edwardh immediately and discovered that the minute the plane had left, the story was all over the media.

The British, who like pomp and ceremonies, turned the whole

thing into a full-scale production for the benefit of the assembled secret agents. British Intelligence walked Mohammad over to Air Algérie in front of everybody. Saleh was sure the plan had collapsed but moments later he was pleasantly surprised. "I called Algeria and was told everything was prepared and a plane was waiting for him at the airport to take him to his final stop," he recalls.

"I spoke too to the top PLO people in Tunis and I asked 'It's still okay?'

"They said, 'Yes.'

"I told them that now the story was out, the Israelis knew everything, and they could hijack the plane in Europe and bring it down to a U.S. base in Italy.

"They said everything seemed okay and the Algerian Air Force would escort us as soon as we were over the Mediterranean."

Saleh talked to the Air Algérie representative in London at about 9:00 a.m. and was told everything would be alright for the noon flight. At about 10:30 a.m., Saleh says, a Scotland Yard official told him politely that there might be a problem. The Air Algérie manager had been taken aside by British Intelligence. "They took him to a security room," says Saleh. "When he came out, he had changed his mind. He was intimidated. He was really shitting his buns."

Saleh says he doesn't blame the British, nor does he blame the Air Algérie manager. He realizes the risk the manager would be taking by allowing Mohammad and his cronies to board the aircraft. His superiors in Algiers were leaving him entirely free to decide, so if anything happened, he would be solely responsible. Here were these three strange men from Canada — a gun-toting Mountie without a valid visa, a man claiming to be a reformed Palestinian terrorist, who for some reason was going to Algeria from Canada instead of the other way, and a wacky, buoyant Palestinian-Canadian restaurateur who appeared to be along for nothing more than the ride. Who knew what plot Mossad, or a rival terrorist faction, or for that matter any of these three men themselves, might have hatched? Who needed the aggravation? And since he was not under orders from Algiers to do anything, why take the risk?

In the end the airline manager didn't have to make a decision; Saleh himself pulled the plug. "Under the circumstances," he said, "the best thing to do was to go back." The discovery of their plan in Toronto changed everything. Edwardh says she doesn't know what pressures were brought on the Algerians in London, or why the Algerians said yes even after they knew the plan had been discovered, and then suddenly changed their minds. The trio admitted defeat and took the next available Air Canada flight back home. It happened to be Flight 857, that afternoon. In fact it was the same aircraft that they'd left Toronto on.

Saleh was fuming all the way, working himself up into a fury against CSIS. He was firmly convinced the agency was responsible for the leak to the media. Inside Pearson airport there were about 100 reporters, photographers and film crew members waiting for the latest instalment in Mohammad's pilgrimage. The RCMP sent a car out to the tarmac to pick up the trio so they could escape the media waiting for them inside the terminal. But they didn't take Saleh with them; they left him behind on the tarmac to find his own way home. Mohammad returned to Brantford, but Saleh walked into an airport full of reporters and poured out his scorn for CSIS for the better part of an hour. Score another point for the Horsemen. At the end of this round in the game, however, the honours appeared to be about even. The Mounties' precious little CSIS-less adventure had ended in a shambles — as travel agents they made very good musical riders — but CSIS was getting all the blame for the disaster. And in Ottawa, the Opposition was having a free-for-all at the expense of a government which couldn't stop Mohammad from getting into Canada, couldn't remove him once he was here, and now apparently couldn't help him out even when he wanted to leave.

"CSIS was not involved in any way whatsoever with the travel arrangements of this particular case," said Solicitor General Kelleher. Truer words he had seldom spoken. The following day he said even more categorically, " . . . CSIS did not leak the news or anything to do with the travel arrangements to the media or anyone else."

Reid Morden, the CSIS boss, attending a conference of intelligence buffs in Kingston, Ontario, two days later, denied absolutely that CSIS had been involved in scuttling the project. He declined to say whether one of his agents had followed Mohammad to London that night, or if he had, what he had done there. Morden told a reporter the leak that thwarted the trip might have come from someone as simple as an ordinary traveller who saw Mohammad at the airport. He didn't explain how an ordinary traveller would know that Algeria was Mohammad's destination.

Immigration Minister Bouchard said that he had personally approved the plan without the help of External Affairs. "When you want a guy out of the country, and you are offered it on a silver platter, you say 'Yes.' We had good reason to believe it would work." Bouchard also refused to say who was responsible for the collapse of the plan. He told the press to ask Mohammad's lawyers, and Mohammad's lawyers kept saying it was CSIS. So attention focused back on the original bearers of the departure news, Shapiro and Zamonsky.

Shapiro, who is in the computer business today, says he regrets ever getting involved in the Mohammad affair. He says he did so only as a favour for Zamonsky, whom he greatly admires. Ever since that day people have been asking him if he is a CSIS agent or a Mossad agent. He does not enjoy it one bit. He is afraid that some terrorist will think he is a spy, and knock him off. Shapiro wants everybody to know that he has never worked for either organization and never will.

Shapiro's pal Zamonsky is a bit more involved in Middle East politics and admits to a bias for the Israeli side. Zamonsky also likes to play with weapons and occasionally drives around in a vintage World War II Sherman tank owned by a friend. He looks after security at one of the larger synagogues in Toronto during the Jewish high holidays making sure, among other things, that those arriving at the door are the true worshippers they appear to be, and when Israeli dignitaries visit Toronto, Zamonsky frequently helps out with security matters and provides other little services. Rather than merely leaving the job up to the RCMP, the Israelis have also asked him to ensure that various buildings on the tour are free of bombs. He admits his presence has raised the ire of the Mounties on occasion. The Israelis do not pay him, Zamonsky says. Their gratitude is reward enough. Unlike Shapiro, Zamonsky says he doesn't regret what he did.

"I received a call from someone I would rather not name, and once I got that call my objective was to cause Mohammad as much trouble as I could. I must have caused him half a million dollars in legal fees that he didn't expect he'd have to pay." Actually, Mohammad's legal bills are being picked up by Canadian taxpayers. After putting his home in hock for $100,000 to pay his lawyers, Mohammad qualified for legal aid to continue his defence. His lawyers, are among the absolute best in the country and charge accordingly.

Zamonsky steadfastly refuses to identify his friend at the airport who tipped him off, and he sticks to his story about the airline ground hostess with the big mouth. He insists she exists, works for Air Canada, and was found by CSIS agents and interviewed. Zamonsky says he does not work for the agency but he believes "CSIS is made up of a clever bunch of guys" who are "well-trained and smart." However, he adds, "they are manacled to the point where they are ineffective, and they can't be effective if their brainpower is dissipated. The guys I've met are well-educated and well-seasoned cops and they're damn smart." He insists that Roger Payne never flew to London to watch Mohammad.

"Roger tells me he wasn't there, he didn't meet any of them, and they don't even know what he looks like," says Zamonsky. "They just think they saw somebody in cowboy boots." Zamonsky says he has a lot of respect for his pal Roger and the way he operates. "His attitude is, 'We're secret. You guys don't know we exist. We're not talking to you'." Finally, Zamonsky says he is neither a CSIS agent nor an Israeli agent, no matter what anyone may think. He is his own man, does his own research and draws his own conclusions.

In Ottawa, despite CSIS Director Reid Morden's assurances that CSIS was not involved and did not scuttle Mohammad's travel plans, Ron Atkey, the chairman of the Security Intelligence Review Committee, announced his agency would conduct an investigation into the airport fiasco. SIRC was set up by Parliament when CSIS was created to examine the agency's activities and report annually on the operations of the intelligence service. SIRC is supposed to act as a watchdog of sorts — after the fact.

A then spokesperson for SIRC, Annie Demirjian, said the investigation would be separate from SIRC's annual report and would examine the role that CSIS had played since the day Mohammad had landed in Canada. But when Atkey appeared on April 14, 1988, before the House of Commons Standing Committee on Justice and the Solicitor General, he summarily dismissed any suggestion of wrongdoing on the part of the agency. "We looked into it and we found it was not the service's fault," said Atkey. "It got a bum rap." In fact, his major concern appeared to be that CSIS had not been brought in on the plan.

Atkey refused to say who, if not CSIS, was responsible. "We're not here to second-guess what went wrong or who screwed up. As far as we can determine things just didn't come off." Atkey never dealt with why CSIS had been left out. As he left the room a reporter asked if it might have been because the government feared CSIS was working with the Israelis. "It's an interesting story," he replied.

The great SIRC investigation that had been promised came to naught. And there was no separate report on the Mohammad affair. The investigation consisted of looking at files that CSIS turned over to the SIRC investigators, and conducting interviews with a few government officials. But the people most directly connected to the affair — Mohammad, his lawyers and Saleh — were never contacted and five months later SIRC wrapped up its findings using exactly thirty-five words in its annual report to Parliament. The two-paragraph exoneration of CSIS read:

"We found that: CSIS did not slip up in the entry into Canada of Mahmoud Mohammad Issa Mohammad; someone did, but it was not CSIS.
Nor did it compromise his attempt to leave the country."

SIRC in essence had repeated exactly what Reid Morden had said and did not provide one shred of information to back up its conclusion.

Those people who were waiting for the SIRC annual report to clarify matters had to wait quite a while. The government did not release the report until after the November '88 election, by which time a whole new crop of MPs with a new set of agendas were in place, so the report caused hardly a ripple. Meanwhile, Mohammad and his lawyers had launched a long court battle that could take years to reach a conclusion.

Mohammad finally found a job not as a businessman but as a program administrator for the International Development and Refugee Foundation, a non-profit organization based in Mississauga, Ontario, which raises money in Canada to relieve the starvation and poverty of Palestinian refugees in Lebanon, the West Bank and Gaza strip. The federal government matches every dollar the group raises on a ratio of three-to-one.

For CSIS, the ending to the Mohammad Affair was not happy. Its reputation and even its loyalty to Canada were attacked. SIRC acknowledged the impact on CSIS in its annual report: "The episode contributed to an atmosphere of suspicion, not to say derision, in which all sorts of allegations about bungling and wrongdoing were floated." Relations between CSIS and the Israelis took a turn for the worse from that moment.

Gaétan Lussier, the former deputy minister, who is out of

government now, says that someday, "maybe thirty years from now," he will write a book about the Mohammad affair. He defends the goverment's decision to keep CSIS out of the Mohammad project "because there were enough people involved." Lussier says Atkey is wrong about CSIS not being informed. "Mr. Atkey doesn't have his facts right. CSIS had been made aware [of the RCMP plan]." Perhaps it was not the official invitation that CSIS would have wanted, he says, but the service was nonetheless informed by the RCMP. Mr. Lussier hesitates to blame CSIS for the failure of the operation. "I'm sure that when certain elements made Mr. Mohammad refuse to get on the plane at the last minute, it effectively created a chain reaction, involving everyone from the captain of the aircraft on down," Lussier says. "As we say where I come from: 'That's probably what made the woodpile tumble.' "

Lorne Waldman, on the other hand, insists that Mohammad and the RCMP are blameless and the fault lies with CSIS. "No more than three Air Canada employees had access to him," he says, dismissing the story about the Air Canada hostess. "And the whole time we were at the airport there was less than half a minute when anyone from the public would have seen him."

Mohammad says: "Just ask yourself who wanted the plan to fail and you'll have your answer."

# "I Did Much Worse for the RCMP . . ."

**T**HE HISTORY OF SPIES and counter-espionage in Canada begins long before Confederation. The French and British repeatedly used Natives as spies and undercover agents against each other and against the Dutch as they fought over the eastern part of the continent. The whites couldn't tell the Natives apart and were easily fooled by the wise "savages" who extracted everything they could in return for information they sold back and forth to all sides over and over again. The Natives were the first successful spies in British North America, and also some of the best double and triple agents ever anywhere in the world. Some of them retired passably well off in Quebec City.

Laura Secord used her cow to get past American lines and tell the British what the Yankees were up to during the War of 1812. She had overheard American officers billeted at her home in Queenston making plans to attack Beaver Dams. Mrs. Secord made the trip to tell her friend, Lieutenant James FitzGibbon, that the Americans were coming. His Indian spies had already told him that, but her visit confirmed his intelligence work. Two days later, on June 24, 1813, FitzGibbon's Indians successfully ambushed the Americans near Beaver Dams, and Mrs. Secord became Canada's first effective non-Native undercover agent, commemorated to this day on boxes of chocolates.

By the late 1860s, the colonial government in Ottawa had its own honest-to-goodness spies and even its own favourite group to spy on. Since Communism wasn't yet a household word, the politicians raised the spectre of the Fenians, an evil horde of Irish-Americans who were hidden just over the U.S. border in secret camps, supposedly waiting for the right moment to launch a sneak attack on the unsuspecting British colonies. The Fenians planned to capture Canada and then trade it back to Britain in return for Ireland's independence. A frontier police force was set up under Windsor, Ontario magistrate Gilbert McMicken, who was something of an undercover operative himself. Several dozen men worked the bars, taverns and hotels on both sides of the border for either Canada or the U.S., since defections were common at the time. Sir John A. Macdonald was a master at using the Fenian menace for political purposes, often including it in his speeches as one more good reason why the colonies should unite into a single country — Canada.

"Henri LeCaron" was the alias used by Thomas Miller Beach, a Canadian who went undercover for the British among the Fenians in the U.S. to find out what they were up to. The Fenians were a disorganized lot, always making public their intentions, and as a result were usually met and repelled at the border. After two decades of espionage, Beach retired and published an account of his undercover activities appropriately entitled *Twenty-Five Years in the Secret Service*.

The Dominion Police force was established by Sir John A. in 1868. McMicken was the first commissioner, and he secretly reported to the prime minister himself. There were indications of a secret slush account in a Montreal bank, and suspicions that McMicken himself may not have been above breaking the law once in a while in the interests of national security — shades of things to come.

The Dominion Police force soon had a sister organization, the North-West Mounted Police, founded in 1873 in response to policing requirements on the Prairies. At first it was a sort of

military organization, based on the principle of taking ill-edu-
cated boys out of farms and small towns, and through effective
discipline and militaristic training, drilling into them certain
values of loyalty, blind obedience and a strange code of ethics.
For years, the Mounties, as they came to be known, had to ask
their superior officers for permission to marry. The smallest
breach of discipline was severely punished. Answering back to
an officer was enough to land a recruit in jail without so much
as the benefit of a judicial hearing. While other police forces
emphasized finding educated recruits, or at least sending them
to college after they joined, the Mounties emphasized making
recruits ride horses in Regina. Less than one percent of all
Mounties are called upon to ride horses on a regular basis, and
yet to this day it remains part of the basic training, known
affectionately as "wearing the saddle."

The Mounties, were entrusted with the delicate task of keeping
the western territories white, English and Protestant. Their dislike of Indians, Métis and the French showed early on. Unlike
other police forces in the East, the Redcoats were given the
power to prosecute and judge as well as arrest suspects and
prevent crime. When the railroad pushed through, they sided
with the railway barons against the workers — the Chinese and
the indentured Irish — and against the Indians, who for some
reason were always claiming it was their land that the railway was
going through. The Mounties helped defeat strikes, protected
strike-breakers and generally were on the side of the employers
in any labour conflict in the nineteenth century. The Winnipeg
General Strike of 1919 persuaded the Ottawa politicians that the
Bolshevik hordes were taking over the Canadian west. In 1920,
in response to the threat of a Communist republic they perceived
in Manitoba, they reorganized the North-West Mounted Police
into the Royal Canadian Mounted Police.

An effective public relations campaign, the feeling of security
that the Mounties afforded to anxious Ontario businessmen, and
the exploits of a few brave Mounties in remote, isolated northern
communities all combined to project an image of dedication,

honesty and integrity matched by few other police agencies in the world. The bright red uniforms were eye-catching, as were the Stetson hats, issued to protect against the hot Prairie sun. These, and a few Hollywood movies, established forever the Mounties' sterling reputation.

At first the Mounties paid little attention to the security side of operations. Had they had any sort of intelligence when they headed out to quell the second Riel Rebellion, they might not have suffered so ignominious a defeat at the hands of the Métis forces at Duck Lake, Saskatchewan. Ten years later, someone on the Force suggested hiring four detectives to deal with under-cover political matters, but the idea was quickly rejected. The Mounties have always been slow to change. In fact they are proud of it; it is part of their mystique. It would take another sixty-one years for the Mounties to set up a special branch to look after intelligence and security matters.

The growth of Communism and the rise of the labour move-ment in Canada after World War I increased the Force's under-cover role. This was the era of the first great Red Scare. The most famous RCMP undercover man during the late twenties was John Leopold, who, under the alias Jack Esselwein, spied on the Communists until he was discovered and booted out of the Communist Party in 1928. Many Depression-era trials of sus-pected "subversives" featured Leopold testifying for the prosecu-tion in his bright red serge uniform against political and labour leaders such as Tim Buck. In those days, it was an offence under the criminal code just to be seen associating with known subver-sives.

Leopold became a hero — and a publicly acclaimed hero at that. This was unusual in the ranks of the Mounties, who tended to be close-mouthed and discreet about their exploits and per-sonnel. The Force discouraged too much probing from outside, and this allowed their occasional mistakes to go unnoticed and undetected by the public for years, sometimes forever; it also helped maintain the illusion that the Mounties "always get their man." Actually, the Force's record at solving crimes or capturing escaped criminals is not much better than that of other police agencies. It's simply that the image of Sergeant Preston mushing across the frozen tundra makes such a great Hollywood script. Leopold, however, was a success. And since he is now deceased, the Horsemen decided it would be acceptable to put his photograph on display in a special section devoted to the "Red Squad" at the RCMP's museum at the Regina Training Academy. There is also on display a letter from the Communist Party officially notifying him of his expulsion from their ranks.

The biggest challenge the RCMP ever had came on September 7, 1945. On that day, Prime Minister William Lyon Mackenzie King learned that the Soviets had established a monstrous spy network in Canada. It wasn't the Mounties who exposed it, but a frightened little Soviet embassy cipher clerk with a fondness for brown-paper grocery bags. Igor Gouzenko came in out of the cold for a long chat with the police — thus starting what became known later as the Cold War. He quickly proved to be the Mounties' biggest security challenge, and their biggest headache. He took risks and complained publicly about bad treatment.

The year after Gouzenko defected, the RCMP set up the Special Branch, making it distinct from the Criminal Investigation Branch. It was given specific counter-espionage and intelligence-gathering sections, as well as units specializing in surveillance, out of which the world-famous RCMP Watchers Section would emerge.

As the Cold War escalated, the Mounties came under increasing pressure to expand their security operations. The Americans wanted more information on spies in Canada and Communist "fellow travellers," as they were called. These included people such as Prime Minister Lester Pearson, his friend Canadian ambassador Herbert Norman, who later committed suicide by jumping off a five-storey building in Cairo, and the entire National Film Board. Many critics believe that the board's creative energies suffered so devastating a blow after RCMP harassment that the Canadian film industry never really recovered. The Americans showed an insatiable appetite for intelligence and classified security information during this time, as they developed increasingly sophisticated methods of treatment and storage.

The focus of the Cold War changed in the mid-fifties. The Americans demanded that Canadian authorities add academics and homosexuals to their list of "subversives." Students, blacks, Natives and women's groups would come later. The Mounties acquiesced. The RCMP security service became increasingly busy, and grew tremendously in size and status.

By 1956, the Special Branch had become a full directorate within the RCMP, an indication of the importance it had acquired as the Cold War raged on and the Red Scare reached a frenzied climax in Canada. Hundreds of careers had been ruined, and some of the best university, cultural and bureaucratic talent in the country hounded out of jobs, and in some cases, off the continent. Already there were noises that gathering intelligence was much too delicate and complicated a task for the Mounties, and that somehow the men in red had been sucked in by the wiser Yanks. In 1954, Mark McClung, who headed a civilian group of analysts within the Special Branch of the RCMP, was asked to conduct a year-long study to find out how the idea of a civilian service would go over.

McClung, the son of suffragette Nellie McClung, was one of the Force's finest analysts at the time. Within a year he produced a report which came to be known as the "McClung Memorandum," which urged setting up a separate, civilian security service, called the Canadian Security Intelligence Organization (CSIO), to handle counter-espionage and anti-terrorism. It would be run by a civilian director and housed separately from the RCMP. Apart from the fact that it would not conduct security screening or look after counter-subversion, McClung's agency was not all that different from what would eventually be established more than a quarter of a century later.

McClung's ideas were ahead of his time. The Mounties

laughed at him, and that was the end of the matter for another fourteen years, until in 1968 Maxwell Mackenzie recycled the notion in the report to the cabinet of his Royal Commission on Security, part of which was rewritten and made public in 1969. It was not appropriate, said the Mackenzie Report, that a law enforcement agency such as the RCMP should be involved in both policing duties and intelligence work; the two were incompatible.

The Mounties fought back. Chief Superintendent Archibald (Archie) Barr, who had just returned to Ottawa to join the counter-espionage section of the security service, vividly remembers what happened: "The entire force was mobilized for one purpose only, and that was to discredit, destroy and knock down the recommendations of the Mackenzie Commission," he says. A special research branch was set up by RCMP Commissioner William Kelly to achieve that end. The group's mandate was to write papers refuting the recommendations and discrediting the Commission wherever possible.

The RCMP did succeed in preventing the "civilianization" of the security service, but Prime Minister Pierre Trudeau forced a compromise on the agency: the security service could remain within the Force, but the RCMP would have to accept a civilian director. Trudeau sent in John Starnes, a former Canadian ambassador to Germany and Egypt. A member of the Canadian Establishment and the descendant of an old Anglo-Montreal grain family, he had been educated in Europe and had served in the Canadian Intelligence Corps during World War II before joining External Affairs in 1948 and rising to the No. 2 job in the department — that of assistant undersecretary of state — where among other duties he was in charge of the department's official link with the RCMP. With him at the helm, it looked as if the RCMP might become a government agency truly accountable to the public.

Then came the seventies.

It was 1:00 a.m., July 26, 1974, a hot summer night in Montreal, but RCMP constable Robert Samson was wearing a raincoat and gloves. Carrying a brown athletic bag containing a package, he walked down a quiet residential street through the wealthiest part of Mount-Royal until he reached 407 Lazard Street, the home of Steinberg's Ltd. supermarket heiress Mitzi Steinberg and her husband Melvyn Dobrin. There was no one around as he slipped quietly into the darkness of the backyard and began fiddling with his package. It suddenly exploded, taking out quite a lot of Mitzi's hedge and large portions of Constable Samson as well. There was only a muffled, deadened noise as most of the explosion was absorbed by human flesh and clothing. Police later estimated that three sticks of dynamite, each ten centimetres long and two centimetres in diameter weighing a total of about half a kilo, had gone off.

Had Samson been bending over the package when it exploded, the full force would have caught him in the face and chest and ripped him in half. As it was, he stood, his clothes in tatters, blinded, burned and bleeding from his forehead, his upper torso, arms, legs and both hands. His right ear was almost severed, and the hearing in his left ear was gone forever. The vision in his left eye would be permanently impaired. The tips of four fingers on his left hand had disappeared and his right hand was ripped apart, hanging loosely at the end of his arm. Only five years of the kind of physical conditioning the RCMP demands from its members saved him from bleeding to death right there in the darkness. He somehow made his way out of the backyard and staggered off down Lazard.

The Dobrins slept through it all. They would not discover the damages — estimated at $1,407 — to their hedge, their central air conditioner and the windows at the back of the house until the light of day. But Notary Lionel Schwartz, who lived around the corner on Kenilworth Avenue and was still awake in his kitchen at the time, heard the noise. He looked out the window and saw a man lurching down Lazard Street. Schwartz concluded it was a noisy drunk and thought nothing more of it, wondering only what was happening to the neighbourhood.

Somehow Samson made his way back to his mother's house in Verdun. He had her call his friend Fernand Barré, who lived across the river in suburban Brossard. Barré took Samson to the nearby Montreal General Hospital, where he told doctors that his friend had been injured in a blast while cleaning his automobile engine with an ether-based solvent. The doctors were suspicious. It didn't take a medical genius to figure out that the extensive injuries to Samson's body were more consistent with those from a dynamite blast than from an ether explosion. Besides, the little bits of metal doctors plucked out of his body looked a lot more like a clockwork mechanism than car parts.

Later that morning, when Constable Samson, who was known to his colleagues as "Sam," did not show up and failed to call in at RCMP headquarters on Dorchester Boulevard in Westmount, his partner Corporal Raymond Langevin became understandably concerned. He telephoned Samson's home and then Samson's mother's apartment in Verdun. Mrs. Samson told him her son had been injured repairing his car. Corporal Langevin rushed over to the hospital to see his buddy but not before alerting his RCMP superiors who, after calling the hospital and talking to the doctors, began wondering whether there was any connection between the Mountie in hospital and the mysterious blast at 407 Lazard that the Montreal police had already begun investigating.

When what was left of Constable Samson had recovered enough to walk and talk, he was brought before the courts. Eventually Robert Samson's sordid, secret existence began to emerge. The man who had been a fairly low-ranking member of the RCMP security service had made friends with some fairly high-ranking people in Montreal organized crime. As it turned out, Constable Samson had been moonlighting for the Mob, and on the night of July 26 he was out on a little after-hours freelance assignment, planting a bomb in Mitzi Steinberg's backyard — just a small bomb, designed to take out a few windows. It might be just enough to convince the Dobrins that it was time for

Steinberg's to consider new policies about buying produce. After a fire commissioner's inquiry and a first court case that ended in a mistrial, Samson went on trial February 16, 1976 in Montreal, before a jury and Judge Peter Shorteno of the Quebec Superior Court. Shorteno, a tough, meticulous judge and a proud Italian-Canadian, harboured a natural dislike of all mobsters, but a particular dislike of crooked police officers. In court, Samson changed his story. It was a bomb blast in the Dobrins' backyard after all, he admitted. He had been there. He had not been injured while trying to repair his car.

He told the jury he had received an anonymous telephone call at his home shortly after midnight, from someone who did not identify himself but who asked to meet him immediately at the intersection of Kenilworth and Lazard. When he got there, he found no one, so he began searching around the neighbourhood, he said, in hopes of finding his anonymous caller. Hearing what he thought was the sound of a gate opening and the scuffling of feet, he wandered into the Dobrins' backyard and spotted a brown athletic bag. Thinking it might have something to do with his meeting, he bent over to pick it up, he said, and it exploded in his face.

Jean Morin, the bright young Crown prosecutor, recognized a tall tale when he heard one and began chipping away at Samson's latest concoction. Morin had a special gift for using ridicule to rip away at a witness's alibi. Under cross-examination he got Samson to admit that he had agreed to meet an anonymous caller on a moment's notice in the middle of the night, without knowing who the man was, what he might want to tell him or why they should meet right away. He didn't even ask his nameless friend why the rendezvous was to be held at such an unlikely spot — a street corner in a quiet residential neighbourhood in one of the wealthiest and best-patrolled parts of town where they would have been the only two men out at that time of night. And Samson, who had always been an obedient Mountie and always operated by the book, had on this occasion chosen to ignore it and had gone to the meeting without telling his superiors, without arranging back-up protection, without even obtaining overtime authorization. For all he knew, the whole thing could have been a hoax or a trap. He hadn't bothered to check it out. Samson was asking the jury to believe he had gone to the mysterious meeting in the unlikely spot, alone, unarmed, unsupported, unauthorized. He hadn't even used his own car; he'd taken a taxi. And he sent it away when he got there. Perhaps it was to make sure he'd have a hard time getting away if something went wrong, Prosecutor Morin suggested nastily. The jury chuckled. Samson's story was coming apart.

Actually, Samson told the court, the caller did offer a reference — one of Samson's undercover informers, somebody called "Henri." Judge Shorteno insisted that Samson give the full name of this informer. And he overruled an objection by the defence that policemen should not have to identify their sources in open court. Samson had no choice. He named his source — Henri Lemire, a Université de Montréal law student who had been his informant since 1972. Prosecutor Jean Morin was not even sure there was such a person; Samson might have been lying about that too. But less than twenty-four hours later Montreal city police brought in one Henri Lemire, alive, well and living in Ville St. Laurent. Better still, he was willing to testify against Samson.

Lemire said that not only had he never given Samson's unlisted telephone number to anyone, but he had never even used it himself. It was always Samson who had called him. Nor had he spoken to Samson for several months. The luckless ex-Mountie's last alibi had disappeared down the drain. Clearly, Samson was having trouble selling any version of his story to the jury — they didn't even believe his explanation as to why he was wearing a raincoat and gloves that hot summer night: apparently he thought it was going to rain. This was greeted with open hilarity.

Finally, irritated by the court's total disbelief in his story, Samson snapped that he'd done "much worse" for the RCMP. Judge Shorteno pounced on him instantly. "Oh yes, what?" And before anyone could stop him, Samson blurted out, "the APLQ, that was us." Judge Shorteno ordered him to explain and offered him protection from incrimination under the Canada Evidence Act.

"Let's say that at a certain time I committed a break and entry," Samson said. Four years earlier he, along with other members of the RCMP security service, some of whom he named, and members of the Montreal city and Quebec provincial police, had broken into the offices of l'Agence de presse libre du Québec, a left-wing news agency. They had ransacked the place and made off with piles of documents from the file cabinets.

The judge ordered a publication ban on this sensational bit of news. He reminded reporters that the remark had been made while the jury was out of the courtroom, during the legal procedure known as a "voir-dire." In fairness to the accused they could not report a word of it until his trial was over. Samson related that he had been there, along with other members of the Combined Anti-Terrorist Squad (CATS), when they broke into the second floor offices of the tiny news agency at 3459 St. Hubert Street in Montreal on the night of October 6, 1972. They stole almost a ton of documents and ripped the place apart to make it appear the news agency was the victim of a rival right-wing *independentiste* group. Samson said there were "other things" the Mounties had done. Crown Prosecutor Jean Morin gave Samson a chance to explain what he meant by these other things, but he refused to.

For the several Mountie observers in the courtroom, when Samson let the secret out, it was as if a bomb had gone off in *their* hands. They raced out of the room to telephone RCMP Headquarters right away. The news media stewed. Since nothing could be published until the trial was over, the Mounties would have a few days to warn everybody to keep their mouth shut, or at least to prepare an explanation and develop a damage-control strategy. It was a major catastrophe. The minister would have to be told. There would be questions in the House of Commons. The left-wing groups would demand an inquiry. The media would dig out their four-year-old files on the break-in and begin nosing around and asking questions. Who knew what they might find?

The jury took sixteen hours to convict Samson. The jurors wondered how such a clean-cut good-looking young man could have done such a thing. But the evidence was overwhelming. Even the chauffeur of Willie Obront, the Montreal millionaire meat merchant that a Quebec inquiry into organized crime had linked to the underworld, was prepared to testify. The prosecution accomplished this feat by showing the reluctant chauffeur several photographs Samson had taken of his fourteen-year-old daughter in somewhat adult poses on nights he took her out, supposedly for rides in his fancy car, after quiet suppers he had had with her family. The jury had heard enough. Guilty as charged. Samson did get off on a second charge of making a bomb. After all, anybody can have little bits of wire in his home. And lots of people buy nine-volt dry-cell batteries at Pascal's hardware store.

Judge Shorteno was still angry when he sentenced Samson two weeks later. What bothered him most was that Samson had never named his client. Who was he acting for? But since this mangled human being before him, who could barely see the judge and kept turning his head to the left to hear him, had never injured anyone but himself, had never collected any money and had already paid a high price for his treachery, Judge Shorteno decided that seven years, not the maximum fourteen years, would be enough.

The news media waited until the end of the trial to write about the break-in. Even then most reporters stuck to the main story — "Ex-Mountie Guilty of Bombing." It was the more immediate story, much easier to substantiate. Samson's claim about the break-in seemed so outrageous that most reporters discounted it as just one more lie he was telling, like so many others he had told in the witness box. Some reporters tried to investigate the story about the break-in by going back to the news agency members who had originally accused police of being responsible, but apart from a few interviews which repeated what was already known, the story went no further.

The Mounties appeared to have controlled the damage. The accomplices Samson had named in court — Montreal Detective-Sergeants Fernand Tanguay and Claude Marcotte and RCMP Sergeant Claude Brodeur — were not talking. Without corroborating evidence, reporters were at a loss. The break-in story hinged on the word of a convicted ex-Mountie who had lied repeatedly in court. But behind the scenes at RCMP Headquarters on Alta Vista Drive in Ottawa, everything was in turmoil. There was hell to pay. Everybody wanted to know if Samson's story was true and if so, who had been in on it.

Lieutenant-General Michael Dare, a former army man who was the new director general of the security service, ordered Chief Superintendent Donald Cobb, the head of the security service in Montreal, to conduct an investigation into what had happened, find out who was responsible and prepare a report for headquarters right away. For Cobb the investigation was easy. He was the officer who had authorized the APLQ break-in four years earlier. Dare was asking the very man who was responsible to find out who was responsible. In an ultra-secret report he filed to Dare on March 15, 1976, Cobb admitted his involvement and said the objective had been to get the membership list of the Mouvement pour la défense des prisonniers politiques du Québec, a sister organization of the APLQ which shared the same offices as the little news agency. The MDPPQ was a fundraising organization, set up to help pay legal bills of convicted Front de libération du Québec terrorists. Dare told Cobb to rewrite his report "with a language that would be more easily understood outside the Force." Cobb got the message. He rewrote his report. "Theft of records" became "removal of records." "Illegal entry" became "entry without warrant." Cobb was getting better as he wrote. "Stealing the documents" became "removing the documents" and a "crime" became "a loss."

There was no mention that it was a major security service operation known as, *Opération Bricole* (Operation Fix-it). Dare got the sanitized report he wanted — one he could present with confidence to then-Solicitor General Warren Allmand, a well-meaning but ineffectual minister whom the RCMP repeatedly misled. (The Mounties had a lot of fun with Allmand during his brief term as solicitor general. He complained later that the Mounties often lied to him while he was their boss.) On this occasion the Mounties got Allmand to tell the Commons with a straight face that RCMP Headquarters never knew about the break-in ahead of time, and that it was an isolated incident. Allmand even tried to deflect the responsibility for the lead role in the break-in to the Montreal and Quebec provincial police by depicting the RCMP as playing only a supporting role in the break-in. Less than a week later, after the Montreal and Quebec police forces had made it clear to Ottawa they wouldn't be taking the rap, Allmand had to admit in the Commons that the Mounties had been the driving force in the operation. Nevertheless, the RCMP had the minister using their vocabulary. The break-in had become an "entry without warrant." Allmand announced to the Commons that a full investigation was under way but did not say it was being conducted by the very man who had authorized the break-in in the first place.

The crisis seemed to be over. The media had plenty else to report that summer. In Ottawa the Liberals were under fire for trying to influence judges. The Conservatives had a new leader, Joe Clark. In Montreal the Olympics were being held amid unprecedented security because of the massacre of Israeli athletes at the Munich Olympics four years earlier. And in November, in what was the greatest political story in Quebec up till then, a general election was held and the Parti Québécois came to power. That left little time or space for reports on what everybody in authority was saying had been just an isolated little incident — what might easily have been called a fifth-rate burglary.

One journalist, however, thought otherwise. John Sawatsky of the *Vancouver Sun*'s Ottawa bureau kept after the story. Sawatsky, a tall, quiet man, did not let go. He kept at it, much as a dog keeps gnawing at a bone until he has gotten at the marrow. The marrow in Sawatsky's case appeared on December 7, 1976 splashed across the front page of the *Vancouver Sun*. Sawatsky had

talked to dozens of rank-and-file Mounties across the country
and come to the conclusion that the cover-up "extended into the
upper echelons of the RCMP in Ottawa." The RCMP superiors
had known about the break-in shortly after it took place "and
knowing the raid was illegal, turned a blind eye to it." The
Mounties had not only robbed the APLQ premises but conspired
to cover it up afterwards.

Canada being a nation of regions, and Vancouver being located where it is, the scoop never had the impact Sawatsky
wanted. Eventually his blockbuster story did drift back East and
joined other bits of information that had been leaking out here
and there suggesting the Mounties knew more than they were
telling. The federal cabinet, which had been discussing what to
do about the illegal activities of the Force off and on for the
previous six years, was not about to open this can of worms if it
was in any way avoidable. The new Parti Québécois government,
elected less than a month earlier in November 1976, did not
share Ottawa's reluctance. It may have had something to do with
the fact that many PQ members had felt for years they had been
victimized and spied upon by the Mounties.

A Quebec investigation produced three names of senior officers who had authorized the raid. They would be offered up as
sacrificial lambs to silence the growing clamour that those responsible be brought to justice. Chief Superintendent Cobb,
Inspector Jean Coutellier of the Quebec Police Force and Inspector Roger Cormier of the Montreal city police would be sent
before the courts. One from each force — it would appear fair
that way. All the other policemen, the ones who had actually
broken in and stolen the documents, would get off scot-free. But
instead of break-in and entry, conspiracy, theft, burglary, damage
to personal property and conspiracy to destroy evidence, which
is what ordinary people who had carried out such a raid might
have been charged with, the three senior cops would be charged
merely with "failing to obtain a search warrant." It was as if
*Opération Bricole* had been perfectly legal and proper and all that
happened was that there had been a small oversight on their way

over — somebody had forgotten to pick up a search warrant.

All through the spring of 1977 reports kept leaking out in Montreal and Ottawa that there was more to the break-in story than Ottawa was admitting. Francis Fox, who had just taken over as the new solicitor general, had said at first that the APLQ break-in was an "exceptional and isolated" incident. Some journalists remembered that back on December 18, 1970, at the height of the police paranoia over the Quebec kidnap crisis, there had been a similar mysterious kind of break-in at the offices of the Praxis Corp., an anti-poverty organization in Toronto. The place had been ransacked and set on fire. Documents were taken and some of the information they contained showed up a year later in a secret letter signed June 15, 1971 by then-Solicitor General Jean-Pierre Goyer. It was based on RCMP information and warned of the existence of an "extra-parliamentary opposition." This was the notorious "enemies list" of the Liberal government.

Six months later, in June 1971, the offices of a left-wing publishing company in Toronto, James, Lewis and Samuel, were broken into and files were stolen. They were later returned by police who said they had been found in a ditch. Then in May, Don McCleery and Gilles Brunet, two Mounties who had been fired in 1973 for refusing to sever their relationship with Mitchell Bronfman, a prominent Montreal businessman, decided the time had come for them to spill the beans on some other dirty tricks. McCleery, a former staff-sergeant and twenty-year veteran of the Force, was a no-nonsense kind of cop who operated by the law of the street. He was one of the few genuine heroes of the October kidnap crisis: it was his hunch to follow a terrorist suspect, dismissed by other cops, that led him to the north-end Montreal hideout where British Trade Commissioner James Cross was being held hostage. Like Samson, and so many other Mounties, McCleery had grown up on the wrong side of the tracks in Verdun, and was not above bending the law a little when it came to the higher calling of protecting national security as he defined it. Brunet, a veteran security service Mountie, had been

McCleery's sidekick for years. After being booted out, they opened a private security firm.

McCleery watched incredulously on television as Fox told the Commons that the APLQ break-in was an "exceptional and isolated" incident. As he explained later, "it was the biggest cover-up since the blanket was invented." He decided to go straight to Ottawa with what he knew — much of which involved his own on behalf of the Mounties, including a theft of dynamite and the burning of a barn that served as a meeting hall for left-wing and radical groups.

McCleery and Brunet met for six hours with Deputy Solicitor General Roger Tassé and Philippe Landry, assistant deputy attorney general, on June 6 and told the two officials about illegal mail opening, "numerous thefts of documents" and "participation and assistance to the Central Intelligence Agency in offensive activities in Canada." McCleery was referring to the time several years earlier that the Cuban consulate in Montreal, the centre of Cuban spy operations in Canada, had mysteriously exploded and burned down. As soon as they heard McCleery's allegations, it was clear to the federal officials that there was no way they could keep the wrongdoing secret. What McCleery and Brunet had told the two public servants, they might also be telling their good friend Conservative MP Elmer MacKay, who was already demanding a full judicial inquiry into RCMP activities. Things were starting to come apart for the Mounties.

The three senior policemen before the courts — Cobb, Coutellier and Cormier, or "the Three Cs" as the news media called them — pleaded guilty, and on June 17, 1977, Judge Roger Vincent gave them all "unconditional discharges," which meant they would not have criminal records and could go right back to their police jobs the next day. In other words, they really weren't crooks after all. The RCMP even paid Cobb's legal bills. And of course, because the men had pleaded guilty, none of the information about what had really happened had to be made public.

There was an immediate massive public outcry from civil libertarians, left-wing groups, editorialists and church and la-

bour organizations. The PQ government was furious. Premier
René Lévesque ordered an inquiry to investigate the break-in as
well as other RCMP crimes in Quebec. To run it, he picked Jean
Keable, a young, soft-spoken, Quebec City lawyer who had once
run for the party in St. Laurent riding, a difficult seat for the PQ.
Keable may have had Péquiste sympathies, but he was motivated
above all else by an enduring love for the law and a respect for
democratic traditions.

The new PQ government hoped the public inquiry into RCMP
activities in Quebec would help dispel a widespread notion that
there was something dark and ugly in its past linking it to the
October kidnap crisis. As well, the PQ wanted to assert itself as a
democratic government and respond to the public clamour and
media outrage over the sentence handed down to the three
policemen by Judge Vincent.

For its part, the federal government feared the Keable inquiry
might uncover the fact that the Mounties had been doing a little
political spying on the side for them. The PQ had by then
discovered that the Mounties had been spying on them for years,
treating Péquistes as dangerous subversives and traitors who had
to be stopped, even if it meant bending the law a little . . . or a lot.

The Mounties demanded that the federal cabinet do something to prevent a PQ government from conducting an inquiry
into their operations, or failing this, that it set up its own royal
commission of inquiry to head off the Keable Inquiry at the pass,
bolster sagging Mountie morale, vindicate the RCMP security
service and present it in a more favourable light — in short, to
polish up the old Mountie image a bit.

Ottawa prepared to do everything it could legally to thwart the
efforts of the Keable Inquiry and frustrate its ability to operate
effectively. The federal government would withhold evidence,
refusing to turn over documents with the excuse that they were
items of national security. And when it couldn't use that excuse,
it resorted to declaring them cabinet secrets. Prime Minister
Pierre Trudeau and his entire cabinet would refuse to testify
before the inquiry. As well, the government would challenge

Keable's jurisdiction before the courts, and openly attack his integrity. It would not stop until it had succeeded in putting the Keable Inquiry out of business a year-and-a-half later.

Finally, Ottawa set up its own royal commission of inquiry on July 6, 1977, headed by Justice David McDonald of the Alberta Supreme Court. His co-commissioners were Guy Gilbert, a Montreal lawyer and Donald Rickerd, a Toronto lawyer.

The three commissioners had interesting backgrounds. Justice McDonald was a former president of the Alberta Liberal Party, having served with distinction from 1965 to 1968. Gilbert was plugged in to the Outremont Liberal establishment and was a friend of Energy Minister Marc Lalonde. Even while he sat on the inquiry investigating Mountie links to Liberal cabinet ministers, Gilbert continued to contribute financially to the Liberal Party's electoral coffers. Donald Rickerd was president of the Donner Canadian Foundation and a friend of Solicitor General Fox. Both had served as directors of the Donner. As spy novelist Ian Adams pointed out in *Canadian Dimension* magazine: " " . . . people who have proven to be stalwart allies of the Liberal Party of Canada are supposed to find out whether the state presided over by the Liberal Party is guilty of using the security services against citizens of this country." Just to be safe, the federal inquiry would report not to Parliament, as other royal commissions usually did, but directly to the Liberal government, which would decide which portions of the report it wanted to be made public. The Mountie secrets the government wanted to keep hidden would remain hidden, all in the name of national security. And in the mandate it handed McDonald, Ottawa made it clear that the federal inquiry would have to be especially careful not to offend foreign intelligence agencies. The McDonald Commission opened public hearings in Montreal in December 1977. The Keable Inquiry had been under way since June. Working almost together at times, the two commissions would produce evidence devastating to the Mounties' hallowed reputation — but it was an uphill battle.

Right from the start, Keable was in trouble. Not only did the federal government withhold documents and witnesses, the provincial Liberals in Quebec pitched in and opened a second front against Keable, accusing him of being a former separatist candidate who was out to make political capital on behalf of the separatists. When that didn't work, they launched a smear campaign against him. Former Quebec Solicitor General Fernand Lalonde, whose officials had conducted the 1976 Quebec investigation into the APLQ break-in, and St. Laurent MNA Claude Forget, against whom Keable had run as a PQ candidate in 1973, took the unprecedented action of openly attacking a public inquiry commissioner while an inquiry was going on. They used the parliamentary immunity they enjoyed in the legislature to suggest there might be something going on between Keable and a vivacious thirty-four-year-old police spy, Carole Devault.

Devault, who was Source 171 of the Montreal police but known more familiarly as "Poupette" (Dolly) to the policemen with whom she worked, picked up $15,000 for two months' work as an undercover police spy among the FLQ terrorists at the height of the October kidnap crisis. She was known variously as Rachel, Suzanne and Severine to her FLQ friends. In 1977 she decided to turn against her Montreal city police handler, Detective Captain Julien Giguère, and tell all to the Keable inquiry. Suggesting sexual involvement, the Quebec Liberals made a big thing out of the fact that during the inquiry Keable was staying in the same Montreal hotel as Poupette, in fact, right down the hall from her. He had even been seen having supper with Poupette, they said. What they forgot to mention was that there were other inquiry officials present at the supper, and that it had ended at a respectable hour after which Keable returned alone to his hotel room to spend the night with his wife, who was staying there with him. Keable, aware that he had to be above all suspicion, retaliated against the Liberals' charges by posing for newspaper photographs with his quite obviously pregnant and smiling wife. That ended the Liberal smear campaign.

Carole Devault soon became the star witness of the Keable Inquiry, revealing how Montreal police had been only too happy to keep the FLQ going after the October crisis was over. She told Keable how she recruited infatuated young adolescents as would-be terrorists into FLQ cells which Montreal police could then control. She also helped prepare false communiqués with the full knowledge of Montreal police. On one occasion they even supplied the paper. When a bomb was assembled in her bathtub, police supplied the dynamite — which may explain why it didn't go off. Devault's testimony was intriguing, but it was only the tip of the iceberg. Over the next few years, the Keable and Mc-Donald Commissions uncovered hundreds of illegal operations by the Horsemen. One ugly thing after another kept crawling out. The Mounties had been systematically violating Canadian law in the name of national security for two decades, even longer.

They had lied, cheated, stolen, committed arson, opened people's mail, held people without warrant, conspired, destroyed evidence, created mischief and deliberately misled other police forces. And when it appeared they might be found out, they had conspired to cover it up to hide their crimes. The Mounties had refined deception to a high art; they had staged a massive invasion of individual privacy and abused the democratic rights of the very citizens they had been hired to protect.

In most cases, the RCMP's crimes were committed in the name of national security — saving the nation from a hidden terrorist enemy which only they knew about. Only rarely was greed or personal advancement involved. It was as if the security service had declared its own private dirty war — a secret little war that it would fight with the same illegal means as the enemy it had defined for itself. Time and again Mounties who testified before the Keable and McDonald inquiries spoke as if they were soldiers at war, not policemen with a duty to maintain law and order. They developed a new vocabulary of martial terms to designate their illegal operations — just like real soldiers have for their military operations. Sexy codes names were invented — Cathedral A (for illegal mail openings), Vampire (a break-in to plant a bug), Puma (surreptitious entry into private homes and buildings), Cobra (setting up a wiretap on a telephone line). They used non-generic code names for specific operations such as *Opération Bricole* (the APLQ break-in) or Operation Ham (the theft of the Parti Québécois membership list.) Featherbed was the name of a hoary old file they kept on the indiscretions and embarrassing private pastimes of federal politicians. Operation Checkmate involved spreading false information about people they didn't like to get them fired, break up their marriages or make them shunned or rejected by society.

The Mounties decided that since the FLQ issued communiqués which sowed fear and confusion; so would they. The FLQ stole dynamite, so would they. The FLQ resorted to arson; so would they. The FLQ spread false rumours about people; so would they. After a while the RCMP security service had become just like their enemy. In fact, they had become their enemy. And when things quieted down after the October crisis, they even went so far as to issue fake communiqués urging *felquiste* supporters to continue the struggle — after all, if the *felquistes* were no longer a threat, the Horsemen wouldn't have nearly so much to do. A lot of guys might find themselves posted out of la Belle Province and into Moose Jaw, Saskatchewan and other well-known hotspots. As well, the government might not be quite so supportive of, or generous with, the RCMP if the Mounties were no longer needed to save Canada from the "French menace." In fact, the notion of "disruptive tactics" to fight the FLQ was countenanced right up to the highest levels of the RCMP and given the tacit agreement of the Liberal administration.

Philip Rosen, in an excellent research paper he prepared for the Library of Parliament in 1984, sets out succinctly how the arm's length relationship between the politicians and the Mounties, which had served Canadian society so well when it came to regular law enforcement issues, presented a difficult problem when it came to intelligence gathering and security work:

The October Crisis of 1970 stunned the government, which found itself with inadequate information as to the nature and scope of Quebec separatism. The government requested the RCMP to undertake a "pro-active" strategy in this area — to try and get advance information as to the intentions and activities of nationalist organizations and, if possible, to prevent or "counter" disruptive acts. This the Security Service proceeded to do with a vengeance. It embarked on an extensive campaign of intelligence-gathering, infiltration, harassment and disruption directed at virtually all stripes of nationalist sentiment in Quebec.

The silence of the politicians sent a clear message to the Mounties. The government did not care how the Mounties did their job, as long as it got done. No questions were asked. Everybody hoped things would work out. They never did. The problem with Mounties breaking the law was discussed in an ultra-secret memo presented to the powerful special inner cabinet of government on November 20, 1970 — at the height of the October kidnapping crisis. It was discussed, but no decision was reached.

John Starnes, the RCMP's director general of security, made an effort to let his boss, Solicitor General George McIlraith, know what was going on without saying too much. They met on November 24, 1970. Starnes told McIlraith point-blank that the RCMP had been carrying on illegal activities for two decades. But Starnes mentioned no specific cases and McIlraith was certainly not about to ask. Starnes even gave McIlraith a memo about it. Nine years later McIlraith told the McDonald Inquiry that he had not read it. The McDonald Inquiry wanted to know why. Failing eyesight prevented him from reading many documents that came his way during his last years in the cabinet, McIlraith replied.

The McDonald Inquiry obtained handwritten notes from a December 1, 1970 meeting of the cabinet committee on security and intelligence at which the issue of Mounties breaking the law came up again, but again no decision had been reached. Later that month, at another meeting of the cabinet committee on security chaired by Trudeau himself, they discussed whether they should provide "some kind of immunity from arrest" for agents who "have to break the law" to infiltrate the FLQ groups. Again no decision was reached. It was only a year later, on September 8, 1971, when the FLQ had almost disappeared, that John Turner, the justice minister at the time, submitted a memo to the full cabinet dealing with the problem of Mounties breaking the law. By then the Mounties were heavily into illegal activities, unchecked, uncontrolled. Turner, trying to justify the RCMP's actions, euphemistically called for "freedom within the law" for the Mounties. For a third time, the politicians passed the buck and no decision was taken. The matter was simply referred back to the cabinet committee on security and intelligence. A series of cabinet memos and other documents released by the Mc-Donald Inquiry in the spring of 1979 showed clearly that the politicians knew what was going on. They simply chose to do nothing. And the Mounties, freed from government control and supervision, resorted to the lowest form of police tactics they knew.

The security service organized a special branch known as "G-Ops" which had written authorization from headquarters in Ottawa and the complicity of Prime Minister Trudeau and his cabinet to implement a program of "disruptive tactics" against whomever they judged to be enemies of the state. Somewhere along the line, this came to mean not only terrorists, but just about anyone G-section decided was a dangerous radical, dissident or reformer. The Mounties had lost the ability to distinguish between terrorism and legitimate political dissent. They spied on labour leaders, labour unions, student groups, protesters, strikers, demonstrators, politicians, church groups, journalists — virtually anyone with whose views they did not agree. Soon they were spying without the slightest moral hesitation on a democratically constituted political party, the Parti Québécois, which operated completely aboveboard and advocated political change through dramatic, though perfectly peaceful, means. It would not be until 1975 that the Mounties would receive specific orders, from Trudeau himself in fact, that the PQ should be treated no differently than any other political party and therefore they should stop spying on it.

When G-Ops' activities became known during the McDonald Commission, the public was outraged. One operation in particular — Operation Ham — shocked the country. Operation Ham took place in January, 1973, only three months after *Opération Bricole*, the APLQ break-in, and it was a massive operation in every respect — sixty-six Mounties, men and machines, outside consultants and at least two dry runs. The Horsemen needed a lot of manpower because they were going after a big target, the PQ whom they regarded as just as threatening to the structure of Canada as any far-left "Commie-sympathizing" terrorist gang. Never mind that the PQ was a recognized political party with entirely legitimate aims that wanted to separate Quebec off from the rest of Canada by due process of legislation. The Péquistes were a problem and the Horsemen were going to take care of them.

Operation Ham was planned with a military precision that would have put the armed forces to shame. The Mounties decided they should enter the offices of a computer data firm, Les Messageries Dynamiques Inc., at 9820 Jeanne Mance Street in the north end of Montreal, and steal computer tapes containing the PQ's membership list. The five dozen men involved included a squad of look-out men from the Watcher Service to act as look-outs, locksmiths to help enter the building, a fleet of unmarked vehicles from the RCMP transport section and the communications people with walkie-talkies and special equipment for monitoring other police frequencies, another team to handle the copying of the tapes, and one last team near headquarters in Montreal to handle logistics and co-ordinate the whole operation. After the Mounties found out the layout of the building, the location of the tapes and the usual patterns of activity on weekends, they staged a series of preliminary break-ins. A first break-in in November to locate and silence the front-door burglar alarm system went off without a hitch. A second visit on November 30, 1972 involved getting past the fancy locks, newly installed on the second-floor computer office within the building.

Finally the big night arrived. Operation Ham was thrown into gear. The Watcher Service sent out five unmarked cars to patrol five blocks deep. Fifteen men entered the building, each with a specific task. They had taken the precaution of stripping themselves of all identity, wallets, watches, rings and clothes labels in case something went wrong and they were caught and had to give false names. Some watched, some picked, some raced upstairs, some grabbed. They took the tapes, fled with them, copied them at a pre-arranged location, MICR Systems Limited in Westmount Square, and then returned, replaced the tapes and wiped the premises clean of any evidence. Everything went off as planned. The duplicate tapes were shipped off to RCMP headquarters in Ottawa where they produced an incredible print-out — six feet high.

The Mounties loved to play games with Warren Allmand. Of all the political bosses they had, he was their favourite solicitor general. They fooled him, they lied to him and they even spied on him. They brought up Warren Hart, an American black who had worked as an FBI undercover agent. Hart, who also spied on black and Native groups for the Mounties, wore a body-pack when he talked to Allmand. The Mounties suspected Allmand because of his mildly left-of-centre views. He was always talking in favour of silly, outmoded notions such as democratic rights, welfare and unemployment insurance.

Allmand told the McDonald Inquiry: "I felt very much betrayed. . . . It appears now that I did not get full answers even when I did ask specifically."

On one occasion Allmand asked the Mounties if they opened people's mail. "No," they replied, but they added that it might be a good thing if the law were changed to allow them to open people's mail. The Mounties explained later to the McDonald Inquiry that the reason they had replied in the negative to

Allmand was because it was not the official RCMP policy to open people's mail, even though it might have happened from time to time. The McDonald Inquiry discovered that the Mounties had been opening people's first-class mail without a warrant for several decades. Prime Minister Trudeau said that if a terrorist were caught every fifth time a letter was opened, it would be "a good average" and added that he was not too excited about " a little mail tampering." However, he was way off in his batting average. In more than twenty years of mail opening, involving thousands of letters, only one terrorist was ever caught through illegal mail opening.

The McDonald Inquiry investigated seven attempts by the Mounties during a two-year period between 1971 and 1972 to use intimidation, even threats of violence and psychological terror, to recruit informers. They might be suspected terrorists, or fringe players, but often they were people who were not themselves part of any suspect group. They just happened to be neighbours, friends or relatives of someone the Mounties had targeted as a suspect for surveillance. They repeatedly violated the right to privacy of individuals and the confidentiality of government records including income tax returns and private medical information. On May 25, 1972 an agreement with the Department of National Revenue was approved giving the Mounties the right to examine supposedly confidential income tax records. In return the department got wiretap information. The agreement was supposed to cover organized crime, but soon it came to include all sorts of other types of cases. And even before the agreement was signed, the Mounties had been systematically going through income tax files, health records, unemployment insurance declarations and industry department forms to dig up dirt on whomever they considered a suspect.

People were picked up off the street and spirited away for intensive interrogation sessions in farm fields or cheap motels near Montreal. The Mounties called it "ego-deflation." G-4 operatives Sergeant Laurent Hugo, a former insurance salesman, and Corporal Bernard Dubuc testified they picked up one man and took him to a motel outside Montreal where they grilled him for fifteen hours. At one point they made him stand in the corner of the room, his face up against the wall, to get him, they testified, into the right "mood" to co-operate.

Torching the barn at Ste. Anne de la Rochelle, Quebec was the most notorious and bizarre of all the RCMP's dirty tricks. The barn, known as La Grange du petit Québec libre, was located on a farm property about ninety-five kilometres southeast of Montreal. The Paul Rose and Jacques Lanctot gangs hid there in the summer of 1970 just before they staged their political kidnappings. Paul Rose had bought the farm through a friend, Yvon Tremblay, using money from one of his scams.

Police first found out about the barn when they raided a Laurentian chalet in June 1970, where they arrested four FLQ members who were preparing to kidnap U.S. consul Harrison Burgess. They found a ten-page document outlining FLQ demands for the release of the American diplomat, 900 kilos of dynamite, $28,260 in cash and the deed of sale for the farm in Ste. Anne. After the Laurentian chalet raid, the CIA began taking a more active interest in Quebec terrorism, and poured men and money into Montreal.

On June 22, 1970, the day after the Laurentian chalet raid, more than a dozen men from the anti-terrorist squad swooped down on the barn but missed the gang members. Jacques Lanctot, who was on the run after the aborted kidnapping of the Israeli consul four months earlier, the two Rose brothers and Marc Carbonneau and Francis Simard — two more soon-to-be kidnappers — had been tipped off. They were all hiding in the attic of the farmhouse. Had they been found that day, the October crisis would never have taken place.

Police searched the place briefly, and then gave up. After that the FLQ terrorist gangs left the farm and no longer used it as a hideout because they knew police would have it under surveillance. In February 1971, when the Roses needed money for court-related expenses, they sold the barn and farmhouse property to the Jazz libre du Québec. On hot summer weekends the farm served as a retreat for Quebec artists, writers, intellectuals and their families. It became a favourite meeting place for radicals and "politico-weirdos" of all kinds, a kind of co-operative commune and community centre. There was nothing secret about it. It was given a big magazine spread in 1971 in *Perspectives*, a French-language counterpart to the long defunct English-language *Weekend* magazine, with a circulation of 500,000.

The barn was a gold mine of information for police. Their files show they saw Bourassa's secretary show up one day in the summer of 1970. They had her fired during the October crisis as a security risk. A future Péquiste cabinet minister, Gérald Godin, was reported to have visited the barn, as well as a couple of ex-FLQ bombers, a few guys with links to Palestinians and even some draft-dodgers. Everybody went to the barn, and, because of its relatively isolated location, everybody had to go there by private car. The barn's location made it particularly easy to keep under surveillance; sometimes police could get licence plate registrations of arriving cars checked out and have the information in their hands before the evening had barely begun. And since people wandered freely to and fro between the barn and the farmhouse, photographing visitors using simple telephoto equipment was fairly easy.

It was not clear why the Mounties decided to burn the barn. Keable and McDonald were told that the Mounties wanted to prevent a meeting from taking place between the Black Panthers and the FLQ. Yet the barn was an ideal spot for the Mounties to cover with a surveillance team. The Keable Inquiry investigated a report that the orders to burn the barn had come from the FBI in Burlington, Vermont, and that the Mounties were only doing the bidding of the Americans, but the inquiry was unable to confirm this. No evidence was ever produced that a Black Panther meeting was ever planned or that one took place.

On the first trip out to Ste. Anne to burn the barn the Mounties' car hit a huge rock on a dirt road, and had to be towed back to Montreal. A few days later they tried again, four of them.

They set out early in the day so they could do all their chores. First they stopped at each of their homes to change into old clothes, then they stopped to look at some country real estate, and then they stopped to pick apples. By then, it was close to suppertime and they were hungry, so they stopped for hot dogs. One of the Mounties — Corporal Blier, who was a big man — had three. Then they stopped at a tavern in Granby, Quebec, for a few beers to wash down the food. Perhaps the hot dogs were not as fresh as they might have been, because Blier got sick to his stomach. (He was not a lucky man. His wife had just left him with their two daughters.) Then it started to rain. Then Blier began to gag. They stopped several times along the way for him to get some air.

It was midnight by the time they reached the gravel road next to the farm, but they were still about three kilometres from the barn itself. Blier stayed in the car while the others got oil out of the trunk. They couldn't remember if they had brought stove oil or motor oil. There is a difference. Blier stayed with the car and the other three headed out in the darkness through the swamp and the fields. Half-an-hour later they were at the barn. Two of the Mounties went in, while a third remained outside as a lookout. They tried to set fire to the concrete floor by pouring oil on it and igniting it. The oil burned, black and thick, with lots of flame and smoke, but the concrete didn't want to ignite. They raced away and watched from a distance. Ten minutes later the fire had gone out. They went back to their car to think up a new plan of attack, but the car broke down. They worked on it and managed to get it going again, more or less, so then they drove very slowly to nearby Magog, Quebec, thirty kilometres away, to get another getaway car from an informer they knew who lived there. They woke him up in the early morning hours and persuaded him to lend them his half-ton pickup truck.

The luckless Mounties crowded into the truck and sped back to the barn. On the way, Blier finally threw up and seemed to feel better for a while. They arrived back where they had parked before. Blier again stayed with the truck; the others again headed out on foot across the fields with a second quart of oil. This time they poured the oil up against the wooden walls of the barn and it caught quickly. Success at last! The loss of the barn was estimated at several thousand dollars by the owners.

Staff-Sergeant Donald McCleery told the Keable Inquiry later: "Don't get the idea we were a bunch of hoodlums burning barns. I was in the security service twenty years and only one barn went up."

It was the Supreme Court of Canada that prevented Keable from investigating the RCMP's methods, techniques and overall security operations. The court told him on October 31, 1978, barely a year after he got started, that he had to confine his investigation to individual criminal acts committed in Quebec, or directly related to Quebec. He couldn't wander off all over the country in search of Mountie wrongdoing. This would have a profound impact on the findings of the inquiry because it forced Keable to focus more on individual activities and individual Mounties, and in fact, more than a dozen Mounties were charged with offences under the Criminal Code. Only one Mountie, however, served any time in jail — Robert Samson, who was ultimately responsible for all the disclosures.

Today Samson lives a quiet life on a farm in Quebec's Eastern Townships. The site, off a dirt road high in the hills, overlooks some of the prettiest scenery in the whole province. Samson's home is a field-stone cottage; he built it himself after he got out of prison. Not far away, leaning up against a barn, is an ominously large wooden boat: big, black and red, it vaguely resembles a giant tugboat, or a modern copy of an antique fishing trawler. It is surely the largest wooden boat in a farmyard anywhere in the Eastern Townships.

Samson is still too bitter, secretive, suspicious and defiant to talk much about the past. He has nothing to say. Even shaking hands appears to be an effort. He has paid his debt to society, and now asks only to be left alone. He survived five years in prison by keeping his mouth shut and he's not about to open it for some book writer from the city. No one's bothered him, he says, neither the Mounties nor the Mob. "Why should they?" he asks. "I've done my time. If I can survive in prison I can survive here." He is still a handsome man, and there is almost a glint in his good eye as he looks towards his boat. Someday, he says, he'll sail it away.

Unlike Keable, McDonald headed a federal inquiry and so was able to be more far-reaching in his probe. He could investigate specific acts of wrongdoing by the Mounties anywhere in Canada as well as examine the Force's policies, techniques, directives and methods of operation. In fact, he could investigate anything that put the security service in the mess it was in. He could even look at the federal government's role in all this, whether it knew about or had even encouraged illegal activities by the Mounties.

After having reviewed countless instances of abuse on the part of the Mounties, McDonald came to the conclusion that responsibility for national security and intelligence should be taken away from the RCMP and given to a new civilian agency. However, protective security — keeping an eye on VIPs, etc. — would still remain the province of the Horsemen. McDonald urged strict control of the new agency by the government — something the Mounties' security service had lacked — plus an independent review agency made up of people from outside government, as well as a joint parliamentary committee with the right to monitor the activities of the agency.

The notion behind the new spy agency was really quite simple. What the Mounties had been doing illegally the new domestic spy agency would be able to do legally, provided it had the approval of a Federal Court judge. At the operations level, out in the street, the new agency would have more freedom and more leeway than the Mounties ever had. Since it would not be a law enforcement agency, it would not always have to be looking for evidence that would have to stand up in court. The new agency would not have to notify people, as the Mounties have to, ninety days after they have been wiretapped or bugged. The new agency would be able to go into people's homes surreptitiously, provided it had authorization from a Federal Court judge and brought along a police accompaniment. Agents could plant bugs, wiretap telephone lines, open first-class mail and poke into private health, employment and government income tax records without ever having to tell a targeted individual what they had been up to. They could do all these things, but there would be enough checks and balances to make sure the system wasn't being abused. There would be no more dirty tricks.

The move to split off security and intelligence from the RCMP should have raised a storm of protest in 1981, as it had after publication of the Mackenzie Report in 1969. But after the beating that the Force's reputation took during the McDonald and Keable hearings, the notion of a new civilian spy agency sounded just fine to a lot of people who otherwise would have been dead set against the idea. And morale among the Mounties themselves was too low to permit any kind of organized opposition. The stage was set for the entry of Canada's new, clean, responsible, civilian security and intelligence service: an organization that would stand as a shining example of probity and integrity — a light unto the intelligence agencies of the world. Everyone hoped.

# "AND NOW FOR SOMETHING COMPLETELY DIFFERENT"

SETTING UP THE NEW CIVILIAN SECURITY and intelligence agency proved more difficult than expected. The Mounties were not about to relinquish their hold over security and intelligence without a fight. The new RCMP commissioner, Robert Simmonds, made a big production out of the fact that the Mounties were putting their house back in order. By late 1982 stories about Mountie horrors from the seventies were already fading into the past. The Mounties have always had a powerful lobby on Parliament Hill, and now it went to work in earnest for them. The Conservative Opposition was soon saying that there was really no reason to set up a separate security service since the RCMP could still do the job better than any civilian agency.

The Liberal government was caught in a bind. It didn't want to alienate the Mounties, but it didn't want to ignore the McDonald Report. After all, the judge had spent four long years of his life and $10 million of taxpayers' money preparing his report. There had to be something worth taking from it. So the government stalled for time. After having held back the McDonald Report seven months until August 25, 1981, the Liberal government waited another twenty-one months before finally bringing out legislation setting up a new civilian security service to be carved out of the remains of the old RCMP security service. It would be called the Canadian Security Intelligence Service (CSIS). People were told it would be pronounced "Cee-sus."

Bill C-157 was presented in the Commons on May 18, 1983 by Solicitor General Robert Kaplan and was immediately dubbed "The Spy Bill." It provoked immediate outrage on all sides because it bore little resemblance to the reasoned, balanced, liberal approach the McDonald Report had urged on the politicians. It was as if the government had written security service legislation for some autocratic country on a far away planet that had yet to discover the concept of civil liberties. The joke going around was that Kaplan had simply borrowed the Soviet legislation on the KGB and translated it.

Where McDonald had urged more public control over the activities of the security service, Kaplan's legislation offered less control. Bill C-157 went out of its way to shield the new spy agency. One clause proposed to give the director of the new security service the right to overrule the solicitor general on security matters. Kaplan said this was done deliberately so the public would be sure there was no partisan influence on CSIS operations; critics replied that the new security agency would be outside government control. Where the McDonald Report had said the new security service agents must not be above the law, Kaplan's bill would have allowed CSIS agents to commit illegal acts whenever they thought it was "reasonably necessary," provided they used "reasonable means." This, it was pointed out, amounted to a licence for CSIS to commit crimes. The Mounties joked that with legislation like Bill C-157, they would never have had to break the law.

The bill allowed CSIS to do almost whatever it wanted, investigate virtually anything it wanted, in any way it wanted, and then tell the solicitor general to mind his own business. It was so draconian that even mentioning publicly the name of a CSIS official would be enough to land someone in jail for up to five years. Of course, with a law like that in effect, the CSIS director's speeches might not get very much attention.

The protest against Bill C-157 came from everywhere — from civil liberties groups, the legal community, human rights groups, provincial attorneys general, the academic community and others. In the Commons both the Conservatives and the New Democratic Party spoke out against the bill. The government quickly realized the bill was so bad that it was not even worth trying to defend. So without a second reading in the Commons, the faulty goods were turned over to a special Senate committee hurriedly formed to try to find a way out of the mess. The man picked for this delicate job was the veteran bureaucrat who had been Trudeau's most trusted man in security matters, Michael Pitfield, the former Clerk of the Privy Council. He would head the committee. Critics were skeptical. They assumed the government was simply stalling for more time and that a Senate committee headed by Pitfield would present much the same legislation Pitfield's people had been responsible for in the first place.

The Pitfield committee sat through much of 1983, hearing witnesses and reading submissions. It worked quickly and issued a report in November, making a total of forty recommendations that corrected some of the worst abuses of the original legislation. The report was called *A Delicate Balance* and offered what Pitfield called "a more appropriate balance between collective and individual security." Many of the recommendations were along the lines of the McDonald Report. The government quietly dropped the original legislation, Bill C-157, and announced that it would try again. It would present a brand new bill in the New Year based on the Senate committee's recommendations.

Bill C-9 was introduced in the Commons on January 18, 1984. It contained virtually everything Pitfield had recommended as well as many of McDonald's recommendations. It was a tremendous improvement over Bill C-157, but the critics said it did not go far enough. Solicitor General Kaplan admitted to the news media that it appeared his second try "isn't a political winner." Like its predecessor, Bill C-9 came down heavily on the side of the security service at the expense of civil rights. For instance, the special five-member independent monitoring committee set up under Bill C-9 to oversee and review the activities of the new security agency would not be allowed to see cabinet documents. That meant that if there was a document the spy boys didn't want the monitoring committee to see, all they had to do was to make sure it was classified as a cabinet document. Then they could be sure it would remain their little secret — just between them and the government.

Animosity between the Liberals and the Opposition was running high over the legislation. New Democratic Party Justice critic Svend Robinson called the legislation "a massive assault on the fundamental civil liberties and privacy of Canadians and anyone visiting our country," and undertook a filibuster to defeat the bill. Political science professor C. E. S. Franks, in a 1984 paper entitled *Parliament and Intelligence and Security Issues*, put the blame squarely on the Liberal government. He said it had made no effort to have the report of the McDonald Commission debated in the Commons:

"Quite the reverse, it prevented Parliament from doing so by not even tabling the report. This was worse than oversight. It revealed a profound mistrust of Parliament by the Government. By having C-157 examined by a Senate committee chaired by one of their own, with the Commons left on the sidelines, the Government aggravated the problem. The Government has consistently acted as though it was frightened of Parliament, and MPs, unlike Senators, were naughty little boys who couldn't be trusted with serious issues like security".

The Opposition tried but failed to stop Bill C-9, which passed with few changes on June 21. Svend Robinson called it "one of the darkest days for democracy in the history of this country." It was given royal assent on June 28 and came into effect immediately. Bill C-9 was the last piece of legislation officially passed by the Trudeau administration before the Commons was dissolved that summer. Shortly after, the Liberals had a new leader, John Turner, and in September 1984, he called a general election which swept the Tories into power.

The new government brought with it the new spy agency. On paper the RCMP's old-style, biased, scandal-ridden security service with its under educated gumshoes was to somehow instantly shed its police mentality and Cold War thinking and be transformed overnight into a new, forward-thinking, unbiased, well-educated intelligence unit. In fact, the RCMP security service simply changed its name without changing its personnel. For many members of the RCMP's security service, the immediate physical changes were not very apparent. Since the new CSIS headquarters was not ready, the RCMP security service members did not even have to change desks. They were still located in the RCMP Headquarters building on what was then Alta Vista Drive in Ottawa. They went on watching the same people they had been watching before. The only difference was that now they were watching them as intelligence agents instead of as police officers.

CSIS was given the RCMP's responsibility for gathering, analysing, storing and disseminating security and intelligence information to approved government departments, including the RCMP. It was told to report on threats to the security of Canada, which were defined as being:

— espionage or sabotage that is against Canada or is detrimental to the interests of Canada, or activities directed toward or in support of such espionage or sabotage;

— foreign-influenced activities within or relating to Canada that are detrimental to the interests of Canada and are clandestine or deceptive or involve a threat to any person;

— activities within or relating to Canda directed toward, or in support of, the threat or use of acts of serious violence against persons or property for the purpose of achieving a political objective within Canada or a foreign state;

— activities directed toward undermining by covert unlawful acts, or directed toward or intended ultimately to lead to the destruction or overthrow by violence of, the constitutionally established system of government in Canada.

CSIS was told that it would not be a law enforcement agency. It would not be allowed to nab spies — the RCMP would still be responsible for that. CSIS agents would not be licensed to carry weapons. If they discovered a spy plot or a terrorist conspiracy in the course of their work, they would have to call in the Mounties. CSIS was to concentrate on advising the government about potentially threatening security situations developing in Canada and abroad that could affect national security and the welfare of the Canadian people. It would report these threats to the Prime Minister's Office or the Privy Council Office, but it would also advise other government departments that needed intelligence information. They would include: External Affairs, which is responsible for passports, visas, foreign relations and external trade; Transport, which is responsible for airport security; Immigration, which is responsible for entry of people into Canada; and Secretary of State, which is responsible for issuing citizenship papers to deserving immigrants. CSIS would operate only in areas where no crime had been committed, but where there might exist the possibility of a crime at some future time. CSIS agents would not be allowed to engage in preventive action. It is difficult to imagine a more cruel mandate for dyed-in-the-wool police officers — to watch without taking part, to content themselves with the shadows while someone else took the limelight.

CSIS responsibilities include looking into the possibility of espionage and sabotage by hostile foreign interests; the possibility of other forms of foreign interference in Canadian affairs, including harassment of certain ethnic communities in Canada and improper advances to Canadian parliamentarians by foreign interests; possible political violence or terrorism such as hostage-taking, kidnapping and bomb threats; and subversion, a harder concept to define that would cause CSIS a lot of trouble later on.

Canadians were asking a great deal of the new service. CSIS would have to tread a fine line, investigating developing situations as long as they remained non-criminal in nature, and calling in the RCMP as soon as something criminal had occurred or was about to occur. The agency would be condemned to defend itself over and over, precisely because of the non-criminal nature of the acts and people it investigated. Any person who suddenly discovered himself or herself under surveillance by CSIS could demand quite legitimately, "What are you investigating me for? I'm not doing anything criminal."

Whereas police officers in Canada function on the basis that they have "reasonable and probable grounds to believe" that a crime has been committed or is about to be committed, CSIS agents function on the basis that they have "reason to suspect" that a crime may someday be committed.

The new spy agency was given incredible powers compared to the restrictions imposed on the Mounties when they handled security and intelligence. CSIS can spy on people, enter private residences covertly, plant electronic listening devices, tap telephone lines for up to a year at a time, and secretly intercept and open first-class mail. It also has legal access to people's darkest, most secret personal records, to the files and data banks of a number of federal departments and agencies and, through a series of agreements with various provincial governments, access to their files, records, data banks, agencies and departments.

In the end, CSIS has access to hospital files, doctor-patient records, mental health records, income tax returns, passport information, and unemployment insurance and welfare records. It can find out all sorts of personal things such as secret alimony payments, old business failures or bankruptcies, political allegiances and secret club memberships. It can just as easily tell an individual he was treated for a social disease in a hospital five weeks ago as show him his income tax returns going back a number of years, or tell him what he whispered to his mistress over the telephone last night. Most astonishing of all, CSIS is never required to inform those people it has spied on, or explain why or for how long it spied on them. Since CSIS is responsible for conducting security clearances on everybody who wants to immigrate to Canada, or obtain Canadian citizenship, or get a job in the public service or in any one of a number of private firms requiring a security clearance, few Canadians find it to their advantage to refuse to co-operate with CSIS when the agency decides to move in on them.

There is one stipulation. For some of the more intrusive techniques, including planting electronic listening devices in people's homes, or tapping telephone lines, CSIS must first of all obtain the approval of the solicitor general and a warrant from a federal court judge. Such a warrant is good for up to a year at a time, with as many renewals as the judge may authorize. And of course, the people spied upon electronically or by the CSIS team of investigators and watchers need never be told.

There are twenty-seven Federal Court judges, but the identity of any judge who issues a CSIS warrant is never to be known publicly, nor are the grounds on which a warrant has been issued, or how many times it has been renewed. CSIS is not bound by the requirement that obliges the RCMP to notify after ninety days anyone on whom it has eavesdropped. CSIS never has to tell. It is because of national security, the CSIS Act says, that everything has to remain secret.

For the government this is an ideal procedure. The solicitor general gets to see all the warrant applications even before the Federal Court judge does. And if the government doesn't like what it sees, the application never gets to the judge. In short, apart from burning down barns and roughing people up, CSIS can do legally everything that the RCMP used to do illegally.

Of course the CSIS legislation left out the major recommendation of the Keable Commission — that before a spy agency or a police force can send in an undercover agent to spy on any sort of organization or group, be it a political party, a cultural association, a labour group, an ethnic community or a religious body, it must first obtain the authorization of both the solicitor general and a judge. Keable wanted this stipulation to impose more control over the use of CSIS moles inside legitimate organizations. In the U.S., this stipulation exists. The FBI is required to obtain a written authorization from the attorney general before it can send in an undercover agent to penetrate an organization. The aim is to discourage systematic targeting of groups on political and ideological grounds. The FBI got into a lot of trouble when it became known that it had sent in undercover agents to spy on Martin Luther King and the black civil rights movement. The Canadian government chose to ignore that lesson and recommendations from both Keable and McDonald.

The new law made CSIS responsible for conducting the government's security clearances — about as delightful a job as cleaning out the Augean stables. More than 70,000 public servants a year have to be cleared for security, proven to be truly loyal to Canada and worthy of being trusted with state secrets and classified government information. Often this information can be no more sensitive than a note to a federal cabinet minister, or an early draft piece of legislation before it is presented in the Commons. Sometimes it can be something as delicate as the federal position on an upcoming federal-provincial constitutional conference, or the Canadian position in free trade negotiations with the U.S.

Security clearances in the federal government have traditionally been divided into three major categories — Confidential, Secret and Top Secret — and one category so secret that no one is supposed to know it exists until they are told they have it (it's called Top Secret — Special Activities). It is believed that no more than two hundred people in CSIS, External Affairs, National Defence and around the prime minister have this highest-of-all security rating which allows access to secrets from NATO and the U.S. But all this is changing as the government is in the process of bringing in a new, more complicated classification system that would divide the Confidential section into a number of sub-categories.

With the adoption of Bill C-9, Canada became the first Western democracy to legislate a mandate for its security service. Most democracies, such as the U.S., prefer to have their security services operate on the basis of directives from the executive of government. The spy agencies prefer that too. It gives them more freedom. The arms sales to Iran and the resulting Iran-Contra scandal in the U.S. could not have occurred as easily in Canada. There is nothing whatsoever in the CSIS mandate that would allow it to sell arms to anyone, especially not a hostile foreign power.

In other ways, however, the American structure offers more protection for civil rights and more control over security and intelligence. In the U.S., the FBI is required to come back before a judge every thirty days to have its electronic eavesdropping authorization renewed, whereas the Canadian approval is good for a year. The FBI must also persuade a judge that the electronic eavesdropping being requested will produce evidence of a crime. In Canada there is no such requirement. The FBI is obliged to destroy tape recordings of telephone conversations of innocent people picked up by the wiretaps — such as friends or members of the family who might have used the same telephone. In Canada, only lawyer-client discussions are destroyed and that is by ministerial directive, not because of a stipulation in the law.

One clause in the CSIS Act defines threats to Canada as any "foreign-influenced activities within or relating to Canada" which are "deceptive" and considered by CSIS to be "detrimental to the interests of Canada." These activities do not even have to be criminal, merely "deceptive." It was pointed out that this could include almost anything, even something as innocent as promoting free trade with the hope that it leads to Canada eventually joining the U.S., or bringing up a couple of National Football League teams from the U.S. to play an exhibition game in

Canada in hopes that it eventually might lead to an NFL franchise and the demise of the old Canadian Football League.

It may sound like semantics, but CSIS, anxious to expand its power, on several occasions took advantage of those words "within or relating to Canada" and interpreted them to mean that it could send a secret agent overseas, which it did on at least two known occasions: once it sent Marc-André Boivin to a peace conference in Copenhagen and on another occasion it sent him to a Soviet bloc country. Critics have pointed out an additional problem as well with the clause. Nowhere does it mention that the "foreign-influenced activities" have to be of a "criminal" nature as defined by the Criminal Code of Canada. CSIS can continue going abroad to spy on activities that are not in the least bit criminal. In the fall of 1989, then-Solicitor General Pierre Blais confirmed that a CSIS "informer" might have gone overseas, and that CSIS employees might have as well, to obtain "information" on matters of interest to CSIS. Blais declined to say — in the interests of national security — how many times CSIS had sent agents abroad, and how many more times it might do so, without having to become a full-fledged, overtly operating foreign spy agency along the lines of the Central Intelligence Agency.

Alan Borovoy, the general counsel of the Canadian Civil Liberties Association, has maintained all along that CSIS should concern itself with threats of espionage and sabotage by foreign nations, and leave threats of subversion or political terrorism up to regular police forces to deal with. Subversion and terrorism should be treated as crimes under the Criminal Code, not as areas of interest for an intelligence agency, Borovoy argues. It makes sense. As a police force, the RCMP is already heavily involved in law enforcement. Adding terrorism, which it already has responsibility for on the criminal side, and subversion would cause little extra difficulty. CSIS in turn would be able to concentrate on intelligence gathering and leave fighting crime up to the Mounties. But the government prefers CSIS to have a larger role.

Another section which gives civil libertarians headaches allows the service to investigate activities by Canadian groups which support the use of violence to achieve a political objective in another country. This section ignores the fact that one person's "freedom fighter" is another person's "terrorist guerilla." Should CSIS have investigated the African National Congress because it advocated violence to overthrow the apartheid regime in South Africa? Where does CSIS stand on the Iranian resistance movement dedicated to overthrowing the regime in Tehran? In the past, some Canadians supported the violent overthrow of the British mandate in Palestine, the Biafran war and the resistance movements within the so-called "captive nations" of Eastern Europe — all causes that are now broadly believed to be good ones. But the CSIS Act allows the agency to pick and choose who it wants to target.

It is still not clear if CSIS helped or hindered the work in Canada of DINA, the dreaded secret police of former Chilean president Augusto Pinochet. Nor is it known whether CSIS follows the Canadian or American position on Nicaragua or whether it provides assistance to the Americans in gathering intelligence on Canadian support for the rebels in El Salvador. Because it has signed a number of intelligence-exchange agreements with various foreign countries, whose identities it refuses to disclose, CSIS has steadfastly refused to say, apart from Eastern bloc countries, who are the good guys and who are the bad guys.

The new legislation also gave CSIS the right to snoop on foreign nationals visiting Canada as tourists, or here on business, or attending a political or scientific conference. The only requirement is that the information CSIS gathered should be of use to External Affairs or National Defence. Any operation has to be approved in writing by either minister.

This means that every diplomat, visiting scientist or member of a trade delegation, whether from a hostile country or a friendly ally, is a potential target of CSIS while in Canada if the information is deemed of use to the country. There has been no great hue and cry from MPs over this section, perhaps because foreigners can't vote in Canada. After all, if foreign visitors don't like being spied on, they don't have to come here. For CSIS, the section is useful. It helps discourage foreign powers from using trade delegations and scientific and cultural exchanges as covers for spy missions. CSIS can conduct surveillance on them just as it would if they had sent in spies disguised as diplomats. For the government, this means that CSIS can legally bug trade negotiators coming to Canada to learn what their negotiating arguments will be. Only a few critics have complained that it is unfair to subject foreign visitors to a more intensive sort of surveillance than CSIS is allowed to conduct against Canadians.

The section also permits something else which is so secret no one dared mention it at the time the bill was presented. It allows CSIS to work with Canada's ultra-secret, multi-million-dollar Communications Security Establishment. The CSE, which is considered the only government agency more secret than CSIS, employs more than 1,700 people, and uses highly sophisticated radio and telecommunications equipment to listen in simultaneously to thousands of embassy, ship and airline telephone and telecommunications transmissions and voice conversations across Canada and around the world. Its headquarters are located in the Sir Leonard Tilley Building near Vincent Massey Park in Ottawa, which from the outside looks like any one of half a dozen ordinary government buildings in the neighbourhood. Inside there is space-age equipment linked to installations at six ultra-secret military bases across Canada that is so sensitive it can home in on two Russian sailors talking about lunch aboard a Soviet freighter off Vancouver Island, or eavesdrop on a businessman in Toronto trying to make a deal with a firm in Spain, or a young man whispering sweet nothings to a girlfriend in England. The CSE functions as a funnel. Everything that is telecommunications in Canada is sucked into it. It needs no judicial warrants because it is part of the military, not part of CSIS. What it picks up can be the most sensitive information as well as the most banal trivia. And CSIS is there to "assist" in this process, the CSIS Act says. It does not say how. Most of the information picked up by

CSE is in the form of electronic data rather than voice conversation. Ninety-nine percent is shipped wholesale, without ever being analysed here, to the U. S. National Security Agency in Fort Meade, Maryland. The Americans in turn tell the Canadians what they think the Canadians should know.

Stuart Farson of the University of Toronto Centre of Criminology argues in a paper called *Canadian Security Intelligence in the 80s* that the government's refusal to put CSE under legislative control is "particularly serious." He warns that "this in many respects makes the whole discussion of wiretap warrants moot to say nothing about a further data bank of personal files which are not governed by the same protection as those of CSIS." He points out that telephone taps are usually no longer required to listen in on conversations since many long-distance conversations are automatically transmitted in digital form from one city to another and then converted back to voice sound. All CSE has to do is plug in to the digital transmission.

The special parliamentary security committee recommended by Judge McDonald in his 1981 report was never set up. It was to have been made up of senior and trusted parliamentarians, such as the various party leaders and senior cabinet ministers, sworn to secrecy and entrusted with monitoring CSIS operations on an ongoing basis. The Federal Republic of Germany and the U.S. have monitoring bodies that involve active legislators. In the U.S. there are both a House of Representatives committee and a Senate committee which regularly review the work of the CIA and the FBI. They both hold in-camera hearings, depending on the sensitivity of the issue they are examining.

In Canada, the government agreed only to set up a special parliamentary committee that would meet, after CSIS had been in existence five years, to review the CSIS Act to see if it needed fixing, and report back to the Commons in July 1990. The government also set up the office of inspector general within CSIS to act as the solicitor general's eyes and ears inside the service. The inspector general would monitor CSIS operations, review files and conduct interviews, check out allegations, look over the CSIS director's annual report to the solicitor general and then report any irregularities or problems.

The only real independent outside protection for the public in the CSIS Act is the watchdog group called the Security Intelligence Review Committee. SIRC, as it is called, is made up of five part-time members, trusted men and women, who have already proven their loyalty and dedication to Canada and have been cleared to the highest security clearance rating — "Top Secret — Special Activities" — obtained, of course, from CSIS. The five SIRC committee members are assisted by a staff of fourteen investigators, researchers, assistants and secretaries.

The SIRC members act as the public's eyes and ears. They monitor and review CSIS operations, examining applications for intrusive operations warrants to see if they have been issued for good cause, and whether they have been used properly. They also act as an appeal body to hear public servants who have been denied security clearances. SIRC investigates abuses, corrects mistakes and suggests improvements to CSIS.

SIRC members speak out publicly on occasion, but they have to remain silent on some sensitive national security issues. SIRC plays a sort of security striptease with the public, showing just enough of CSIS operations, the good and the bad, to satisfy people, but not so much as to upset CSIS, which can always accuse SIRC of having compromised national security by revealing too much about its activities.

Once a year SIRC publishes an annual report, parts of which are made public, parts of which remain secret. Usually SIRC discovers abuses after they have been leaked to the media or been raised in the House of Commons. Occasionally SIRC discovers something on its own and investigates.

SIRC is very useful to CSIS, because it eliminates the need for the CSIS director to defend the agency publicly every time an allegation of abuse or criminal behaviour is made. SIRC is responsible for a great deal. Not only does it have to keep an eye on CSIS — an organization more than 100 times its size — but it is also the appeal body for immigration or citizenship security clearance denials. SIRC must review the solicitor general's policy directives to CSIS. Many of SIRC's investigations involve frequent CSIS disasters and foul-ups that are exposed in the news media. In spite of their heavy responsibilities, the five SIRC committee members work only two or three days a week on average, usually one SIRC member per appeal panel, and are paid on a per diem basis — $425 per day.

SIRC is not much — part-time watchdogs without access to cabinet documents who can reveal very little of what they find out — but it is all the public has in terms of independent reporting on CSIS. Voters can hardly expect the solicitor general to point out the shortcomings of his security service. Usually he spends his time praising it and saying how well it is working since he took over. It is left up to the news media or the Opposition politicians in the House of Commons to show the other side of CSIS.

The makeup of SIRC is unique. To ensure that SIRC is not too close to the government, the two major Opposition parties nominate two of the five SIRC members. The first committee was appointed in November 1984. Its chairman was Ronald Atkey, a Toronto immigration lawyer with a civil rights background who served briefly as immigration minister in Prime Minister Joe Clark's Conservative government.

Atkey, a tiny, quick-witted man with an accessible disposition and a good sense of humour, seemed ideally suited for the job. However, not everyone was happy with the appointment, and Atkey had to fend off criticism that his Toronto law firm, Osler, Hoskin and Harcourt, continued to represent immigration clients while he was SIRC chairman hearing immigration security appeals. Atkey said there was no conflict of interest since he would never chair a hearing involving any of the firm's clients. He served exactly five years to the day as SIRC chairman and resigned in November 1989, two months after he registered as a lobbyist for the Daiwa Bank of Canada, a subsidiary of the giant Daiwa Bank of Osaka, Japan.

The Liberal nominee was Jean-Jacques Blais, a lawyer and former Liberal cabinet minister who had had first-hand experience with security issues. Blais was solicitor general while the Mounties' dirty tricks were being revealed before the McDonald Commission in 1978. He had also been postmaster general in 1977 when the Mounties had been illegally opening people's mail with the help of his officials. Nobody told him what was going on, Blais complained to the Commons. While he sat on SIRC hearing security cases, Blais also worked as a registered lobbyist for Thomson – CSF, part of the French military consortium trying to sell a string of nuclear submarines to Canada in the late eighties. Blais said then in an interview that he never let his work as a lobbyist interfere with his work as a SIRC member. Nor was there even a possibility of a conflict of interest because he never gave his client any information about Canadian military or security matters that he picked up as a SIRC member. In fact, Blais points out that he never once judged a case that involved either Canada-France security matters or Canadian naval security issues. If a case had come up, another committee member would have conducted the hearing.

The NDP appointment was Saul Cherniack, a former Manitoba finance minister in Premier Edward Schreyer's first NDP administration. Cherniack, who later served as Manitoba Hydro chairman, had been in the Canadian Army Intelligence Corps during World War II and was the only appointment who had any intelligence background at the operations level.

The fourth committee member was Quebec City lawyer Paule Gauthier, the only woman on the committee and a former Quebec branch president of the Canadian Bar Association. She earned a reputation among the staff as the hardest working of the five committee members. Gauthier and Prime Minister Brian Mulroney go back a long way: they dated a couple of times while they were both at law school at Laval Université in Quebec City.

The final appointment was Frank McGee, who served briefly as a minister without portfolio in John Diefenbaker's last cabinet in 1962.

In its first annual report in 1985, SIRC reported that it saw itself as a group of "detached outsiders" who had "a genuine curiosity sprinkled with a healthy dose of skepticism." Together the committee members had a total of thirty-nine years in Parliament and legislatures. They bragged later that their committee felt "this constitutes a pool of knowledge and insight which enables it to pursue its oversight and complaint functions with intelligence and sensitivity to the competing interests at stake." Clearly they were not wanting in self-confidence.

Then came the job of staffing the new security service. CSIS officials dismissed the thought of putting advertisements in the newspapers: "Wanted — secret agents, spies, analysts. Must be loyal, fearless, and know how to use scissors." CSIS officials decided they would get too many James Bond types, so they did something else. They relied on the old RCMP security service to provide the warm bodies they needed, despite the fact that Justice McDonald had gone out of his way to point out how inadequate these people would be — poorly educated, biased and unsophisticated. Never mind, the government pressed the entire RCMP security service into duty as civilian spies. In one fell swoop ninety-five percent of the RCMP security service became the bulk of the CSIS force. The other five percent found jobs elsewhere in the RCMP or retired. The RCMP immediately lost 1,772 employees. And CSIS suddenly had more than three-quarters of the staff it would need to start off.

A great many Mounties who went over had never asked to become civilian spies. They were gumshoes, not newspaper-clipping analysts. They could catch a pickpocket, terrorize a stool pigeon, or more to the point, spot a terrorist with a bomb in an airport, but they couldn't name the various warring Lebanese factions, let alone analyse their political thought or predict their possible future behaviour.

Right away they began saying they had nothing to do. They missed their old ways and the buddies they had grown up with in the RCMP. There was actually plenty for them to do, if only they'd read up on some political material, but all they knew was that they had no crimes to solve, no suspects to round up. So they sat on their hands and did nothing. CSIS was given a whopping budget of $115.9 million for its first full fiscal year, 1985-86, about twice what the government had predicted the new service would need to start up. The RCMP's total budget reflected the loss of the security service. It decreased by $45.5 million to $828 million the following year.

The government blamed CSIS's inflated first-year budget on high start-up costs, but the following year the budget did not go down. It went up again, and again the year after that, and every year since, even in the latest era of Finance Minister Michael Wilson's exemplary budget cuts. For the 1990-91 fiscal year, CSIS was given a whopping 28.7 percent budget increase over the previous year. CSIS spending will reach $190 million in 1990, $32.7 million more than the $157.3 million it spent in 1989, even though *glasnost* is in full swing in the Soviet Union and the Canadian government is cutting hundreds of millions of dollars from needed government social programs in order to keep budgetary increases to less than five percent. Everybody goes second class — except CSIS. Once again, as in the past, no explanation has been given as to why CSIS is gobbling up more federal funds. The service is specifically exempt by law from having to make details of its financial spending public.

The ex-Horsemen who joined the fledgling security service got a sweetheart of a deal. They could stay with the civilian spy agency for two years, and if they didn't like it after that time, they could transfer right back again to the Mounties without losing salary, seniority or benefits. And of course, RCMP Commissioner Robert Simmonds said he would co-operate with CSIS.

Everybody had high expectations for the new service. The advance publicity pumped out by the government was all so positive. The Mounties had been so inadequately trained and set in their ways, and these new civilian spies would be so educated, so smart, so modern, so analytical, and so fair and democratic. Surely, they would do Canada proud.

\* \* \*

The man who became CSIS's first director was Thomas (Ted) D'Arcy Finn, then forty-six, a boyish-looking, Ottawa-born, well-connected bureaucrat who came out of the security and intelligence side of the Privy Council Office. He was brought along under the tutelage of his friend and protector, Senator Michael Pitfield, who has shaped the careers of so many public servants. Pitfield and Finn went back a long way. They were in the naval reserve together in 1958 and it was Pitfield who persuaded Finn in 1971 to give up a law career to join him in the Privy Council Office.

Finn was the complete company man, discreet, loyal and dull. He is best remembered in the PCO for his long, boring memorandums on esoteric constitutional themes. His affection for long, large smelly cigars appears to have been his only eccentricity.

In 1972, Finn headed off for a six-year stint in a couple of other government departments but returned to PCO in 1978 to act as secretary to the cabinet committee on security and intelligence, the most secret of all cabinet committees. Three years later, he was handed the thankless job of convincing Justice David Mc-Donald to allow large sections of his report to be cut — in the interests of national security, of course, — about 800 pages in all.

When Fred Gibson was appointed chairman of the Security Intelligence Transitional Group in 1981, Finn took the No. 2 job and became executive director of the SITG in order to get some hands-on security and intelligence management experience. The plan was that the older Gibson would step aside graciously at the proper moment. But within a year Gibson was gone, promoted to deputy minister of justice, and Finn took over as No. 1 at SITG, which became CSIS on July 16, 1984.

Finn lived in the Billings Bridge area of Ottawa with his wife Marg, their four children and two German shepherd dogs in a large, three-garage home. They did not have any special security protection, only the special RCMP alarm senior public servants are given in Ottawa. (The alarm rings at the RCMP, rather than merely around the house.) Their home was located on an elegant cul-de-sac not far from where the new CSIS headquarters was supposed to have been built, although it never was, at the corner of Kilborn Avenue and Bank Street.

Finn liked to spend weekends with his family. He played an occasional game of golf and once told a *Maclean's* magazine interviewer that his golf partners had teased him about the possibility that his golf ball might be bugged. It would be like him to feel obliged to add earnestly, "It wasn't."

He had come a long way from his lower middle-class Irish-Ottawa background as the son of the hard-living, tough-talking Ottawa *Citizen* reporter Joe Finn, a man whose practical jokes had made him a legend in the local press establishment. The Finns were an old, Irish-poor Ottawa Valley family. Ted grew up in the Sandy Hill district of Ottawa. In those days, you could hear the chimes from Parliament Hill. Born in 1939, he remembers how, during his younger years, his father was away a lot of the time, first for six long years during the Second World War, and then later as a reporter.

Young Ted was a great deal different from his father. You would not want to believe everything the elder Finn told you, but you knew you could believe everything his son said. He worked his way through law school thanks largely to a comfortable inheritance that a relation of the Labatt family had left his wife Marg, who had worked for her.

Finn the bureaucrat was a quiet, polite, athletic-looking man of medium build with straight, unmanageable sandy hair and a pasty complexion. His large, clear-framed glasses gave a strange magnified look to his blue eyes and the total effect reminded people of Andy Warhol.

In an immensely insightful and almost prescient portrait of Finn, in which she praised him for "an extremely high sense of values, common sense and compassion," Charlotte Gray, writing in the March 1984 issue of *Saturday Night*, warned that "there are serious reservations about Finn's appointment. The first is that he has never headed a large organization. He was noted in the PCO more for loyal response to Pitfield's direction than for management skills or imaginative strategies. . . . whether he will exercise the necessary leadership is less certain." Gray was right on the money. Within three years, Finn would be gone, destroyed as much by his inability to head a large organization as by forces conspiring against him.

Finn's right-hand man at SITG had been RCMP Chief Superintendent Archibald (Archie) Barr, Chief Superintendent, Policy Development for SITG. Barr had been in charge of the task force that had been so important to the RCMP in keeping the lid on the findings of the McDonald Commission. So when CSIS was set up in the summer of 1984, Finn brought him along as one of his five deputy directors.

Like so many other senior RCMP officers of his era, Archie Barr came from a poor Prairie farm background. He first dreamed of being a Mountie when he was still a boy growing up near St. Adolphe, Manitoba where his father worked on a horse farm owned by the Richardsons, a millionaire grain family from Winnipeg.

One day two young Ukrainian-Canadians who worked as farm-hands borrowed a canoe from a neighbour and went out on the nearby Red River. Neither of them had handled a canoe before, and neither could swim. The canoe rolled and both of them drowned. Two Mounties showed up and immediately began dragging the river for the bodies. One youth was found right away; the other came up a few days later. The tragic death of the two farm-hands and the way in which the Mounties had searched for their bodies combined to have a profound impact on young Archie. Mounties did dangerous, exciting and serious work, he concluded, exactly what he would like to do some day.

He saw more of the two Mountie constables that year. They would show up unexpectedly at school after classes from time to time. Archie and his older sister Lil would climb up into the patrol cruiser and be driven home. The constables' motives were not altogether altruistic. Mounties were paid only once a month back then, and if they didn't budget properly, they could go hungry between paycheques. If that happened, they often looked to local residents to supplement their diet with free produce. They knew Mrs. Barr was a soft touch, especially after they had driven her children home from school.

In 1953, young Archie dropped out of high school after grade 11 to help support his family, and like so many high-school Prairie drop-outs at the time, he turned to the Mounties for a job. Barr was regarded as bright and promising and within two years he had been accepted by the RCMP's fast-expanding Special Branch. It was the height of the Cold War and there was plenty for a Mountie to do. Young Barr could chase Communists with the best of them. He was assigned to the Sudbury district which, at the time, was rife with espionage. Sudbury produced most of Canada's nickel, considered a vital metal in the space race developing between the two superpowers. Nearby Elliot Lake, where the Americans had obtained the uranium for the first atomic bomb they dropped on Japan, was a sensitive security area of major interest to the Soviets. There was also an air base at North Bay. "They had some very arcane interests," he recalls.

Barr arrived in Ottawa in 1961, and within two years had made it up the ladder to headquarters as a desk officer. At the time there was a pitched battle within the security service as to whether it should be removed from the RCMP and set up as a separate civilian agency. Barr sided with the minority who said it should be civilianized. "I was an aberration," he admits today, "an operations man who believed in civilianization." But he was wise enough to keep his opinions to himself.

Barr was soon promoted to sergeant and spent the whole of the 1970 October Crisis working as a desk officer on the international side of counter-espionage. He says that if the security service had been providing adequate intelligence to the politicians about the FLQ in 1970, the War Measures Act would have never been invoked.

Indeed, it was the application of the War Measures Act that brought the terrorist crisis to a climax. The kidnappers of Quebec Labour Minister Pierre Laporte believed negotiations were no longer possible and retaliated by killing their hostage. Only much later would the federal politicians realize how little support the FLQ really had, and how disorganized they were. The RCMP had fed the politicians inadequate intelligence reports.

It was pointed out afterwards that if the senior officers in the security service at headquarters in Ottawa had spent less time resisting civilianization and more time trying to understand what was happening in Quebec, things might have turned out entirely differently in 1970. Barr says it was when the Mounties realized after the crisis how inadequate their security operations had been in Quebec that they tried to correct the problem, and this is what led to the "excesses and abuses" known commonly as the Dirty Tricks Era of the RCMP.

Soon afterwards, Barr was promoted to the rank of inspector and was picked to run the controversial Operation Featherbed, which was so secret that regular security service members were barred from its offices, and even today only a handful of people really know what was in the file. By 1976, Barr was in charge of Policy, Planning and Co-ordination, which in effect was the secretariat of the director general of the security service. He had reached the rank of superintendent and had in fact become an administrator.

Then came the sudden, sickening series of revelations about RCMP illegal acts, and Barr headed the security service task force set up to tell McDonald what he should know about the RCMP's dirty tricks. Barr prepared evidence, rounded up witnesses and got to know not only where the skeletons were kept, but also which ones should be dusted off and presented publicly.

Superintendent Barr came out of the McDonald Inquiry with his reputation intact. Two of the three McDonald commissioners rejected an allegation that he had advised a Mountie at one point during the inquiry to change his story. But apart from that one dissenting opinion, Barr was squeaky clean.

On July 16, 1984, the 1,772 members of the RCMP security service traded in their red serge for grey flannels. (Actually, the more fashion-conscious Mounties are fond of light brown summer suits. This runs contrary to a persistent myth that they like to wear "full Winnipegs" — loose-fitting checkered black-and-white sports jackets, white polyester slacks, and matching white belt and white shoes with socks of any colour but white.) Not much changed on the day the security service became CSIS. Someone remarked that the new agency was "the RCMP without the Musical Ride."

Since they didn't yet have their own building to move into, the new CSIS employees mostly stayed exactly where they were. More than half of the staff of 2,300 employees had been working at RCMP Headquarters, a former Roman Catholic seminary which had suddenly become vacant when religious vocations dwindled in the fifties. The building had been sold to the RCMP for a good price.

On the morning of July 16, most CSIS employees just went to work as usual. They didn't even change desks or filing cabinets. There was a brief swearing-in ceremony to fulfil the requirements of the CSIS Act. New letterhead arrived a couple of days later, but that was about all, apart from an order to turn in RCMP-issued firearms. The staff would still be using RCMP forms, manuals and equipment for several more months, even years in some cases. Only in 1989 and 1990 would they finally get their own training and operational manuals. Even the agreements with foreign countries under which they exchanged information were those that had been signed by the RCMP and would still be in the RCMP's name for several more years. It was easier to keep on pretending to foreigners that they were Mounties rather than trying to renegotiate those agreements.

It would be almost a year before CSIS would be moved to its new headquarters in the East Memorial Building on Wellington Street. And even there, the agency would have to share the building with Veterans Affairs and an organization appropriately known as the Commonwealth War Graves Commission.

Ironically, the last people to use the empty offices at the East

Memorial premises before CSIS were members of a visiting Soviet delegation. The entire building was given a thorough sweep for microphones before the service moved in. The Mounties who were in charge of sweeping the East Memorial building did a fine job. They had to, even though they may also have allowed their feelings for the new service to show: they left huge holes in the plaster walls here and there all over the place where they had entered to make sure whatever was registering on their equipment was not a hidden microphone or transmitter. The new occupants did what slum-dwellers usually do: they moved large pieces of furniture in front of the holes. It is always easier than trying to get the landlord to make repairs.

Archie Barr picked up a broom and swept his own office because somebody had neglected to set money aside for office cleaning. The new recruits saw their bosses sweeping out their own offices and thought that what was going on inside them must be so secret that no cleaner could be trusted to enter that area.

CSIS was set up under an executive committee made up of five deputy directors, all of whom were White Anglo-Saxon Protestants. There was not one Francophone, one ethnic minority, one woman among them. It never struck any of them that this might not have been the best of all possible selections. Four out of the five deputy directors were ex-Mounties, and they were all ex-security service Mounties. Not only were these four ex-security service Mounties, they were all ex-Featherbed members. They had all worked together on that holy of holies, that most sacred and secret of all RCMP security service files — the Featherbed file. The fifth man came from the Justice Department. He was William MacIver, a former assistant deputy minister of justice. The next two men down the line, James Warren and Ian Mac-Ewan, were also old Featherbed men. You just couldn't get away from Featherbed. Just going near that old file did wonders for one's career.

Archie Barr would be Deputy Director of Requirements, which

meant he was supposed to say what it was the agency should be doing in operations. In the old RCMP style he would be called the "DDR" and that was how he would sign his memos to subordinates.

Ray Lees would be Deputy Director of Operations (DDO), which meant he was to say how the service would carry out its work.

Harry Brandes would be the Deputy Director, Intelligence (DDI), which meant that he would produce the intelligence reports to facilitate operations.

John Venner would be the Deputy Director, Support (DDS), which meant that he provided the support operations — personnel, equipment, etc.

William MacIver, the Deputy Director, Administration (DDA), would make sure the whole thing ran with everything else in place from recruitment to paying the bills to making promotions.

The four ex-Featherbed people together had something approaching eighty years' experience in security and intelligence work. It would have been impossible to find in all the intelligence and security community in Canada anyone who had more knowledge of who the spies were and where the secrets were hidden. "Buddies" is not a good term for them. These men had competed and worked against each other, even investigated one another.

Even Finn could almost be called a Featherbed man, although he was never in the RCMP. He admits that while he was assistant secretary to the cabinet, there were frequently questions from MPs about the Featherbed file, so one day he made a point of using his position in PCO to find out what was in it. Refusing to say what he found, he also says that it had never occurred to him there was something strange in the fact that four out of five of the CSIS deputy directors were from Featherbed. "I never had any concept of a Featherbed Mafia at CSIS," he says.

This remark shows how out of touch Finn was with ordinary CSIS employees. Down in the trenches, there was often talk about "the Featherbed Mafia" running CSIS. It is only natural that employees on the lower rungs of any organization talk about promotions. CSIS is no different than any other bureaucracy in this respect. It didn't take long before the Featherbed connection was noticed — how four men who all worked on the same Top Secret file about politicians and bureaucrats all made it into the higher echelons of a new spy agency set up by politicians and bureaucrats.

"Sure there was a Featherbed Mafia," says Barr. But who else could have been appointed? The government could hardly have chosen men from the Dirty Tricks side of the security service.

Finn declined to say whether the Featherbed file followed the RCMP security service over to CSIS or whether it was one of the files that stayed behind with the Mounties. In any case, he says, it doesn't matter. Anything of value it might have contained was milked long ago. There's not much left that would be of use today.

The five-member executive committee set up to run CSIS quickly turned into a nightmare. It was perhaps one of the worst administrative set-ups ever thought up for a security and intelligence service. Finn says there was nothing wrong with the system, but then, he was the one who dreamed it up.

The committee was set up in such a way that the area of responsibility of each deputy director overlapped with the next. "This was done by design," says Barr. "The way the service was designed was to have these overlaps so that [one deputy director] could overrule part of what the other [deputy director] was doing. It was structured so that the director of the service could never be held captive by one deputy director."

Beneath this, an elaborate system of committees and subcommittees was set up to cover virtually every task and responsibility of CSIS. "We had more committees than Carter has pills," says Barr.

What happened could have been foreseen. They soon began going around in circles and were at each other's throats in the boardroom all the time.

"Deputy directors were overruling each other all the time. Ted was always the mediator, seeking the middle ground," recalls Barr.

Meanwhile, far down below in the ranks, a most serious rivalry was building up, this one between the two major CSIS centres outside of Ottawa. Montreal and Toronto were competing against each other for the distinction of being the major CSIS centre outside the capital. Traditionally, after headquarters in Ottawa, Montreal had been No. 1 in importance and size for the RCMP security service, with adequate funding and personnel, particularly during the FLQ era in the 1970s. As the terrorist threat subsided, some senior officials in Ottawa decided that the security service in Montreal was a little heavy, especially at the top. RCMP Headquarters began exercising closer control over allocations to the Montreal operations.

In addition, the security service personnel in Montreal were hardly in Ottawa's good books after the shame they had brought to the Force in the early part of the decade. When CSIS was formed, the negative view of the Montreal personnel persisted. Security service officers who had been involved in illegal activities continued to live under what Finn called "a cloud." Gradually headquarters clamped down, and Montreal was left with less and less independence.

At the same time, major changes were taking place elsewhere. Toronto was emerging as the new capital of industrial espionage in Canada. The Golden Horshoe area in Southern Ontario, where so much of Canada's research and development were taking place, was a treasure trove of the sort of secrets today's spies are after. (The second major target area for this kind of espionage was — and is — Silicon Valley North at Kanata, Ontario, on the outskirts of Ottawa, which is handled by a separate and steadily expanding Ottawa region CSIS branch. The joke among Eastern bloc diplomats serving in Ottawa is that "a day in Kanata is worth a week at Canadian Defence Headquarters.")

In addition, major social changes were taking place. Toronto had replaced Montreal as the "ethnic" capital of the country, and keeping an eye on ethnic community intrigues in Canada — especially ones that led to terrorism — is a big part of CSIS's work.

In 1984, the Quebec region of CSIS, based in Montreal, accounted for nineteen percent of all CSIS employees. At the time, CSIS had roughly 2,300 employees. Gradually staff was cut back in Quebec and employees were quietly transferred to headquarters in Ottawa and not replaced.

One reason that branch offices are no longer as important in counter-espionage is the increased reliance on computers and more modern telecommunications. The latest developments allow counter-espionage agencies to centralize their operations. Wiretaps, for instance, no longer have to be monitored by agents with earphones sitting nearby. A wiretap against two Sikhs (CSIS has heard a lot of conversations in Punjabi since June 23, 1985, the day an Air India flight was shot down) who are chatting over supper in a Montreal restaurant does not have to be listened to by an agent physically located in Montreal. There is nothing that prevents CSIS from sending that communication to a Punjabi-speaking translator in another city. In fact, the translator may be listening to the conversation in the comfort of her own home, and translating what is being said as it comes in, with another agent standing nearby in case the information has some urgency.

The same is true of documents, which can be sent by wire or facsimile transmission in a matter of seconds to analysts in another city. And analysis, report production and computer-terminal work can all be done from a central location. Only human surveillance and face-to-face human source contact still have to be done on location.

The number of people at CSIS headquarters in Ottawa has been growing by leaps and bounds. The staff is estimated to have increased by about fifty percent since 1984 and now stands at close to 2,000 people. Today, four out of five of total CSIS staff (about 3,000) are located in Ontario, more than half in Ottawa and most of the rest in Toronto, which has passed Montreal as the No. 2 centre after Ottawa. The Quebec staff accounts for only eleven percent of total personnel, almost half what it was six years ago when CSIS was set up.

In addition, in May 1985, the CSIS branch in Toronto moved out of its old, inadequate location borrowed from the Mounties on Jarvis Street and into a spanking new Harbourfront office tower. It occupies the top four storeys of a twelve-storey building opposite the Harbour Castle Hotel, not far from the CN Tower. The offices are guarded by the latest in closed-circuit cameras, heat sensors, light detectors, sound alarms and a variety of other ultra-secret devices to ensure the place is tighter than a drum.

So as to attract top talent to Toronto, headquarters decided that employees in Toronto would be paid more than CSIS staff who did the same jobs, but happened to be located elsewhere in Canada. The justification was that this was due to the high cost of living in Toronto. Staff in Montreal perceived it as just one more example of how Toronto was the favoured child of the service. Again Ottawa ignored the grumbling, and by 1990 the discrepancy between Montreal and Toronto due to special allowances had reached as much as $8,400 a year.

CSIS in Toronto was favoured in another respect. The service bought, for use by its employees in the region, a fleet of about thirty cars. They chose automobiles of different shapes, sizes and colours and did not register them all at the same time, so at least the licence plates were not in series. But then they decided to park them in a fenced-off part of a public lot, accessible only to drivers with a special CSIS plastic card. This ensured that any agent of a foreign country who was watching would know exactly which were CSIS cars. And since the CSIS cars stayed on the lot at night, after the rest of the public lot had emptied, it was even easier to spot them.

Some of the cars were used for operations, while others were used for travelling by CSIS officials; some were used for deliveries, others for driving around visiting secret agents from foreign agencies, usually the FBI or the CIA. It was cheaper than renting cars under an assumed name, which is what the FBI and the CIA do, running up horrendous bills.

After some kids began writing "CSIS spies" in the dust on the trunks of some cars, agency officials decided that it might be time to make their automobiles less conspicuous. So employees were assigned responsibility for various cars, and were allowed to take them home at night. At least they would be off the CSIS lot. The "representatives of hostile foreign intelligence agencies," as CSIS officials like to call enemy spies, would have to search all over town if they wanted to confirm that a car they had seen earlier in the day belonged to the agency.

It sounded like a good idea, but it wasn't. CSIS employees quickly realized what a great thing they had going — free transportation back and forth morning and evening, with CSIS paying for the gasoline. Now they could save money and move to Barrie, Hamilton or Ajax, or wherever they wanted to go where housing was cheaper than in Toronto — and there are lots of places where housing is cheaper than in Toronto. CSIS gasoline bills shot up to new and dizzying heights.

There was also another effect. All those kilometres added up, and not just because of travelling to and from work. There was often some place to go at night with the company car, which was cheaper than using the family car. Some agency employees sold their second cars; some even considered selling their first cars.

Like many private firms, CSIS sells its company cars after 100,000 kilometres, and all the travelling on the side at night suddenly racked up a lot of kilometres. Those 100,000 km cut-offs began arriving a lot faster. At one point, CSIS was buying a new car every eight days. Things were getting way out of hand. Finally, the agency changed its policy, and CSIS cars are now parked in various places downtown.

Cars weren't the only embarrassment CSIS had to contend with. For an agency whose work was supposed to be carried out in secret, CSIS seemed to go out of its way to attract attention. In fact, lack of organization and professionalism made some

CSIS employees ridiculously easy to spot in any crowd.

Take, for example, the question of accommodation. CSIS arranged a special government rate at the Plaza de la Chaudière, a fancy hotel in Hull, for visiting CSIS officers. It was a smart move in a way because it saved taxpayers lots of money. The problem was that there was a taxi stand across the street from CSIS headquarters.

Taxi drivers are always exchanging information about fares and destinations freely among themselves. It didn't take them long to figure out that smartly dressed, athletic-looking young men with short haircuts, coming out of the East Memorial Building and carrying briefcases and travel bags, were going either to the airport or to the CSIS hotel in Hull. Just to show off, some of them would ask a CSIS officer as he got into the taxi whether he was going to the hotel in Hull or to the airport.

The startled CSIS employee would ask the cabbie how he knew, and the cabbie would reply calmly, "Where else would a CSIS agent carrying a bag be going?"

After a while special rates were set up with other hotels, but visiting intelligence officers were still being asked, "How's the spy business?"

Eventually, visiting CSIS people were told before leaving the building to walk a couple of blocks past the chatting taxi drivers at the stand before hailing a cab for the airport. But you can't fool a hungry cabbie looking for an $18 airport fare that easily. For that kind of money he will easily follow a customer a block, two or even more, and wait ten or fifteen minutes if he has to.

The trick is to follow from a safe distance, and when the CSIS officer decides he's far enough away and looks around for a taxi, there's the cabbie, who is smart enough to pretend he just happened to be cruising past. Every business has its own security and intelligence procedures.

To CSIS's credit another hotel is used for informers and undercover agents. They do not claim the special government rate, and they register under false identities.

CSIS agents aren't the only ones who have preferred hotels.

For some unexplained reason, the embassies of several East European countries in Ottawa have tended over the years to use the same few hotels for the spies they bring into Ottawa. There is nothing secret about this. Several Soviet spies who were busted produced the names of hotels where other Soviet agents had been staying. It always seemed to be the same places, even going back to the fifties. In those days the Peter Pan Motel on the outskirts of town was a favourite of theirs.

The Eastern bloc nations compound this security blunder by booking some of their diplomatic visitors into the same hotels. Even the hotel staffs are aware of it, and journalists have long known about it as well.

One of the cruellest jokes CSIS management perpetrated on young intelligence officers during its first year of operation was the decision not to allow them to have identity or business cards. They were never told why — simply forbidden to have them.

Some officers suspected it was so they would work harder. Without cards they would have to identify themselves as best they could. It would force them to be more inventive, show more initiative and develop their ability to bluff their way into a situation.

Others thought cards were forbidden so that their identities would always remain secret, for the same reason they were told to get unlisted telephone numbers. Some said that if they were given business cards with their names on them, they would soon be passing them out in bars and at parties to impress friends. This often happened in the case of young RCMP constables, and CSIS managers didn't want their flock going the same route as the Mounties. Some joked that without any ID, if they were ever captured by the KGB they could deny everything and no incriminating evidence would be found on them. CSIS employees were told in the early days that whenever anyone asked what they did for a living, they were to reply, "I work for Solicitor General," and leave it at that.

The answer was supposed to be enough to deflect suspicion and strictly speaking it was not a lie since CSIS does report to the solicitor general of Canada. But it was such a strange answer — "I work for Solicitor General" — even though in Ottawa bureaucratic language it is quite permissible to drop the article "the" in speaking of a government department, as in "I work for Justice" or "I work for PCO." However, it would have been easier to maintain cover if CSIS employees had been able to say something like "I do analysis work in the solicitor general's department, you know, trends, developments, policies, activities, so on."

In fact, there are thousands of other government employees who work in the department of the solicitor general, but they usually specify where they work within it. It quickly became a standing joke in Ottawa that anyone who said "I work for Solicitor General" was really a CSIS employee.

The vague answer syndrome reached comic proportions at the federal government language school on Carson Road in Ottawa's east end. This was the notorious language mill where thousands of federal public servants had to go for their six-month language courses. Most of the students were middle-aged unlingual Anglophones trying to learn enough French to qualify for the all-important "B" levels which would keep them in the promotion stream in the public service. Most of them didn't like being there, but had no choice, so they usually tried to make the best of it with a little banter and camaraderie.

Whenever a new class was starting up, the French teacher would ask the students to identify themselves and say why they were there: *"Qui êtes-vous?"* and *"Où travaillez-vous?"* the teacher would ask. Most of the students would look like middle-aged public servants out of central casting. Their answers would finally emerge in extremely fractured French, and would go something like, "Bonjour, mon nom est John and je suis dans policy, planning and system management, Public Works, and je veux mon damned B level."

The men would wear open-neck shirts, slacks and loafers and sweaters on colder days, and they would come with government-issue pens and notepads. But always in the back of the class, there would be two or three identical-looking, white, Anglo-Saxon, athletic young men with short-cropped hair, wearing suits and ties and well-shined shoes, and carrying identical government-issue briefcases. They would always arrive together and on time, and never grumble or say anything disparaging about either the course or the teacher, or look hung-over, or be impolite to their fellow students. "It was like having those Christian missionaries who come to your door beside you all day long," grumbles one jaded old bureaucrat who took the course.

These guys were completely out of character with the rest of the class. Everybody knew who they were. Asked to introduce themselves, they might say, "Bonjour, mon nom est Phil and je travaille pour Solicitor General," which would send the rest of the class into fits of laughter.

The French teacher, not aware of the buzz word, would invariably listen and wait attentively for the rest of the answer. And wait, and wait. Finally she — most of the French teachers were women — would ask, *"Que faites-vous au travail, Phil?"*

There would be a pause. Phil would look desperately at his straight-faced CSIS colleagues, then back at the smiling teacher and at the other snickering students and reply, "I don't know how to say, 'I can't tell you.' "

The teacher, thinking that Phil didn't know how to describe in French what he did, would ask him to say it in English so they could work it out together in French.

"No, I'm sorry, I can't tell you in English either. I'm not allowed," Phil would answer.

Finally, one of the other students would explain: "He can't tell you, Madame, because he works for CSIS, and at CSIS they're not allowed to say they work for CSIS." This would invariably break up the entire class. Even the CSIS guys would laugh sometimes.

There were other times when it wasn't so funny, when CSIS

field officers had to identify themselves to people who had never heard of CSIS and wanted to see some identification before agreeing to answer any questions. In the early days more than one CSIS field officer had a door shut in his face when he said, "I work for Solicitor General and I'd like to ask you some questions."

Frequently they would be confused with other types of door-to-door solicitors. "I'm sorry, we don't want to buy anything," was a frequent reply. "And just what are you soliciting for, young man?" asked one friendly woman. One apartment janitor simply pointed to a sign besides the front door and snapped, "See that sign? NO SOLICITING."

The most difficult question a CSIS operative would get was, "Are you with the police?" If they answered yes, they could be in big trouble because it is a serious offence in Canada to impersonate a police officer. It happened once in the first year, during a surveillance operation in Winnipeg, and the CSIS field officer was caught. The RCMP were furious, but the whole thing was hushed up. The man's name was never made public and no charges were laid. SIRC chairman Ron Atkey explained to the Commons Justice and Solicitor General Committee in June 1986 that the "unlawful conduct" incident had been handled "internally" by CSIS "to our satisfaction."

The temptation to impersonate a police officer was great. After all, many of the new CSIS employees had been RCMP officers for ten and even twenty years. "Hello, I'm from the RCMP," was an almost automatic reflex, especially since that phrase would have worked magic and opened so many doors for them. It was frustrating not to be able to use the RCMP name any more, and in many cases the work they were doing was not very different from what they had been doing previously in the RCMP. In some cases it was just the same: interviewing the same Communist sympathizer to fill up exactly the same file in the same drawer in the same filing cabinet in the same office.

Not being able to identify themselves as Mounties made the work of CSIS field officers particularly difficult when they had to work in ethnic communities where suspicions of persons in authority were understandably quite strong. For many new Canadians, their trust began and ended with the fabled red-coated Mounties. This "Solicitor General" business sounded too much like somebody from Revenue Canada, or worse still, Immigration Canada, coming around to snoop. The fact that they couldn't carry CSIS identification made CSIS people even more suspect. Some people won't let a water meter reader into their home without first seeing identification. Some CSIS agents resorted to keeping with them the office and home telephone numbers of an old friend in the RCMP who could vouch for them if there was need. "Ya, he's okay, you can talk to him."

Eventually, sometime in 1985, CSIS management relented and said that some CSIS employees could have business cards. But to save money, because there was such a turnover in staff and in positions during the first year, they were issued plain cards with only the name of the agency at the top, and told to fill in the blanks when necessary. When asked for identification, CSIS agents would whip out a blank business card, fill it in and hand it over to the person who demanded it. It didn't always work. They soon learned the trick of typing in their name and telephone number on a few blank cards before leaving the office.

Finally, after two years of this monkey business, all CSIS employees were issued proper identification and business cards with their names and office telephone numbers printed on them. And sure enough, just as CSIS management had feared, the cards began showing up here and there. One was found tacked up to the wall of an Ottawa Italian restaurant where it is the custom for patrons to leave their business cards on the bulletin board for other patrons to know they too patronize the establishment. Someone had scribbled above the name on the CSIS card, "For a good time call . . . " and below it someone else had added, "Speak Russian."

# No Way to Run a Security Service

T HE NEW SECURITY SERVICE SET OUT to attract the finest of civilian recruits — university-educated, sophisticated and responsible. However, from the beginning, the agency's recruitment techniques were, to say the least, unusual and disorganized.

Susan Angus figured she would be a natural as a CSIS agent. After all, she had done similar work in Prime Minister Pierre Trudeau's office two years earlier. In 1983 and 1984, the attractive, auburn-haired political assistant had worked in a not-very-well-known section of the PMO called the "Op Watch." It occupied a little office in the Langevin Block across the street from the Parliament buildings.

"Op Watch" — which meant Operations Watch or Opposition Watch depending on who was asking — had been set up to investigate the personal background of the newly chosen Conservative Opposition leader Brian Mulroney, and if possible dig up some dirt on the fast-rising politician. Angus recalls it was run by David Crenna, who was listed officially as a "senior policy adviser" to Trudeau. She says it was the brainchild of Tom Axworthy, Trudeau's principal secretary, who set up the unit before she got there, possibly prior to the 1983 Conservative leadership convention. There were as many as ten people involved.

Op Watch collected information on Mulroney's background, his personal life, his real estate holdings, past business dealings and the occasional forgotten gaffe, anything that could be embarrassing politically. No detail was overlooked. A useful scandal, ticking away like a time-bomb, could be hidden anywhere. A tip came in one day, Angus remembers, that there might be something interesting in Mulroney's real estate holdings, and a member of Op Watch was sent to Chicago where the information was supposed to have been located. He found nothing, however, and returned home.

At one point in fall 1983, Crenna went down to Washington to get files from the Securities and Exchange Commission on the Cleveland-based Hanna Mining Co., the giant American company which controlled the Iron Ore Company of Canada that Mulroney had run before he became Conservative Party leader. And a government official was assigned, at taxpayer's expense, to go to Montreal and do a title search on Mulroney's former home in Westmount. He discovered that Mulroney had obtained his million-dollar home from the Iron Ore Company for one dollar "plus other considerations" which were never made public. That sort of sweetheart deal is not unusual in the world of big business, but politically, it wasn't the sort of information likely to endear Mulroney to thousands of Canadians struggling to meet mortgage payments. The news was quietly leaked to a Montreal paper.

The existence of the Op Watch unit was finally made public in February 1984 by *Globe and Mail* reporter Lawrence Martin, who broke the news in a front-page story, including the fact that Angus had been working out of an office in the PMO while she was still collecting unemployment insurance benefits. She was quickly put on a full-time salary and assigned to other duties, helping look after Trudeau's Mount-Royal constituents.

When Toronto lawyer and businessman John Turner became Liberal leader in 1984, Angus was one of the few Trudeau veterans invited to stay on, and even after the Liberals' 1984 general election debacle she was kept on staff. But by June 1985, she realized things were not improving in Turner's office, and so she began looking around for another job.

CSIS was looking for investigators, so Angus applied. She was called in for a personal interview in early June and asked the usual sort of questions about her family background, previous work and education, as well as the names of three references. She included people working in the PMO. Angus passed the first stage but it was rough. First off, she had to deal with a series of questions about her private life. Because they are involved in security clearances, CSIS interviewers have a right to be probing in a way that no regular employer would ever be permitted. They wanted to know how she spent her leisure time, if she had any boyfriends, what sort of relationship she had with them, and the degree of intimacy in these relationships. If the interview had not been clearly, specifically and only for the purposes of conducting a security clearance, these questions could not be asked under protection provided under the Canadian Human Rights Act.

Angus recalls saying that she had been going out with a man. "What do you mean 'going out'? " the interviewer asked. "You know," she replied. "Could you describe the relationship?" he pursued.

She explained that she had a normal healthy and complete relationship of the sort that men and women are known to have. He seemed to have gotten the message, but then he asked politely, "Is it just men?" "Yes," she answered. *"Just* men."

The interviewer asked about her family background, indebtedness, basic financial information, her political views, her leisure activities and her previous addresses and employment going back ten years.

She mentioned that she had visited China as a tourist when she was still at university in 1976. That interested the interviewer. She added that she had even written a letter afterwards to a Chinese interpreter she had met on the trip, but the woman had never written back to her. The CSIS interviewer wanted the interpreter's name and address. Unfortunately Angus did not have it with her. The interviewer wasn't pleased, nor was he particularly interested in the work she had done in Op Watch. What he really wanted to know was whether she knew any diplomats.

Unfortunately, the Op Watch office wasn't the sort of place where you'd meet an ambassador, so Angus had to admit she really didn't know anyone like that. Never mind, she passed the first hurdle and was sent on to a second-level interview in June 1985 to be tested on a series of spy scenarios.

One scenario was the old test about the spy's suitcase in the restaurant. The subject is told that a person she has been assigned to follow leaves a suitcase behind in a restaurant. What do you do? Rush up quickly and open it? Pick it up and hide it in the restaurant before the person returns? Pick it up and leave discreetly by the back door? Telephone headquarters and ask what to do? Forget the suitcase and stick with the subject you were assigned to follow, hoping to alert headquarters before the person being followed comes back for it?

There is no right or wrong answer. The forgotten suitcase could be a diversion by the subject to give you the slip. Or it could be disinformation — even a bunch of fake files. Or it could be a bomb, and it might be the last suitcase you ever open. If you decide to ignore the suitcase and stick with your subject, as you were assigned, you could find yourself coming back into the restaurant two minutes later and watching a very relieved spy pick up the suitcase he is happy to find still at his table, while you end up hating yourself forever.

No matter how the applicant responds, it tells CSIS something about what sort of agent the applicant would make. The purpose of the test is to gauge how the applicant would handle unexpected situations.

Angus was given a variation of this scenario. In her case it was an attaché case left behind in a supermarket line-up. She cannot recall how she answered the test, but it was apparently enough to satisfy her interviewer who told her she had a lot of common sense.

Occasionally CSIS applicants are given trick questions like this: "What would you do if you were ordered by your CSIS superior to kill someone?" The "correct" answer is simple: "CSIS does not ask its investigators to kill anyone." Blind obedience is a virtue in the public service, but at CSIS, blind obedience stops well short of murder, and this question is used to root out the would-be 007s.

In fact the best answer, the one that would get you the brownie points, would go like this: "Since CSIS doesn't go around killing people, I would know something was wrong, so I would pretend to agree to follow the order but discreetly report that superior to someone higher up as soon as I could." You don't get extra points for saying the superior was: (a) "probably joking;" or (b) "probably drunk as usual." But you might get extra points for answering that the superior was "probably a KGB double agent trying to set up the service."

Angus got a different trick question. The interviewer asked whether she thought it would be alright for the CSIS director general, who normally reports to the solicitor general, to confer directly with the prime minister about the Air India tragedy which had occurred two days before her interview. Angus replied with a straight face that it would be an excellent idea. Score one point for her. That very morning CSIS director Ted Finn had met with Mulroney to discuss the Air India bombing. At CSIS, the director general is always right. No one gets any points for second-guessing *him*.

Angus added that she had read about the meeting in the morning papers. Her interviewer was impressed. At CSIS, you have to be informed on current events. Ninety percent of what CSIS knows comes from what it calls "open sources." That includes the news media, newspapers, magazines, periodicals, learned papers in every language and on the most arcane subjects, radio and television reports and their transcriptions in dozens of different languages and, increasingly, data banks of all kinds. CSIS is a giant clipping operation, an endless filing cabinet, an overflowing net of information. It sucks and scoops and filters.

The charge made frequently against the old RCMP gumshoes who came over to CSIS was that they never read the papers. They didn't know what was going on in the outside world from one day to the next. And if given the papers, chances were they'd turn to the sports pages. They were more interested in the crime news than in the international section. Occasionally they can still be caught reading skin magazines in their offices. One of them was asked a question by his superior recently, and his answer indicated he thought Myanmar was a new type of plastic.

After her second interview Angus was contacted by CSIS agent W. A. (Bill) McDowell. She found a CSIS card in her hallway with his name on it, and a message that he wanted to speak with her. Pure CSIS style. Don't pick up the telephone and call, sneak over and slip a card under the door.

It seemed the problem was her references. Angus was taken by surprise — anyone in the PMO is usually considered a good reference. No, that wasn't the problem. The people whom she had given as references were too old, McDowell told her. "Don't you have any younger people as references?" She gave him the names of three younger people, although none of them held any high positions in the PMO. McDowell happily went off to interview them.

The problems with her superannuated references behind her, Angus went on to the third level of testing. When CSIS was first set up, interviewers asked candidates a lot of strange questions that came from psychological tests they obtained from the U.S., which, more than any other country, influences how CSIS recruits, thinks and acts.

One of these tests was called the California Psychological Inventory. It was given to CSIS candidates who had reached the third-level interview, after they had answered all those questions about their boyfriends, girlfriends and sexual preferences, and had played a few scenarios about the suitcase in the restaurant.

The "California," as it was commonly called, was an endless series of written questions about morals, ethics and dreams, which candidates were required to fill in on their own time.

Third-level candidates were also asked to write a concise, one-page summary of a report about a complex series of obscure incidents that took place in an office situation. The whole thing was subject to a time limit; its purpose was to test each subject's skills at analysis, as well as the ability to write clearly, effectively and quickly. Unfortunately, Susan Angus failed this third-level test, and so never got a job at CSIS.

Anyone who wanted to become a CSIS employee, or to advance within the organization, had to undergo any number of rigorous — and at times extremely arcane — tests. Members of the watcher section, known as "surveillants," who wanted to progress to the level of intelligence officers, were obliged to undergo a special psychological test. One of the questions asked was: "Do you prefer Washington or Lincoln as president?" Since this was a psychological test question, there was no right or wrong answer. American psychologists believe that most Americans see Washington first as a military leader and second as a statesman, while Lincoln is seen primarily as a statesman and secondarily as a military leader.

The problem with using this question in Canada is that most Canadians don't make that distinction. American history is taught from a different perspective in Canadian schools. To Canadians, Washington and Lincoln are both seen as good American presidents who helped their country through difficult times. So the question has little relevance as a test for a prospective CSIS intelligence officer who was born and raised in Canada.

For an American, it's an excellent question. It is a particularly brilliant question to ask of prospective FBI candidates because extensive psychological testing has shown that many Americans who harbour racist, anti-black sentiments also have a subconscious aversion to Lincoln. They resent him without knowing why. The deep, dark reason, the psychologists say, is because he was the American president who helped blacks out of slavery. With Washington, on the other hand, who kept slaves on his plantation, such bigots have no negative feelings.

As irrelevent as the Washington-Lincoln question may have been, CSIS erred even more when it came to administering a similar one to its French-speaking applicants. Instead of asking to choose between Washington and Lincoln, it substituted a question prepared by the authors of the test for use in France. It asked, "Do you prefer Pasteur or Lyautey?"

Now, every Canadian schoolchild knows who Louis Pasteur was, but very few Canadians, French- or English-speaking, know that Louis Hubert Gonzalve Lyautey was a superb French general, a reknowned humanist, a noted writer, a noble spirit and French colonial administrator. He believed in equality of all peoples, and served as war minister for a brief time in 1916-17. In Canada the good general is unknown. Who would Francophone applicants have picked? Why, of course, the scientist they knew over the general they had never heard of. The Security Intelligence Review Committee quite properly singled out this aberration in a report it presented to the solicitor general in March 1987 as an outstanding example of CSIS's inability to understand the Francophone element in its ranks.

CSIS could easily have used the same Washington-Lincoln question in both English- and French-Canadian tests. Francophones know as much about Lincoln and Washington as Canadian Anglophones. At least the question would have been equally irrelevant in both languages. But then, CSIS is often so close to the American security agencies, such as the FBI, the CIA and the National Security Agency, that it fails to grasp the nuances of being Canadian, let alone French Canadian.

One CSIS watcher did say later that he felt insulted that he was being asked to compare American presidents rather than Canadian prime ministers as his heroes, but he did not dare complain because he wanted the promotion. At CSIS, the political spectrum is so clearly defined that anyone voicing anti-American sentiments is immediately suspect. Being anti-American at CSIS is next to being pro-Communist — the greatest sin of all. Admitting you are a Communist or a Socialist is enough to get you booted out of the service.

*    *    *

One of the strangest controversies in the history of CSIS personnel management has been the continuing battle with the Security Intelligence Review Committee over the agency's continued
use of the polygraph, or "lie detector test," as it is often erron-
eously called, on its recruits and employees.

SIRC describes the machine as an unreliable piece of pseudo-
scientific junk which belongs "on the garbage heap" and that its
continued use is an insult in a democratic and free society. CSIS,
which is not obliged to follow any of SIRC's recommendations,
kept right on using the polygraph machine. For the first four
years of its existence, the agency had a Freudian fascination with
using the polygraph to get recruits to answer what it called
"lifestyle" questions. Crudely put, what interviewers usually asked
the sensitive, long-haired young recruit was if he had ever had
homosexual relations. And what they usually asked the pretty
young woman recruit was how many men she was sleeping with.
This somewhat prurient interest on the part of the agency now
seems to have died down. CSIS recruits may or may not be sleeping
around, but at least they no longer have to share it with a machine.
CSIS concentrates its attention solely on their "loyalty."

The polygraph has been discredited almost everywhere in the
world: British Prime Minister Margaret Thatcher, for instance,
ordered her intelligence services to stop using it in 1988. But in
the U.S., where such luminaries as J. Edgar Hoover and Senator
Joseph McCarthy swore by it, both the FBI and the CIA still use
it on their employees, and they like intelligence agencies that
want to do business with them to also use it.

As much as ninety percent of the foreign intelligence that CSIS
receives comes from the Americans, because most British and
NATO information comes through the Americans, not directly
from Europe. (The remaining ten percent trickles over from a
security liaison officer who picks up something abroad, or an
occasional tidbit from the RCMP, or the Foreign Intelligence
Bureau at External Affairs.) And so, whether it wants to admit it
or not, CSIS is bowing to American pressure in continuing to use
the polygraph.

For the first two years of its existence CSIS added an interesting quirk to the "science" of polygraph testing. It tested Francophones with questions only in English. "Oui, oui," the Francophones would answer, or "Non, non," depending on what they guessed the question might have been. Sometimes their answer had no relationship whatsoever to the questions asked. Then CSIS began using a translator to act as an intermediary. Alas, no studies were done by CSIS on the results of polygraph testing using intermediary translators. Finally, about a year ago, CSIS hired a French-speaking psychologist to administer the polygraph tests in French.

The big problem with the polygraph machine is that it registers physical manifestations of emotions of every kind; it registers annoyance and fear in exactly the same way as it registers guilt. The only thing the needle indicates when it jumps is that here is an area which concerns the individual. It does nothing to spot the guy who has been stealing everything he can from the office supplies cabinet but who thinks it's perfectly alright to serve himself in that way. Guilt is in the mind of the individual, and the polygraph does not make moral judgements.

CSIS's own director, Ted Finn, took a test himself that convinced him of the machine's usefulness. The psychologist who tested him included a question that Finn agreed he would answer one way one time and another way a second time. The question was, "Have you ever done anything that you would be embarrassed about?" Finn wondered what the question was getting at, but he took the test twice, answering "Yes" the first time and "No" the second. On both occasions the "trace results were virtually the same," Finn says. The psychologist replied, "Here is a question where you have a problem. I would say, 'Here is an area we should examine further.'" Finn says the machine could not tell whether he was lying but it did show he had given answers which indicated "an area that should be looked at further."

Noting that the polygraph is not used for security clearances in the public service because it isn't accepted by management or staff, Finn says that when used on CSIS recruits it is "one test among several but not more useful that any other test." He feels that although it wouldn't spot a liar, it could indicate an area that should be looked at further in a personal interview.

SIRC, which has been trying to stop the agency's use of polygraphs for years, says that no matter what CSIS's intentions are, the tests are used as more than an investigative tool at CSIS: they do influence who is hired.

CSIS personnel officials and CSIS recruits talk of "passing" or "failing" the polygraph test. Nobody says, "Oh, I think I got the job because I raised all sorts of interesting areas to probe further."

Annie Demirjian, the former research co-ordinator for SIRC, says the Americans are the ones insisting on polygraph testing and CSIS doesn't believe in it any more than SIRC does, but has to go along with them. She adds, "The day the Americans stop using polygraph testing is the day CSIS stops using it."

SIRC said in its 1986-87 annual report, "New recruits were put through polygraph examinations, covering both lifestyle and loyalty, as a condition of employment. CSIS tried to dress its program up in a lab coat by calling it a 'pilot project', but this is merely a disguise." In fact, CSIS has been calling it a "pilot project" for years, and claiming the use of the polygraph is "under study."

When asked recently about his plans for polygraph testing, Morden smiled and replied he had no idea when the "study" would be completed.

Curiously enough, the test is one of only a few CSIS procedures that has not produced complaints from CSIS staff. It's as if they liked the idea of sitting all wired up to a machine just like in the movies and being asked all sorts of personal questions. That's exactly the sort of work many of them hoped to be doing for CSIS after they were hired. SIRC knows this. In fact, an early report conducted by a SIRC task force interviewing CSIS recruits produced exactly this response. It asked the thirty-three graduates of the first graduating class at the Sir William Stephenson Academy how they felt about the polygraph testing. "No complaints

were made, and many interviewees commented on the professionalism in which it was delivered." These were the same
recruits who did not hesitate in the next breath to criticize
virtually everything at the school including their professors, their
accommodations, the poor quality of the food at the base, the
length of the courses, the subject matter and the lack of adequate
instruction in French.

That first generation of Academy graduates who had no complaints about the polygraph are working for CSIS now. Someday
soon it will be their turn to decide whether CSIS should keep on
using the polygraph machine.

Susan Angus may not have made it through all the CSIS testing,
but Stephen Beatty did. He was bright, young, tall, blond and a
good scholar. If there was ever an all-Canadian boy at the agency,
then Beatty must have been it. He had the determination and
tenacity that it takes to become a top-level athlete and represented Canada in rowing at the 1984 Olympic Games. What more
could CSIS want? Today he looks back at the two and a half years
from the fall of 1986 to the spring of 1989 that he spent with the
security and intelligence service as some of the most disappoint-
ing and frustrating days in his life.

Beatty grew up in Woodstock, Ontario and went to the University of Western Ontario where he studied international affairs
and looked forward to a career in the foreign service. In 1983
he enrolled in a master's program at the University of Pennsyl-
vania because Penn had an excellent rowing program. He trained
and went to the Olympics where the Canadian team finished
seventh, as good a showing as had been expected considering
what they were up against. After the Olympics, Beatty returned
to Canada, got married and landed a job on Parliament Hill as
an assistant to Conservative MP Bruce Halliday at $32,000 and
change a year. Not bad for a first job at twenty-five years of age.

But a year later he was looking for something else.

"I wanted something intellectually stimulating as well as international in scope," he says. He saw ads for CSIS. "They were

looking for Ivy League types. My master's topic at university had been on CSIS so I knew what to expect — balancing security of the state against liberty of the individual." He was in for a surprise.

Beatty was among 1,200 Canadians who applied to work for the agency in 1986. With his qualifications, he had little trouble getting hired. CSIS sent out someone to interview him. "The guy I met was an old boy, former RCMP. You could read him like a book. You knew right away what he wanted to hear you say. He wanted to hear that you didn't expect to be a manager right away, and were willing to put in your time." That's exactly what Beatty told him.

Beatty was then subjected to the same kind of highly personal questions that had been given to Susan Angus. Among other things, he was asked if he preferred to sleep with women or men. Many candidates were bothered by these questions, but they didn't worry him. He found out later that female candidates were asked questions of an even more intimate nature, such as whether they had ever had a sexual relationship with more than one partner at the same time.

At the next level he encountered the spy scenario which he refers to as the "situational." "For instance, let's say you're tracking a Soviet diplomat and he steals something in a store — he blatantly shoplifts in a department store and gets picked up. What's your reaction to that?"

One reaction would be to ignore it, it's probably a trap to see if he is being followed. If it isn't you can always deal with it later, after he's been charged. However, that would be the wrong reaction, says Beatty. "Do you approach him? The answer is 'Yes, of course, approach him' because one of the theories is that deliberate and obvious shoplifting is an attempt to make contact. He knows he's being tailed and wants to talk to his watcher."

Beatty is actually right; this is a behaviour trait frequently displayed by potential defectors — almost as if subconsciously they could convince themselves that they had no choice but to defect since they had already been compromised. There are dozens of stories about Soviet KGB agents going around diplomatic cocktail parties, dropping little hints and deliberately placing themselves in compromising situations to attract attention before they defected. To anyone outside the strange little world of spies this is incredible behaviour. Why not just come out and say, "Hi, my name is Ivon and I want to defect." But that would be so unusual that it would be quite likely a deliberate plant.

The situationals that interviewers throw at applicants are designed to test their ability to react to and analyse a situation. Many large multi-nationals are using similar tests on applicants. "There is no right answer or wrong answer to some questions," says Beatty. "They throw them at you to see if you are at least going to think of one of the variations and be able to explain why you chose that one."

They asked some bizarre questions as well, he recalls. For instance, they asked him if he thought he was Jesus Christ. He replied, "No" — it was the right answer. The issue of Beatty's divinity having been settled, CSIS sent him off to spy school.

The service's elite spy school, the Sir William Stephenson Academy, was located at the time at Camp Borden, north of Toronto. Somebody once remarked how fitting it is that the training academy for CSIS, which spends much of its time spying on behalf of a well-known "friendly foreign intelligence service," should be named after someone who himself had become famous for his espionage activities on behalf of a friendly foreign intelligence service. Sir William was the famous Second World War spymaster known by his code name "Intrepid," who headed the British espionage, economic and secret propaganda operations for North and South America.

Winston Churchill had put Stephenson, a wealthy Canadian businessman, in charge of the British Security Co-ordination Office in Rockefeller Center in New York, where he oversaw all British propaganda efforts in North America aimed at countering the American isolationists and getting the U.S. into the war quickly and in a big way. Stephenson was immensely successful at what he did, and highly decorated for his efforts later on. He was knighted in 1945.

Soon afterwards, a number of books began appearing, written by various authors, that glorified Stephenson beyond anything he had done. Perhaps these books were fulfilling a deep-seated need by some to find real-life heroes in the espionage business. The adulation continued unabated for the next forty-five years. In fact, David Niven played Stephenson in a TV mini-series entitled *A Man Called Intrepid*.

Unfortunately, Stephenson came down with a form of senile dementia and retired to Bermuda in 1968. Many spy-struck writers visited him there, and he became a sage — the original Old Man of espionage books. But by this stage in his illness, he could no longer distinguish between fact and fiction, and he misled a number of people. Even the RCMP Security Service contributed to the Stephenson cult, mainly because it needed a hero and Stephenson happened to be Canadian. The man who had been called Intrepid died in 1989, aged ninety-three.

It was all fact and very little fiction at the Sir William Stephenson Academy when Beatty showed up in fall 1986. The school had been set up the previous year, in August 1985; Beatty was enrolled in the third six-month course.

He remembers the Academy as being "impressive, with portable classrooms, crammed with just about the latest in everything needed, with semi-circle layouts and seminar-type rooms, with the best audio-visual equipment, and white-boards all the way around the room — the sort of thing you can really work with."

There were a total of sixty-nine teachers and guest lecturers. Some taught just one hour every six months while others taught almost every day, depending on their courses. "The teachers had been chosen as winners," Beatty recalls. They had entered a competition and the ones chosen were automatically promoted from an IO-3 to an IO-4 (Intelligence Officer-3 and Intelligence Officer-4). "They knew how to massage people and groom them for certain situations. We also had outsiders in every week, a wide range of people all the way from Alan Borovoy to right-wing profs from American universities, and real lectures in political analysis, not just red-baiting."

Borovoy, the general counsel of the Canadian Civil Liberties Association, taught exactly one hour on civil liberties every six months, but CSIS was proud to cite him repeatedly to the news media as being a lecturer because he was a well-known critic of the agency and was popular in civil libertarian circles. CSIS took great care never to name any other guest lecturers it brought in, especially not the right-wing American professors. It said *their* names had to be kept secret for security reasons.

The program included courses on the Criminal Code and the CSIS Act, how CSIS had been set up, its objectives, how it operated and basic information on counter-espionage, counter-terrorism and counter-subversion, the three main functions of CSIS at the time.

"We learned how each of the five components of CSIS worked, how threats are defined, how work is assigned. We had people come in and talk about geo-strategic politics, for instance, over a two-day period. Someone who was specialized in Eastern Europe would come in and talk to us for two days.

"Some people criticized the school as too many hijinks and too much glitz," he says. One day they brought in an explosives expert who loaded up an old car with dynamite and blew it up, even though CSIS agents are not supposed to be involved in blowing up people's cars. But Beatty argues it wasn't as silly as it sounds, because CSIS agents might find themselves someday sitting in on a counter-terrorism planning meeting with police representatives. If everybody in the room except the CSIS officer has seen a car bomb go off and knows what the effect might be, he could lose his credibility. As well, even though CSIS agents aren't allowed to carry guns in their line of duty, they had to qualify to the Marksmen level, using 9-mm hand-guns, with twelve hours of training spread over six months.

The living conditions could not have been better, says Beatty, who has lived in a lot of college dormitories in his life. "Top-notch, everyone had individual suites with air conditioning, television, radio, private bathroom with showers, their own computer terminal." In addition, there was office space for staff, a common lounge and living facilities for visiting officials and guest lecturers. It may have been Camp Borden, but boot camp it was not. The Academy even outstripped CSIS headquarters in equipment. At HQ, they were still fighting over terminals two years after the agency had been set up.

Physical activity had not been on the program the first year, but by the time Beatty arrived, it was on the course three times a week, and extra activity was encouraged at the surrounding military base's extensive recreational facilities.

SIRC sent a study group to the school for a two-day visit in the spring of 1986, and SIRC Research Director Jacques Shore wrote later in his report that he found the facilities "impressive" and the atmosphere positive.

There were some problems. Many students at the Academy who were interviewed as part of the SIRC study said they could have done without the course on "effective writing." Part of the problem was the old RCMP mindset that still pervaded CSIS. A course in how to write effectively is excellent for the RCMP training school in Regina because the RCMP plucks its recruits out of high school. But for men and women who already have a couple of university degrees and an extensive background in academic writing, such a course was not nearly as important as getting more hours of investigative technique and more study of criminal law and the CSIS Act. Only 15 of the 869 class hours, just slightly more than they spent shooting guns, were spent learning federal statutes, the Criminal Code and the CSIS Act. As well, the Academy could have done with a decent library. Books were obviously not a priority.

The biggest mistake of all, however, was that the Academy did not offer a French course. CSIS had set up an entire spy school without a single class taught in French. It was the oldest RCMP mindset of all, going back to the days when the Mounties were an English-only corps and Louis Riel and the Francophones were the enemy. Out of an estimated 3,000 applications CSIS selected only one Francophone for the first spy school class of thirty-three students. It was not an oversight, because six months later CSIS picked only two Francophones for a class of twenty students. The lone Francophone in the January 1986 class had to struggle as best she could in English. There was not a single document or sheet of course material in French for her to use. Only two of the sixty-nine teachers and lecturers could speak French. Clearly CSIS was not interested in having many Francophones in its ranks.

Because of its obsession with secrecy, the service insisted on keeping secret the actual number of students and the cultural makeup of each class. The excuse CSIS gave was that revealing the number of students enrolled at the Academy or saying how many were women or Francophones might help the Soviets in their spying activities. For the same reason, CSIS argued, it would not reveal how much the Academy was costing annually.

It would take at least another year before CSIS's insensitivity towards Francophones was finally exposed. In any bureaucracy, secrecy provides a temporary advantage to the bureaucrats. The trouble was that by the time the language situation at the Academy was discovered, it was too late. CSIS had a full-blown language crisis on its hands, and the school was quickly shut down. Senior officials said the Academy was closed because of lack of money, but they never said how much it had cost, nor how much they lacked, and whether they could have used more money to keep it open.

In 1988, the Academy reopened in the more bilingual confines of Ottawa, offering courses in both official languages. It also accepted a higher proportion of Francophones, women and members of ethnic and visible minorities. But the harm had been done.

There was one thing that happened at the Academy in the fall of 1986 that Beatty says is really worth noting. A student was expelled at Christmas under mysterious circumstances and was never heard from again. The whole thing was hushed up. There had been a number of drop-outs at the Academy. And some students had failed — a handful every year. It happens in the best of schools. But this was different. This student was good in class. He showed no signs of wanting to quit, and yet he was suddenly gone. There was speculation that he had been suspected of being a Soviet mole who had somehow sneaked past the recruitment screening process. He was either discovered quite by accident, or as a result of a tip from a Soviet defector in Montreal at the time, Yuri Smurov, a Soviet national who was an official at the International Civil Aviation Organization and brought some information about Soviet spy networks with him when he came over.

Whatever the reason, eighteen months later the Canadian government would be expelling a total of seventeen Soviet diplomats in the biggest spy expulsion episode since the days of Igor Gouzenko. One of the charges whispered against the Soviets was that they had tried to penetrate CSIS. There would be no details. If more was said, the Soviets might be able to figure out which penetration CSIS had found out about. And it may well have been the case of the student expelled from the Academy.

An attempted penetration by the Soviets to plant a mole so deep inside CSIS would have given Finn and his cronies nightmares. It would have been enough to warrant closing down the Academy until they could figure out how it had happened and completely revamp the recruit screening procedures. The only problem with this theory is that, although the Academy *did* close soon afterwards, there has been no noticeable change in recruit-screening procedures. CSIS is not any more or less rigorous.

Beatty the rookie arrived at CSIS headquarters in Ottawa in spring 1987 with his spy school diploma in his hand. He was full of great expectations. Back at the Academy the graduates had been conned into believing they were the "cream of the crop" because they had been chosen from among 1,200 applicants. They were told repeatedly they would be the stars of the new civilian security service.

The new intelligence officer discovered CSIS was in a state of turmoil and disorganization. For two and a half years it had been mired in chaos and confusion under director Ted Finn. The Mountie old boys' club that ran CSIS under him had been unable to adapt to a changing political reality. It had failed to grasp the notion that hiring civilians, Francophones, women and minorities was in, and hiring old Mountie buddies and ex-cops from municipal forces was out. Their management approach amounted to: "Do it because I tell you to do it." Somehow, in 1987, that failed to motivate new civilian recruits. As a result, cynicism was rampant.

CSIS was under a constant barrage of criticism from the public and parliamentarians. It appeared to be making mistakes at every turn and was being blamed even for things over which it had no control — everything from failing to solve the mystery of the 1985 Air India jumbo jet crash, to not knowing ahead of time when the terrorist attack on a Turkish diplomat would occur. CSIS had allowed or enticed a number of prominent undesirables to waltz into the country and now was paying the price.

Solicitor General James Kelleher confided to Montreal *Gazette* reporter Terrance Wills that CSIS Director Ted Finn was not to blame, that he had merely inherited the mess from the RCMP security service and was really trying to improve things. "There's an old saying: When you're up to your behind in alligators, it's hard to remember you came in to drain the swamp," Kelleher said.

CSIS didn't respect him. Kelleher demanded to know from the agency whether anything embarrassing was being kept from him; he was forever being hit by unexpected Opposition questions in the House of Commons.

Occasionally Kelleher would hold little confession sessions, as he called them, with the Executive Committee at CSIS to find out if anything embarrassing had happened. The committee members despised him and mocked him behind his back. Even the lower ranks didn't like him. "We called him 'Mr. Haney,' you know, the junk dealer in *Green Acres,*" laughs Beatty. The re-runs of the venerable show are still a hit with CSIS agents.

Kelleher repeatedly told senior CSIS managers that it was his neck on the line, not theirs. In the end, it was Finn and his five deputy directors who lost their heads. As for Kelleher, he survived until the wise and merciful electors of Sarnia voted him out in the 1988 general election.

CSIS management, unable to speak French, had allowed a feeling of alienation to grow in the Montreal headquarters until it erupted, in 1986, into a major linguistic crisis that raged unabated for almost a year. Montreal was in open revolt against the Ottawa headquarters, and sent a flood of internal telexes all over the capital. There was a series of leaks in Ottawa and Montreal exposing the inner workings of the service, revealing who was being watched, where, when and why. Two senior CSIS officers in Montreal sued a superior in civil court for telling them where to get off with their "fucking French rights." The Montréal office filed 1,600 protests over language discrimination against Ottawa headquarters. When it came to sensitivity on language issues, CSIS was described as being in the Stone Age.

Ottawa headquarters was in a state of disorganization. It still had no comprehensive security screening policy, no operational manual of its own, no security clearance data bank, no computerized personnel list, and only a very rudimentary operations data bank. It relied on the FBI and the CIA for most of its foreign intelligence. And it did not even have its own office — it was spread out over eight office buildings in Ottawa. The major branches kept running messengers from building to building carrying Top Secret red file-folders in brown canvas bags.

When the graduates from the Academy stepped into this maelstrom it was understandable that no one noticed they had arrived. They were hardly welcomed with open arms. The ex-RCMP officers who ran CSIS treated Beatty and his fellow students as "the graduating class of Intrepid High." They made it clear to them that they would have to put in their time, telling them that it would take at least eight to ten years before they would be considered fully trained intelligence officers.

Beatty thought he had been trained sufficiently to head into the field right away. Failing that, he should be given a foreign posting, he figured, on account of his university training in international affairs and his successful stint at the Academy. Instead, he found himself, like so many of the other Academy graduates, stuck behind a desk in the security clearance section, assigned to reading boring security clearance reports on public servants. All the interesting field office jobs had gone to ex-RCMP members, as had the thirty foreign postings for security liaison officers.

Beatty should have noticed the "double standard" earlier. Even SIRC chairman Ron Atkey confided in 1986 to *Toronto Star* reporter John Picton that when he had visited the Academy for an inspection, some ex-RCMP instructors were going around wearing stylized "S" ties which they said could be worn only by former RCMP security service officers. And yet CSIS was supposed to be the new civilian security service in which former Mounties would not try to lord it over civilian recruits.

"What a way to hit them over the head early," Atkey remarked. "The new people may well be feeling like second-class citizens."

If he missed the double standard at the Academy, at headquarters it struck Beatty smack in the face. He discovered that, contrary to what the ads said, not all intelligence officers were equal. Some had negotiated higher salaries for themselves. Beatty, who had taken an $8,000 pay cut from his Parliament Hill job to start out in CSIS as an IO-1 at $25,000, discovered that some recruits with identical academic qualifications were starting out at $28,000 a year. If he had known that, he would have asked for at least what he had been making in his previous job.

The second thing he discovered was that ex-cops who had never spent a day in their lives at the Academy were being brought in as full-fledged intelligence officers at higher pay and higher positions than his. Ex-Mounties were coming in the back door through a "direct entry program" and "a modified entry program." They were immediately given IO-3 status at $38,000 a year, the equivalent of a ten-year headstart on Beatty. They might have been good cops, but never having been to the Academy, what did they know about being intelligence officers? In addition, their academic qualifications sometimes went no further than a high school diploma. In 1985 and 1986, a total of thirty-nine ex-Mounties were brought in as intelligence officers. Every last one of them came in at the higher IO-3 level.

Beatty wondered how useful it had been to compete against 1,200 other people and then spend six months training in Camp Borden if he ended up having to take a back seat to an ex-RCMP officer.

At this rate the number of ex-Mounties in the service would be increasing, not decreasing. To make matters worse, CSIS had shut down the Academy, the one place that was producing civilian intelligence officers, just after Beatty had graduated. CSIS management said at first it was because they had run short of money; they added that they didn't need the school because they didn't have any more openings for intelligence officers. But they had just hired sixteen more ex-cops as IOs in the last quarter of 1986 on the grounds they needed intelligence officers in a hurry. They *said* it was easier to hire ex-cops right away than wait six months for another class of graduates. But nothing they were doing (or saying) made much sense. "They were just dumping people into the service who lacked the qualifications," says Beatty. "It was the old story of who had connections."

CSIS announced that the service urgently needed bilingual officers, so a group of ex-cops was hired — bilingual ex-cops this time. Then CSIS said it was putting more emphasis on counter-terrorism and so urgently needed experienced investigators — ex-cops again!

Ron Atkey had another explanation. He told *Globe and Mail* reporter Victor Malarek that CSIS was simply balking at becoming a truly civilian organization. "It's police officers first and university graduates second," he said. " . . . there's a definite mindset at CSIS. I think there is a group within senior management who sees civilianization as a crock. . . . "

Atkey pointed out that the whole purpose of setting up CSIS as distinct from the RCMP had been so that Canada would have a civilian-based security and intelligence service with an attitude different from that of the Mounties, not so that Canada would have a new security and intelligence service made up of ex-Mounties.

In 1985 and 1986 CSIS chose almost half of its 103 new intelligence officers from among ex-cops. By spring 1987, CSIS had hired only seventy-three civilians as intelligence officers at IO-1 level. After three years in operation, out of a total staff of more than 2,000 persons, there were fewer than 100 civilian intelligence officers at CSIS. At this rate, somebody joked, CSIS would be civilianized by the year 2028.

The service seemed to be going backwards. With the Academy shut down, it would be more difficult than ever to find qualified civilians. It was a shame, Atkey said, because the civilian graduates had been doing better than the ex-cops. SIRC conducted interviews with the thirty-three graduates of the first class at the Academy and found them to be progressing at a much faster rate as intelligence officers than their police-trained colleagues.

"It takes a new civilian intelligence officer two to three years to get to the level where it normally takes five years for the cop to get," said Atkey. Needless to say, that remark did not endear him to CSIS management.

"When I arrived, I found a vacuum in the organization, in policies, in communications and even in intellectual orientation," says Beatty. "In a nutshell, it didn't work."

Beatty sat at his desk in the security screening section amazed at how primitive the screening procedures were. "It was a total disaster," he says. "It was all on index cards and big red legal-size files — one on every single soul that has a security clearance in the federal government. These things were trucked around in bags. It was tedious as the dickens." Some middle management were bucking computerization of the security screening for the most self-serving of reasons. Their status depended on the number of persons working for them, known as PYs, or person-years.

They didn't want machines replacing the PYs, because that would reduce their status.

And yet, for a modern security and intelligence agency, computerization of security screening files is indispensable. If a security leak occurs in Section "A" of Department "Y", you have to be able to push a button and get a list of all the people in Section "A" who had a security clearance that gave them access to the information that has been leaked. At CSIS, no such lists were available. Every time there was a leak, staff would have to obtain a list of everybody who worked in Section "A" — sometimes they even had to use the federal government telephone book to try to put one together. Then the files would be called up alphabetically and each one located and fetched by hand from the stacks and examined one by one. It could take weeks instead of minutes.

"With computerization you can identify right away who has had access to the leaked information and then pull those files from the computer and see who has a weakness or a difficulty," says Beatty. "You could weight a profile of maybe ninety or so characters and then go after these people rather than having to go through the whole department alphabetically every time."

Beatty was floored by the inadequacy of the system. And it is not any better today than it was when he left CSIS in 1989. Former Academy friends who are still plodding along in security screening told Beatty recently that, although there has been some modernization and some computerization in the security screening branch, they are still using the old red file-folders and still lugging them around from office to office.

The young officer was never allowed out in the field to conduct security screening interviews. He was told that interviewing was "a senior investigative responsibility," and he was a merely a "junior." So his job as a junior was to sit in the office and analyse the reports that came in from the seniors, the security screening investigators, most of whom were old ex-RCMP detectives hired on contract to conduct interviews for CSIS.

"I was put in the perverse position of having to analyse their

responses. When I wasn't happy, I would have to ask the field
investigator who was maybe fifty-five years old that he had to go
back and find out this, this and this," recalls Beatty. "So all of a
sudden, I'm locking horns with some fifty-five-year-old who says
to me, 'I've been down this road, son, for thirty years.' And I'm
saying, 'No, I'm sorry, but I need this information.'

"The calibre of the people in the field was a disaster. It's a
nightmare. They were hiring old gumshoes. It should have been
a breeding ground for new intelligence officers."

Some of the office procedures were out of the last century.
"You thought typing pools had gone out of existence?" asks
Beatty. "Not at CSIS. They still have typing pools there. You come
in and you write down your report and you take it over to a typing
pool to get it typed. You put it in the in-basket and then the typist,
who types all day, types it up and then you come back and you
proofread it, and you make your changes, and you hand it in.
Pretty scarey, eh?"

Beatty says he checked recently with former colleagues still in
CSIS and the typing pool is still there. Strangely, though, there
were never any security leaks in the typing pool, as far as he
knows.

The operational files, the ones about spies, terrorists and
political groups under surveillance, had already been computerized when Beatty arrived, but the system struck him as being very
outdated.

"You can punch in 'Iranians' for instance and get all the
material dealing with Iranians. The basic thing is there." The
problem is that there are no policies as to what kind of information on Iranians should be entered. Every investigator filing a
report decides what should go into the system and that leads to
inconsistencies and omissions, as well as overly detailed entries
of trivia.

"There has to be some analysis," says Beatty, "so that you're not
just collecting garbage." He suggests an intermediary stage so
that field investigators would not decide personally what should

go into the system; they would show their reports to a senior official, an IO-4 or an IO-5, who would be the co-ordinator for "that little sphere of intelligence." The senior official would decide what was important enough to put in the system.

Beatty wasn't happy in security screening, but he discovered there was nothing he could do about it. Every time he asked to be transferred, he was told he couldn't leave because they needed him. There was a big political crisis over the security and immigration screening backlog.

"I was in for almost three years," he says. "I never went out into the field." Nor did any of the other twenty graduates in his class. "They kept us in there. It was a human resources disaster. The personnel department had no control at all over where you worked."

Each director had his own fiefdom. Senior officials were loathe to let anyone leave for fear of eventually losing precious PYs. Intelligence officers who wanted to be transferred had to persuade the director of the branch they wanted to go to that he should take them, and then go back and persuade the senior official in their branch to release them.

Some CSIS intelligence officers were having serious emotional problems. Beatty recalls a Francophone who had come over to CSIS as a transfer from the RCMP security service. He had such severe mental problems that he should not have been at work. As it was, he was in and out of hospital a great deal. As far as his colleagues could make out, his problems had something to do with illegal activities that he had taken part in on behalf of the RCMP during the October Crisis. He had done "some things that bordered on the criminal" that he had never gotten over.

In 1986, CSIS did not have an employee assistance program for the fifteen percent of the staff that was estimated, by a special SIRC investigative study group led by lawyer Jacques Shore, to be suffering from emotional problems. Four years later SIRC complained again in its annual report that CSIS still does not have a proper employee-assistance program.

Beatty recalls another intelligence officer, a former RCMP security service officer who had let a couple of ex-Nazis, one a former SS officer, into the country in 1983 after the federal government had specifically barred their entry. Some government officials had lied and destroyed documents which would have prevented the two suspected war criminals from being cleared to enter Canada. The former Mountie was named in a 1986 study prepared by historian Alti Rodal for Judge Jules Deschênes's Commission of Inquiry on War Criminals in Canada. He had been described by his RCMP colleagues as "quite right-wing" and regarding "the war crimes issue as being blown all out of proportion by the Jewish lobby." The Conservative government censors blacked out the ex-Mountie's name — in the interests of national security, of course — when an expurgated version of the Rodal report was finally made public a year later. But his CSIS colleagues knew who he was, although CSIS management and the RCMP, as well as the government, refused to disclose his identity even after NDP MP Svend Robinson demanded to know who the man was and what disciplinary action had been taken against him.

Then-Solicitor General Kelleher replied that because "it happened under a previous regime" — the Liberals were in power in 1983 — CSIS had "absolutely no comment." SIRC chairman Ron Atkey promised to investigate, but the issue was quietly shuffled aside after the initial publicity had died down.

Beatty says that inside CSIS the incident caused quite a furor at the time. "They wanted to remove the guy, but then he started talking about who else he felt knew as much as he did — even if they didn't. He said, 'Hey, this person and this person also knew about it, and I'm taking the whole deck down with me.' " He named two very senior people at CSIS who were still in positions of authority. "He could paint them with this brush even if it became one person's word against another's," says Beatty. "So the shit hit the fan everywhere. And obviously this guy was let off the hook."

Current CSIS Director Reid Morden said in an interview

recently that the man in question has retired. He declined to say whether CSIS had finally been able to get rid of him, or whether he had left CSIS of his own will.

As for all the talk coming from SIRC about how CSIS should go abroad to collect intelligence, it is nothing more than a sick joke, says Beatty. There is no way CSIS could do it, even if it wanted to. The agency has only thirty-one security liaison officers abroad, but would need at least eighty to do a half-decent job. "There's no question that we should have intelligence officers posted in every embassy around the world, collecting open information, but my God, we haven't got people who know how to do that yet."

This is too bad, because the kind of intelligence that will be most needed during the next decade will be about business, economics, and industrial and technical processes. This is the one area where CSIS counter-intelligence is untrained, and unwilling to develop. According to Beatty, "The view from the desks is so restrictive and myopic that unless something has to do with politically ideologically driven covert activity, these people won't look at it."

In fact, most of the CSIS officers on the various East European counter-intelligence desks don't even know the language of the country for which they are responsible. A SIRC study conducted in 1986 revealed that CSIS didn't think training intelligence officers in languages other than English and French was justified in terms of the expenses in time and money, because the intelligence officers "would often lose their language skills" anyway. So they operate in English and French, usually in English, and use translators. SIRC has discovered that it sometimes takes up to twenty days for CSIS translators to crank out a translation.

There is no way the agency is ready to send anyone abroad, says Beatty. "If you go abroad as an intelligence officer you have to be pretty smooth and pretty diplomatic to survive. These guys would paint themselves into a corner in three weeks."

In some areas where CSIS should be well-informed, it is woefully weak. One of the most flagrant recent examples Beatty mentions is the case of Canadian engineer Gerald Bull, the sixty-two-year-old genius and master gun-maker who was murdered, execution-style, by two quick bullets to the base of the neck as he opened the door to his Brussels apartment on March 22, 1990.

Bull, who was born in North Bay, Ontario, was the world's leading authority on super-heavy artillery. In 1968, he founded Space Research Corp., located on a well-guarded, isolated mountainous site straddling the Quebec-Vermont border, to fulfill his dream of building a cannon so powerful that it could actually launch a satellite into space without the use of a rocket. By 1990 he had been having trouble with the law in Canada and the U.S. for more than a decade, after being exposed in the late seventies by a CBC television documentary for selling super howitzers to South Africa in violation of a Canadian embargo on the sale of arms to that country. The super-guns were used to hurl deadly projectiles hundreds of kilometres, to attack with devastating accuracy civilian populations in neighbouring Namibia and Angola.

In 1980, the Americans moved in and put an end to Bull's North American operations. He was tried, convicted and sentenced to six months in jail by a Vermont court for violating the American embargo on arms sales to South Africa. But Bull didn't seem to care to whom he sold his super-weapons, nor how they were used. He sold guns to China, Spain, Israel, Iraq, and possibly half a dozen other countries as well.

Bull's death came as Great Britain intercepted a shipment of what it said were parts of a super-gun, possibly the longest cannon ever built — more than forty metres long — believed to be destined for Iraq, which is thought to be seeking a Doomsday super-gun to launch either a small nuclear bomb or a super-deadly cannister of germs into Israel. Somebody got to him ahead of delivery. But why, if the gun was already made and on its way to Iraq?

There are at least half a dozen intelligence agencies around the world actively investigating the Bull murder, trying to figure out how it fits into the geopolitics of Europe and the Middle East.

Naturally enough, some came to see CSIS. After all, Bull was a Canadian, and this is where he got his start and where his family and his roots still are.

"I happen to know we knew very little," says Beatty, who is furious about it. "That is very unfortunate, because while we're mucking around with some candy-ass things that won't amount to a hill of beans, we're losing our international credibility because we don't know jackshit about a Canadian who is a major player."

Two CSIS officers went to Montreal recently to interview Michel Bull, the dead engineer's son. He was pleased to co-operate and answer questions because the family has insisted all along that Bull never did anything wrong and was not building any super-gun for Iraq, just shipping some metal chimney sections for the country's petrochemical industry. Michel Bull gladly spoke to the two agents, but he said later he was stunned by how little they knew about his father or his activities in Canada or Europe.

Part of the reason for CSIS's ignorance of the Bull affair is that the Bull file would have been one of those inherited from the RCMP security service, for whom what South Africa did or didn't do in Canada was not exactly a matter of burning interest. CSIS is paying today for the RCMP's sins of omission a decade ago.

To appease the complainers after he replaced Finn in 1987, Reid Morden announced a new career planning policy. CSIS employees were told they would be given something called "The Social Contract" which would tell them everything they needed to know about what they should be doing. The document finally came out — with a burgundy cover and a gold crest on it. Everybody in the service got one, but few employees were impressed. "It was a glossy brochure," says Beatty, "that looked like something you get in airplanes with a little mint stick — 'thank you for flying with CSIS' — and that was supposed to be your contract for the next ten years."

In January 1989, Beatty was asked to identify what policies

existed for security screening. He discovered that even then, after almost five years in operation, CSIS had no comprehensive document on security screening policies. The agency was still working with memos, agreements, directives and material left over from the Mountie regime; in effect, operatives were winging it, trying to deal with sensitive issues as they came up. He didn't think this was any way to run a security service.

In 1989, he decided he couldn't take it any more. He couldn't support his wife and child on the salary he was making, and he didn't relish seeing ex-Mounties with less education and training than he had earning so much more. The chaos at CSIS angered him and he felt the personnel management was abysmal. So he left the agency and headed back to his old Parliament Hill job. He has not regretted it.

Beatty and others like him may have been appalled by what they saw as disorganization and poor management, but whole sections of CSIS were even more demoralized. Even now, only about 500 of the 3,000 employees of the agency are unionized, and they tend to be purely clerical workers — secretaries and clerks. The rest must fight battles for promotions or better working conditions on their own. Take the case of the "SURs."

In every organization there are certain people who have to do the donkey work. In the spy business, these are the surveillants, or "SURs" as they are called. They are the watchers, the people who "tail" targets of investigations — nameless, faceless people of every shape, size, age and personality. Only two things are required of them — that they do exactly as they are told without being seen, and that they keep quiet about it afterwards. They are badly paid, ill-used and, for security reasons, they are seldom told what they are doing, whom they are watching or why. If they are spotted, they have to report back immediately to their superiors, but spies aren't always kind enough to indicate that they have noticed their surveillants and will go through the motions of whatever operation they had under way without bringing it to completion, leaving the surveillance team wondering whether they missed the meeting or the exchange of information somewhere along the route.

A surveillant can be an old lady with a heavy shopping bag walking along the street, or a man asleep in a parked car, or an unemployed youth on a park bench. If CSIS is lucky, a surveillant may even be that tired-looking factory worker on the subway train — the one with the hidden microphone who is standing barely inches away from two men sitting together talking.

Surveillants do all sorts of dull things, such as waiting at bus terminals to note and report back the time of arrival of a man whose picture they have been given, what car he got into, or whether he took a taxi. They usually work in teams, but sometimes they're alone. There may be as many as a dozen or more of them on a big operation. When it's over they go home without asking questions and wait until they are called another day.

They may have to go to the local post office to buy stamps on the same day as a man with red hair and a slight limp comes in to empty a postal box. Their assignment will be to note which box it was he emptied. Or they may have to sit pretending they are asleep in a car on a side street for two hours and wait until a red car with a Quebec licence plate with two digits — "7" and "4" — passes by. Then, hoping it's the right red car, and that it was really red, not just maroon (and was that really a "4"?), they will call in the information and go home, wondering if they were right because if they weren't, somebody down the road is going to be watching the wrong car. Many surveillants are either retired people or unemployed, or have the sort of work that allows them to take time off at strange hours during the day or night. Most of them, however, are on full salary.

Very few SURs have much formal education. Not all of them fit easily into society. They do the work because they are told that they are part of something important, and that what they are doing is worthwhile, whatever it is. They can be used in all sorts of ways. It is not just CSIS or the RCMP who use them. Foreign powers also use a type of surveillant within Canada. They sometimes call them undercover security guards. The Israelis may use surveillants in Canadian airports to protect their El Al flights and the flights of other airlines going to Israel. The Israeli surveillants, sometimes quiet old men or women, or young couples in each other's arms, will deliberately line up in passenger check-in queues behind suspicious-looking characters, observing them all the way up to the ticket counter before signalling discreetly at the last moment, if they see anything that would require a real security investigator to step up, by saying quite politely, "Could you please come over here to this counter for just a moment, sir? It's about your ticket." Combined with the ever-present visible Israeli security and the not-so-hidden closed-circuit-cameras, these surveillants play a vital role in preventing terrorist attacks at Canadian airports as well as after aircraft leave the ground.

On the rare occasion when both are used in the same operation, surveillants do not interact with undercover agents. Each is not supposed to know the other exists. So they do not — as they do in the movies — nod to agents, stroke their noses at them in a meaningful recognition or even wink knowingly. If one ever did, an agent would likely call in immediately: "Pull that lousy SUR out of here. He'll blow the operation."

If a CSIS officer even *thinks* he's seen a surveillant during an operation, he'll notify his operations centre immediately. "If I've spotted him, they'll have spotted him. Get him out of here." A compromised surveillant is a liability.

The identity of CSIS surveillants is so secret that an intelligence officer who even tries to find out the identity of a SUR will immediately come under suspicion. Only the identities of undercover agents and informers are more secret than SURs. There is a good reason: the lives of undercover agents and informers may be at stake, especially in counter-terrorism cases. The lives of SURs are seldom in danger; they are protected from physical harm by their anonymity.

The surveillant service works out of its own office, separate from the rest of CSIS operations. Its members do not fraternize with other CSIS employees. Nor are their cars parked in the same location or gassed at the same gas stations or repaired at the same garages as regular CSIS cars. Surveillance cars are frequently repainted, to avoid recognition. Some are old bangers — they have to be; some are hot wheels; some are clumsy-looking old trucks. They have to be bought at different times, in different places, and their licence plates must be out of sequence with those on other surveillants' cars.

Attached directly to each CSIS district or region, SURs must be experts on their area. They must know every nook and cranny, every back door, every traffic tie-up, every bridge, every one-way street, every back alley. They have to, because a spy on an operation may run through a series of dry runs three or four times before choosing an escape route. Spies often deliberately delay their arrival at a checkpoint, or double back along a street, or send out an advance man — called a counter-surveillance officer — just to check out if there is surveillance ahead along the route.

The moment spies suspect they've spotted surveillance, they will abort their operation, whether it is a vital meeting with a secret agent or an information pick-up. An operation can always be rescheduled. A good spy network takes years to put in place.

Surveillants aren't the people doing things on the street — changing a tire, washing windows — because these activities attract attention, especially if they go on suspiciously long. Much better to put a surveillant in the second-floor window of a cheap hotel. The SUR becomes just another tired-looking face staring out the window at the world going by, the kind of face that everybody sees but no one notices.

Most surveillance today is done from cars, following targets for two or three blocks and then pulling away and reporting time, position and direction. Cellular telephones, special transmitters and other fancy electronic gadgetry have given the advantage to surveillants in recent years. But spies, to make certain they are not being followed, will often stop at a green light or pull over into the only parking spot available on a busy street. The surveillance car caught in the traffic flow may not be able to stop in time to avoid having to drive by and risk being recognized.

Last year in one major city, a car being followed closely by surveillance ducked in front of a large parked truck. "We've lost him," declared the men in the car coming up behind.

"But *we* haven't," a calm, low voice said over the communications network going into the operations centre. "He just pulled in front of us and is parked almost on our front bumper." Such surveillance through cities is rare because most spies prefer lonely country roads, where it is easy to double back, pull off the road or create a diversion to find out if someone is coming up behind. Suburbs are also favoured locations for detecting surveillance: it's easy to pull into an empty shopping centre parking lot on a Sunday afternoon, and check if everyone is coming up behind.

There is nothing glamorous about being in surveillance. It can mean sitting in a restaurant at a window table nursing a coffee or a drink for an hour or more, not knowing whether the target car has gone by or not.

SURS have been among the most disgruntled of CSIS employees. Many of them expected, after years of plodding service with the Mounties, to have a chance at more prestigious and interesting positions as intelligence officers when CSIS was set up. They were to be bitterly disappointed, left on the sidelines as old RCMP cops and new civilian recruits fresh from the Academy moved in and took over the best jobs in the agency.

When CSIS finally relented to pressure and told the SURs they could take tests for "conversion" to jobs as IOs, they were asked to sign the following statement: "I understand that as an employee of the Service I may at any time be required to relocate anywhere in Canada dependent on the needs of the Service."

It would have been fine if everyone else in CSIS had been asked to sign the form, but no one had (and in fact, ex-Mounties had special non-transfer clauses in their contracts). SURs took this as a veiled threat — "We'll promote you alright. But then we'll send you to the Yukon." And SURs in Montreal were particularly incensed: psychological tests for promotion were in English only; if they wanted to take them in French, they had to wait six months for translations, putting them even further behind in the chase for jobs.

The Francophone SURs protested, sent letters to their MPs, appealed to the Commissioner of Official Languages, identified themselves and went to the media. They produced internal documents and directives. The Montreal headquarters was leaking like a sieve.

A SIRC team sent in to investigate their grievances concluded in 1987 that they had every reason, in the absence of clear policies about personnel, to be upset. Incredibly, it took CSIS five years to issue a detailed policy statement describing career paths and conditions for SURs trying to enter the IO stream. By then, many had quit and gone to work for the private sector — or back to the RCMP, which employs them in anti-drug work, criminal investigations and a discreet little security intelligence directorate the Mounties don't talk about much these days.

And then there are the Francophones. From the beginning, CSIS has had trouble speaking French, even though twenty-eight percent of its employees were Francophone. Matters came to a head in April 1987, when Ted Finn faced the Standing Joint Committee of the Senate and the House of Commons on Official Languages.

The parliamentarians on the committee were well-informed. They knew there had been 2,075 documented protests alleging systematic violations of the Official Languages Act by the Ottawa headquarters of CSIS since the day the service had been set up almost three years earlier. Headquarters had insisted repeatedly on using only English in internal communications with the Montreal headquarters in open violation of the Official Languages Act.

The previous evening, a group of sixteen Francophone CSIS employees in Montreal had been the focus of a Radio-Canada news item which revealed a number of the linguistic anomalies and Official Languages Act violations at CSIS. And earlier in the day the protesters had been quoted extensively on their grievances in a number of newspaper articles.

Their complaint was that they were being forced to work with

English-only operational plans: the Academy had been run as a unilingual English-language training centre; French was not essential even for a posting to the CSIS office in Paris; and unilingual Anglophone investigators were being sent regularly into Quebec to conduct investigations. This last criticism prompted the committee chairman, Charles Hamelin, a Conservative MP from Charlevoix, to remark, "If I were Moammar Gadhaffi, I would not hesitate to dispatch Francophone spies to Canada in order to avoid being spotted by your totally English agency." CSIS held the dubious record of being the only government agency without an official languages policy, as required by law, almost three years after being created.

The sixteen operatives who had been interviewed the previous day had signed a protest letter and sent it to the committee. It was a daring move on their part — appealing directly to Parliament. By writing the letter they had put their jobs on the line. It was an act of frustration as much as of hope — frustration because to them it seemed that two years of official protests through the usual channels, including interviews with news media, appeals to the Commissioner of Official Languages and a couple of internal investigations, had produced nothing; and hope that the politicians might finally have an influence on CSIS headquarters.

Director Finn admitted total responsibility right off the bat. He was contrite, he was apologetic, he promised to do better, but it was still not enough. The parliamentarians insisted that he come up with a comprehensive language policy for CSIS, not just individual programs in branches here and there, depending on their linguistic makeup.

Finn's excuse was that between 1984 and 1986 he had been too busy setting up CSIS to give an Official Languages Program all the attention it deserved. He only got around to appointing a chief of official language services in May 1986, about the same time as the first two Francophones were appointed to senior management positions.

To his credit, Finn had tried to impress on his assistants the importance of at least trying to be bilingual, sending memos to that effect as early as May 1985. But the memos had been ignored. In August 1986, he sent a memo to his five deputy directors, identifying bilingualism as one of four priorities for the coming year. But again it had little effect on the staff at headquarters. They made one concession to the boss, however. They sometimes put "French to follow" at the bottom of the English-only memos they sent to Quebec. And sometimes a French version did follow a couple of weeks later. Then again, sometimes it didn't. One Francophone manager in Montreal used to translate the English-only directives himself and read them out in French — as if they had come in that way — to his employees rather than fan resentment by passing around the English-only version.

Finn pointed out that the situation was not as bad as it seemed, because 1,700 of the complaints dealt with one specific issue — English-only travel notices. These are five or six lines of standard-ized wording, alerting region and district offices that certain potential targets will be in their territory. In Canada, (as in the U.S.), diplomats from Soviet and Eastern bloc countries are under severe travel restrictions. In most cases, they are not allowed to venture, without prior permission from External Affairs, more than forty kilometres from Ottawa or Montreal, two cities where they are posted. They must make their travel re-quests to External Affairs several days ahead of time, extensively documenting where they intend to go, how they intend to travel and why they are going there. External Affairs passes the request along to CSIS for security considerations and CSIS decides whether the trip is acceptable.

Sometimes CSIS goes along so that it can lay on surveillance. Occasionally, the agency will recommend that External Affairs veto the trip on the grounds the area is one of intense strategic importance, off-limits to diplomats from non-allied countries. Canadian and American diplomats are under similar restrictions in the Soviet Union.

Every time a trip by a Soviet or Eastern bloc diplomat is

approved by External Affairs, a "travel notice" is sent ahead by CSIS headquarters to the closest office. Diplomats of other countries may also figure in travel notices, as may foreign nationals and officials of international agencies visiting Canada. Each notice advises the local office of the estimated time of arrival, the officially stated purpose of the trip, the suspected purpose if there is one and other useful particulars, such as where the individual is expected to stay, who the individual may meet, and so on.

Under the federal government's official languages policy, all travel notices sent to Montreal should be either in French or in both French and English. (By the same token, a member of headquarters staff, even if he were a Francophone, could not send a unilingual French message to Toronto.) And yet in 1984, 1985 and 1986, more than 1,700 English-only travel notices were sent to Montreal, despite repeated protests from Francophones. What shocked the parliamentarians the most was the fact that the messages kept going out in English only, even after all the protests. Weren't they getting tired of receiving all those protests in Ottawa? Or were they trying to make a point? Sending out bilingual travel notices would have been fairly easy, a matter of changing the standard form using a lexicon of a few hundred words and a few computer keyboard strokes.

In a way Finn was lucky. The parliamentarians never found out that CSIS had been administering polygraph tests to Francophones in English only. They would have had a field day with that one. Nor did they find out that two months after CSIS was established, just when they were passing out all the good jobs, Finn had ordered a two-year moratorium on language training for his senior officers. It meant that unilingual Anglophones could hold bilingual jobs and did not have to learn French because they were supposedly desperately needed to set up CSIS.

The moratorium also effectively shut out bilingual managers, who tended to be Francophone, from most of the senior positions requiring bilingual people. "CSIS appeared in the eyes of

Francophone employees to be turning back the clock," said the SIRC report. "Not surprisingly, some of them got the impression that their language rights would remain hostage to the Anglophone majority unless they formed a cabal so effective that the Service could not ignore them."

The moratorium on learning a second language was finally lifted in September 1986, and dozens of CSIS employees in Ottawa immediately rushed out to learn a second official language. Before the month was out, eight had enrolled in the full-time six-month French course at the federal government's Carson Road language school in Ottawa, and fifty others had enrolled in evening courses of the Public Service Commission. Five more were off for courses in a private language school. However, almost three years after its creation, forty percent of the bilingual jobs at CSIS headquarters were still occupied by unilingual persons.

Other things were going on that the parliamentarians did not find out about during their meeting with Finn. When a secret document came in to CSIS in a foreign language, it was translated and passed around. When it arrived in French, it was also translated and passed around, sometimes without the original French version attached. Sometimes only the English version would be passed around — to Francophones. They had to work with an English version of a document they would have understood much better in the original.

On one occasion a Francophone intelligence officer in Quebec was struggling with an English-only document that had arrived — until, upon closer examination, it began to look familiar. Finally he recognized it as an English version, amended and altered, of something he had originally written in French.

Finn's meeting with the Official Languages Committee was a stormy, occasionally acrimonious one. At one point, it was even suggested that Finn take an oath to swear to tell the truth. This supreme insult was, in fact, voted down, but Finn was visibly shaken. Finally, the parliamentarians extracted a promise from him that the next batch of recruits trained at the Academy would be bilingual. The MPs seemed happy until Finn pointed out that now that all the available jobs had been filled, they would not be needing any more recruits for a while and that the Academy would not reopen that fall.

Whatever Finn's good intentions were, his actions had alienated virtually all the Francophones in CSIS. It wasn't until 1989 that they finally, grudgingly, began to trust management.

An observer watching all the management failures, linguistic biases, labour disputes and operational confusion at CSIS might think that the agency is a lost cause. But there are a few signs that things are improving. The new management, personnel and operations manuals are a step ahead. And hiring policy, compared to other government departments, has become positively enlightened.

Very early in its life, for instance, CSIS was immunized against homophobia, the terrible affliction that had so greatly hindered the security and intelligence gathering abilities of the old RCMP security service for two decades. After some prompting from Opposition MPs in the House of Commons, SIRC chairman Ron Atkey wrote to CSIS director Finn in March 1985 asking for information about the service's policy on hiring homosexuals. Finn replied two weeks later that CSIS did not have a formal policy on hiring homosexuals, and that each applicant would be treated on an individual basis.

The letter was tantamount to saying the agency was prepared to hire gays and lesbians. Today, this does not sound like a very dramatic statement, but back then, it was a great leap forward. After all, CSIS was built on the remnants of the old RCMP security service, which used to hunt down homosexuals in the public service, chart their movements around Ottawa on a wall map, and even set up a special branch, called "A" Branch, to investigate all homosexuals living in Ottawa just in case some of them might someday want to apply for a job.

In the old days the RCMP often used "national security" as the major excuse for not hiring homosexuals, even though fewer

The man who "founded" CSIS: RCMP Const. Robert Samson
(left) confers with his lawyer in October, 1974. Samson, a member
of the Mounties' Organized Crime Squad with reputed Mob
connections, detonated a bomb at a Montreal supermarket heiress's
home in July, 1974. Not only did this "dirty trick" maim Samson,
it blew the lid off many RCMP activities – and set in motion the
forces that would create CSIS ten years later. *(Canapress)*

Quebec City lawyer Jean Keable conducts a public inquiry into
RCMP activities in Quebec. The inquiry, which began in June, 1977,
was a major factor in the federal government's desire to establish
an all-civilian intelligence agency. *(Chuck Stoody/Canapress)*

Senator Michael Pitfield (right) introduces Ted Finn, head of the Securities Intelligence Transitional Group (SITG), to a 1983 session of the special Senate Committee on security. Pitfield's report, *A Delicate Balance,* helped pave the way for the creation of CSIS. *(Canapress)*

Ted Finn swears an oath of secrecy before Liberal Solicitor General Robert Kaplan to become the first director of CSIS. Four years later, in 1987, Finn resigned in the wake of the Atwal affair. *(Paul Chiasson/Canapress)*

Punjabi cabinet minister Malkiat Singh Sidhu recovers from the wounds he received May 25, 1986, from four Sikh separatists who attacked him on Vancouver Island. CSIS agents had advance word the Punjabi minister might face "a rough reception" during his B.C. visit, but failed to alert the RCMP. *(Rick Loughran/Canapress)*

Harjit Singh Atwal waves to supporters in September, 1987, after he and Piara Singh Natt were freed after spending more than one year in a B.C. jail. The two had been charged with the attempted assassination of Punjabi politician Malkiat Singh Sidhu but were released after it was found CSIS had bungled in getting a wiretap warrant. *(Bill Keay/Canapress)*

Career diplomat/bureaucrat J. Reid Morden succeeded
Ted Finn as the director of CSIS in 1987. Politically
astute, he's bolstered morale in the organization,
initiated major administration changes, and shown an
ability to "contain situations." *(Ron Poling/Canapress)*

In 1986, Pei Chi Chang – better known as Patrick Chang to his Canadian friends – was the highest ranking Taiwanese government official in Canada. CSIS wanted him deported and on March 3, 1986, he left Toronto for Taiwan. No official explanation has ever been given.
*(James Lewcun/The Globe and Mail)*

Ryszard Paszkowski, a former KGB agent, hijacked a plane from Warsaw to Munich in 1982. He eventually ended up in Canada and in 1985 CSIS directed him to spy on Eastern Bloc spy operations. Paszkowski lived in an Edmonton, Alberta, walk-up apartment for a time. *(Canapress)*

This advertisement appeared in several newspapers
across Canada in fall 1989.

than one in ten Mounties did security and intelligence work. After CSIS was set up, the RCMP had to come up with a new excuse. Security considerations would hardly wash, so they hit on an interesting new angle. They didn't want to hire homosexuals, they said, because they didn't want them beaten up or harassed by local toughs on weekends in places like Cranbrook, B.C. It was a variation on the same excuse the Horsemen had given a decade earlier when they resisted hiring women. They didn't want drivers laughing in the faces of RCMP women constables pulling them over on the highway. Only after they had been forced to hire women did the RCMP notice that not too many people tend to laugh in the face of any police officer pulling them over on the highway, least of all one who is carrying a sidearm.

The RCMP and the armed forces have always had problems accepting the gays and lesbians into their ranks. CSIS, however, never had to deal with this kind of problem, thanks to Ted Finn's open mind on the matter and his quick resolution of the issue soon after CSIS was set up. One of the reasons he was so open about this issue may have been that he came from the Privy Council Office, where the notion of excluding anybody on the basis of sexual orientation would have been foreign to the people who worked there.

Finn's momentous decision sent a message down through the organization: it was okay to hire homosexuals. Gays and lesbians began joining CSIS, not in droves, but in rough proportion to their distribution within the general population. When asked on the probing CSIS recruitment questionnaires and during interview sessions if they were homosexual, the recruits who were would by and large answer truthfully and, depending on how this related to other factors, would be accepted or rejected.

The issue has gone far beyond the service's hiring practices. When a CSIS investigator happens to be a homosexual, the chances of sexual orientation being misrepresented as a major security risk are greatly reduced. Even the office humour changes tone. If there is a chance the boss may be gay, it's remarkable how the kinds of jokes that are told around the office change. It has almost the same effect as when the boss happens to be a woman, or a Francophone. Eventually at CSIS, the humour around the office will change even more if it ever happens that the boss is a black or a Sikh. But that is still in the future. One step at a time for CSIS.

The agency has never had a policy of systematic discrimination on the basis of race or colour, although for the longest time, no effort was made to attract anyone from visible minorities or ethnic communities. It was only in 1986-87 that CSIS began to realize what it was missing out on.

Even after the Air India crash in June 1985, the agency did not seem to care much that it did not have a single full-time officer who could speak Punjabi. And when Armenian-Canadian terrorists attacked the Turkish embassy in the same year, CSIS did not have a single Armenian-Canadian intelligence officer. Part of the intelligence work, which involved speaking Armenian, had to be done through translators. Now the agency has two officers from each of these groups.

Recently CSIS got its first black intelligence officer, a graduate of the six-month training course in Ottawa. A Haitian-Canadian who speaks fluent French, his colleagues refer to him good-naturedly as "Can't Miss." They kid him about considering a sex change and becoming Jewish if he wants to make director by next year.

Humour aside, it's encouraging to see how, in five years, being black and speaking French have gone from being handicaps to being perceived as assets at CSIS.

# "GREETINGS FROM THE POLISH EMBASSY"

CSIS'S HIRING POLICIES may have become relatively enlightened, but the service has continued to make some very serious mistakes in other areas. Take the story of Ryszard Paszkowski, whose recruitment and subsequent treatment by CSIS were so badly handled that a potential coup in international espionage became a disaster. Paszkowski could have been one of the most effective spies Canada ever had, but now the case has rebounded awkwardly and is turning into an embarrassing international incident.

Basically, what happened is that CSIS recruited a Polish hijacker in 1985 and sent him on a spy mission into the Polish embassy in Ottawa. It was a violation of international conventions and flew in the face of CSIS's claim that it is a purely defensive security and intelligence agency, never involved in covert operations against foreign countries on their territories.

Now Paszkowski, who has gone public with his story, says CSIS helped him in a complicated plan to use him as a double agent in a 1986 Polish-East German terrorist plot to put a bomb aboard an Air India plane flying out of Europe in 1986 in order to discredit the Canadian Sikh community.

The tale begins in Krakow, Poland in 1961 when a six-year-old

boy who lived alone with his father came home one day crying
that bullies had been hitting him. His father told him, "Never
come home to me again crying that you were beaten up." The
father's words had a strong impact on the boy, who vowed then
and there, "No matter how much it hurts, I will never cry. And
nobody is ever going to fuck me again." A Polish Scarlett O'Hara,
no less.

Young Ryszard was tall, athletic, dark-haired and good-looking. Good at school, he had a welder's certificate at seventeen.
At eighteen, he was conscripted into the Polish military, the Sixth
Pomorska Airborne Division. It was not long before he attracted
the attention of the Polish secret service, the Sluzba
Bezpieczemstwa (SB), who saw him as a potential recruit. He
showed such talent as an intelligence officer that, three years
later, at twenty-one, he was sent for nine months of training in
spy technique at the famous secret KGB training school in a
secluded villa in the woods outside Lesnov, near Kirov. The KGB
course offered there, a sort of graduate program for Soviet spies,
is also given to the most promising spy recruits from satellite
countries. Paszkowski was part of a group of Poles and East
Germans when he took the course in the fall of 1976.

By comparison to Lesnov, the Sir William Stephenson Academy is kindergarten. While the CSIS recruits are listening to Alan
Borovoy talk about civil liberties, the KGB recruits at Lesnov are
learning four ways to make a lethal bomb from commonly
available materials, and eight ways to kill a man without making
inconvenient noises.

The nine-month spy course features training in language,
lifestyle and something the Soviets call "training of the heart,"
which means obtaining blind obedience from its recruits. The
instructor and the recruit will stand alone in the middle of the
interior courtyard of the villa; the instructor will suddenly throw
a rifle into the arms of the unsuspecting recruit and then point
to an old lady in black with a babushka crossing the other end
of the courtyard and yell: "Shoot!" To pass the test, the recruit
must shoot immediately. There are only blanks in the rifle, of

course, but occasionally the old lady will fall down "dead," just to scare the daylights out of the instructor and traumatize the recruit forever.

Paszkowski says he would rather not discuss in too much detail what he learned at the KGB school until he is sure that the Gorbachev administration will be around for some time. He was trained in terrorism, murder, mayhem, how to make bombs and how to fool lie-detector tests. He also learned a number of ways to kill a person. "I learned to kill a man using only a toothbrush," he says, refusing to elaborate.

Paszkowski, the graduate returned to Poland and was promoted to sergeant in the SB, assigned to monitor the French and American consulates in Krakow. But in 1981 martial law was invoked and he had no taste for what he was doing as an intelligence officer. Besides, the government suspected him of secretly helping Opposition groups. So he and a friend, Franciszek Sarzyenski, who worked in a shop but was also with Polish intelligence, decided it was time to get out. In early 1982, they took off on travel visas to neighbouring Bulgaria, but were caught, badly bitten by a guard dog and ordered to return to Poland. Polish intelligence should have known right then that they had a problem on their hands, but they didn't. It was a big mistake on their part.

The pair tried a second time in August 1982 and made it to Budapest. There, on August 25, they boarded a LOT Polish Airlines flight to Warsaw. Once aboard, using the skills the KGB had taught him, Paszkowski had no trouble fabricating a most realistic-looking bomb out of red wax candles, insulating tape, wires and a battery he had been carrying. He and Sarzyenski produced their "bomb" and demanded to be taken to Munich. The pilot took one look at the candles and did exactly as they demanded. In Munich they promptly requested political asylum, which the West Germans granted to them immediately; however, the pair had to serve a four-and-a-half year sentence for airplane hijacking.

Sarzyenski decided he would serve his time and stay in Germany afterwards, and today he lives quietly outside Munich. But not Paszkowski. Using prison escape methods the KGB had taught him, he had no trouble escaping from Bernau, a minimum-security prison, on July 20, 1984. While in prison, an East German who had befriended him had said he knew some people who would help Paszkowski if he could escape. Now that he was out, he contacted them only to discover it was a set-up. They were really his old friends in Polish intelligence, and they wanted him back. Either he did what they said, or they would turn him in to the West German police. They meant it. Paszkowski had no choice but to go along. So he took the fake Swedish passport they gave him, and the several thousand American dollars as well, and agreed to head off to France to kidnap two people and take them to the Polish embassy in Paris. He followed their instructions as far as Strasbourg, but there his conscience got the better of him. Paszkowski was a cowardly spy at heart; he was never cut out to be a killer or a terrorist. So he gave the Poles the slip and headed south to Marseille where, he recalls, "I sat in the sun and spent their money."

Then, having decided that Canada was such a free and accessible country, he hopped a boat to Italy and went calling on the Canadian embassy in Rome. Paszkowski has never had trouble crossing borders at will. After telling officials at the embassy that he was a Polish refugee, he found himself ushered in to meet an RCMP investigator and laid out his life's story for him, including his stint at the spy school at Lesnov. He says that all the Mountie, whose name he can't remember, promised him was that "we might be able to help you, if you can help us."

The Mountie told him to go back to France, lose his Swedish passport and show up at the Italian border, telling officials he was Robert Fisher, a Polish truck driver who had escaped from Poland with the help of other truck drivers. Paszkowski says he followed the instructions to the letter, and soon found himself in custody in a large refugee camp at Latina, where he was processed as Robert Fisher. He points out that "Fisher" is a good alias because it is a common name in Poland, and also fits in nicely in Canada, where he was headed.

After spending forty days in the refugee camp, he was beginning to wonder about his Mountie friend, until suddenly the Canadian refugee selection committee arrived and right away picked him out of the crowd. They gave him a train ticket to Rome, and there gave him an airline ticket to Toronto and on to Edmonton. He flew out of Rome on December 11, 1984. Since he had no passport, the embassy gave him a Canadian-issued travel identity document and told him he would be met at the airport in Toronto.

It was the Mounties who cleared him in Rome to go to Canada. Although CSIS had been responsible for immigration security clearances for five months by December 1984, in many places, such as Rome, the transfer of responsibilities from the RCMP had not yet taken place. CSIS would make its first contact with its new agent, "Fisher," in Canada. Later it would be able to say in all honesty that it had not recruited him in Rome. It had hired him legally in Canada. That was important because the CSIS Act expressly forbids CSIS from operating covertly abroad. Recruiting spies in foreign lands would certainly be considered in that category. For their part, the Mounties could always pretend that they didn't know who "Fisher" was when they cleared him for security in Rome. It was safer than letting him into Canada as "Paszkowski."

His flight was met in Toronto by a woman who welcomed him in Polish and gave him a parka that fit him perfectly. These smart Canadians think of everything, he thought. He was pleased. The woman also gave him Canadian money. After a two-hour stop over he boarded his flight for Edmonton. It was midnight by the time he arrived there. This is a very big country, he thought. An immigration official who spoke German met him at the airport and took him by cab to the Pan-Am Motel.

The next morning the same cabbie who had driven him the night before showed up unannounced and drove him to Immigration Canada offices. Clearly these Canadians knew what they were doing. Bob Kawami, the immigration official who had met him at the airport, processed his papers and gave him information on life in Canada. "They organized everything," he recalls. Kawami lined up a language school for him and told him to learn English and settle into the large Polish-Canadian community in Edmonton. He enrolled him in language courses at the Alberta Vocational College in January 1985.

"We'd meet once a week or twice a month," recalls Paszkowski. "He'd give me instructions. We'd work together." Immigration Canada officers never mentioned CSIS by name, but left no doubt they were relaying messages from the people who wanted him in this country. They told him to stay put. He would be contacted eventually, he was told, when he would be of use to them. In the meantime, he was told to build up his profile in the Polish-Canadian community in Edmonton.

He worked for a while at Northwest Spring and Machine Ltd., and then a job was lined up for him in the garage at Maran Construction Equipment Ltd., through one of the owners, John Boyko. At first Paszkowski washed trucks and changed oil; later he did light mechanical work. At the garage, he continued to use the alias Robert Fisher. He soon became one of the hardest-working, most popular workers in the shop. General manager Ernie Jacubo recalls that "he was the best worker we had back then in the shop. And I'm not saying that just because I'm Polish." Certainly none of his fellow workers suspected that he was an undercover agent establishing an elaborate cover. Zygmunt Paszkowski — no relation — who runs a geodetic surveying firm in Edmonton, hired the undercover agent he knew only as Robert Fisher to work occasionally as a helper on survey crews. "I helped him buy his first car and his first television set, and he paid me back every cent I lent him," he says.

CSIS intelligence officers would show up at the garage occasionally to have Fisher fix their cars on the side and he would talk with them. CSIS was waiting before baiting the hook for the Polish intelligence services. This was a delicate operation. If CSIS didn't act slowly, discreetly, the Poles wouldn't bite. The word was put out in the Polish community that "Fisher" might be somebody else. It would only be a matter of time before the Poles, who ran a fairly extensive intelligence network in Edmonton to keep an eye on Polish immigrants there, figured out who Fisher really was. And then they would try to get their errant spy back once again.

Finally, in May 1985, CSIS approached him, Paszkowski says, and directed him to make contact with a Polish intelligence agent active in the Edmonton area — a university professor — who sometimes came in to the garage to have his car fixed, and who had befriended Paszkowski. One day the professor came in and said, "I bring you greetings from the Polish embassy." Paszkowski says he reported the remark to his CSIS handlers, who knew they had a bite on their line. They equipped their agent with a microphone and transmitter and told him to arrange another meeting with the professor as soon as possible. He did and the two men met several more times. CSIS monitored every meeting. They talked of many things, but nothing in which the professor, who has since returned to Poland, compromised himself.

Paszkowski says that CSIS knew sooner or later the Poles would try to blackmail him into going back to work for them. If they didn't, it would be because they suspected he was working for CSIS and they didn't want to have a double agent on their hands. Finally, at one meeting — according to Paszkowski — the professor admitted he was with Polish intelligence and asked him to go to the embassy in Ottawa. Paszkowski says CSIS knew that this was big and that the Poles were hooked solid because Polish intelligence would not bring someone to the embassy unless they had something major in mind for him and were really sure that he was not working for the Canadians. He also says CSIS was very happy with him. It had a fantastic opportunity to plant him as a Canadian double agent right in the middle of a Polish spy network in Canada.

The problem was that Paszkowski didn't want to go to Ottawa.

He was afraid. The risk was too great. What if he were discovered and caught inside the embassy? It was Polish territory, and the RCMP couldn't help him there. His handler at CSIS, Nick Maduck, and his boss, a big, good-looking man named "Earl," met him repeatedly at the Chateau Lacombe Hotel in Edmonton and insisted that he go, Paszkowski recalls. They assured him that it had all been cleared with External Affairs Minister Joe Clark, he says. He didn't believe them. But he claims they were paying him $2,000 a month at this time, and it was hard for him to refuse. He finally agreed and made his first trip to the Polish embassy in September 1985. CSIS had helped him arrange a cover story to give him credibility with the Polish embassy. He registered at the Park Lane Hotel near the Rideau Canal under the name Edmund Busch.

The clerk greeted him by saying, "Oh, Mr. Busch, you must be with the RCMP party." Paszkowski almost died on the spot. It was a simple case of mistaken identity. The Mounties happened, by pure coincidence, to have a group staying at the hotel. (The Soviets frequently use the hotel too.)

The next day, after a CSIS handler from Ottawa named "Kent" had fitted him with a microphone at his throat, wired to a switch in his pants pocket and a transmitter and battery attached to his leg and ankle, "Mr. Busch" went to the Polish embassy at 443 Daly Avenue. He was shaking with fear, terrified that the Poles might search him. They didn't. Most intelligence services no longer search suspects for hidden transmitters. That is considered old-fashioned. They simply walk them past an X-ray machine or a special scanning device that picks up whether somebody is broadcasting. Nothing the Poles did later indicates they suspected or detected anything that day. But the risk was very serious. If the caper had failed, if Paszkowski had been found out and they had held on to him, tied him up and made him talk, it would have been a huge diplomatic incident. "Canadian Spy Caught in Embassy with Microphone." They could have called in the news media, displayed the equipment, and paraded their spy. Or else they might have asked External Affairs quietly how much Canada was prepared to pay them to hush up the whole affair and let the spy walk out of the embassy quietly. Poland owed Canada $3.8 billion in outstanding loans at the time. It is even higher now.

That day, Paszkowski says, he met Stanislaw Pisarski, first secretary at the embassy, for the first time. Pisarski is a tall, intelligent, friendly man in his early fifties, with a ramrod-stiff military bearing, but a most charming Polish riding-school manner. His delightful wife Elzbieta was the hit of cocktail parties while they were in Ottawa. Pisarski's previous posting had been at the United Nations in New York, where the American press had identified someone in the Polish delegation as being a colonel in the SB. CSIS certainly knew about him. He had been under surveillance by CSIS when he had been to Edmonton on a "vacation" in 1985. According to Paszkowski, Pisarski is really a colonel in Polish military intelligence.

Paszkowski says Pisarski simply told him he knew who he was and asked him if he was available for work. He was too smooth to insult Paszkowski with blackmail. "Pisarski knew everything," says Paszkowski. "He used the old Polish system of talking, speaking very friendly to me."

The secretary told him they would be needing him in Europe, and that he might be asked to go to Rome to take part in an intelligence group that would be doing some *marozrabialaby*, a word rarely heard outside of the Polish intelligence service, which translates roughly as stirring up trouble in another country. It appeared they trusted him. But Pisarski was not specific about plans. He told him to return to Edmonton, await instructions, and not try to contact the embassy; someone would be in touch with him. He also gave him a visa application that he could say he had been to the embassy to pick up if he was stopped afterwards and asked what he had been doing there.

Shortly before he was called back to Warsaw for another posting in the fall of 1988, Pisarski said in an interview that he had never met anyone called Paszkowski while he was in Ottawa, and that none of the conversations Paszkowski speaks about ever took place.

CSIS had been listening to their conversation in the embassy, says Paszkowski. "Kent" was so excited that he broke normal security precautions and was waiting for him back at his hotel. Paszkowski was furious. What if the Poles had been following him?

CSIS insisted he call back Pisarski to find out when he wanted him to go overseas. Paszkowski says he realized then how mistaken he had been about CSIS. The Canadian intelligence service didn't know what they were doing. They were placing his life in jeopardy. That was when he decided he was heading back to Edmonton right away.

The incident had shown sloppiness on both sides. The Poles had been remiss not to check his background more thoroughly before bringing him to Ottawa, and had taken quite a risk in exposing someone they might have had plans for by bringing him to the embassy, but CSIS was being just as short-sighted when it suggested that he try to force the Poles' hand. This certainly wasn't the way he had been taught the craft back at Lesnov, Paszkowski thought. "Canadian intelligence, they are new, fresh, they are like a young woman," he says. "They are like children. They want to make something very fast."

Paszkowski returned to Edmonton, and for the next six months he had only occasional chance meetings with Polish intelligence agents on the street or in his home. They considered him one of their people. A Polish agent who acted as a courier used to meet him at a prearranged time every month or second month under a large clock in Calgary and hand him expense money. He usually got $2,000 or $7,000 per meeting, he says. CSIS as well was paying him, although all he ever got from CSIS was about $2,000. Before each one of his Calgary trips, he always tipped off CSIS and every "drop" was monitored. The Poles insisted that he carry a gun for protection on his trips to pick up his expense money in Calgary. Paszkowski says he thought this was funny since there were enough CSIS agents around on every trip to ensure everybody's protection.

He still had his job at the garage. He says that after CSIS spoke to his employer, John Boyko, he had no trouble getting the time off — two or three days at a time — that he needed for his trips to Calgary or Ottawa and occasional "undercover assignments," the nature of which he refuses to discuss.

Based on what he learned from his year as an undercover agent with CSIS and from his contacts with Polish intelligence, Paszkowski estimates that there are about 100 Polish agents active in Canada. He says he doesn't have much respect for the efficiency of the Polish spy organization after they let a Canadian agent into their embassy so easily. In fact, he says the Polish intelligence service is about on a par with CSIS — neither of them is very professional and both rely on a neighbouring superpower for their expertise. After he got back to Edmonton, CSIS put him under tremendous pressure to go back to Ottawa unannounced and press the Poles to send him to Europe. His handler, Nick Maduck, especially, kept pressuring him. They used to meet regularly in a room that CSIS rented in the Chateau Lacombe Hotel. And on one occasion Maduck's boss, "Earl," came to the meeting to plead the CSIS's case.

Finally, although he knew he would be breaking all the rules and might be compromising the whole operation, Paszkowski agreed at CSIS's insistence to fly to Ottawa. He arrived in the national capital on April 11, 1986 and again booked into the Park Lane Hotel. He warned CSIS one last time. How would it look to the Poles — when a supposedly impoverished Polish refugee, whom they are paying good money to lie low in Edmonton and do virtually nothing, travels to Ottawa at his own expense and in defiance of their express orders, and insists on being sent to Europe? Would they not be suspicious?

In Ottawa he reluctantly telephoned the embassy but was told that Pisarski could not see him. CSIS made him telephone again. This time he was told that Pisarski was in Toronto. Nick Maduck pressured him to call the consulate in Toronto to arrange a meeting, but Paszkowski refused. He tried to explain that if he had made any attempt to contact the consulate in Toronto, they would have known for sure he was a double agent.

Information obtained later by CSIS showed that Pisarski had been in the embassy in Ottawa all the time. He just didn't want to see Paszkowski. And in pushing him to call the embassy, CSIS was only reacting to tremendous political pressure on the agency at the time. Several Conservative MPs, including Pat Boyer of Etobicoke-Lakeshore, had been urging CSIS to move against the activities of Polish intelligence services in Canada. The Polish consulate in Toronto was undergoing a major expansion, almost doubling in size. And the thirty-five diplomats accredited to Toronto at the time, the MPs said, made the city a major centre of Polish "subversion."

Paszkowski went back to Edmonton determined to have nothing more to do with any cock-eyed plans to force himself on the Polish embassy. Without telling CSIS, he contacted three other foreign intelligence services in Canada about the Polish embassy's offer to send him back to Europe as a spy. One of them was Mossad, which he dealt with via an Israeli friend in Edmonton he identifies by the alias "Daniel Asher."

Asher actually came to him, he says, because he had made some contacts in Lebanon and, almost immediately, Asher was onto him asking who these people were and what intentions they might have. Paszkowski was impressed by the efficiency of the Israeli network, and the two men became friends.

But CSIS too was on to him, and they knew as well that on April 15, 1986 Paszkowski had also contacted the CIA and Italian intelligence agents in Canada and offered his services to them as well.

Soon afterwards, a meeting was arranged with representatives of the CIA, the Italian and the Israeli intelligence agencies operating in Canada and officials from CSIS headquarters to discuss what should be done with Paszkowski. As we shall see, the world of international espionage in Canada is small and rather incestuous.

The word came to Paszkowski in Edmonton through a Polish intelligence contact in Calgary that he was to fly to Rome and make contact with the East German embassy in the eternal city.

He was even given enough money for the trip. The Poles were still thinking Europe, back where he had skipped out on them. They and the East Germans were very big in European terrorism at the time — giving protection, money and arms to Baader Meinhof and other terrorist gangs. They needed somebody with skill and training, like Paszkowski, to help out. Now it became obvious why the Poles took the risk of bringing him to the embassy: they couldn't care less about whether CSIS saw his face. They wanted him for Europe, not Canada. They did have something very big for him. He would be underground with a totally new identity.

"They knew what I could do," says Paszkowski. "They wanted me to go back and do it." He could have kicked himself for not realizing it earlier. "What is there to spy on in Canada?" he chuckles.

He had no intention of going to Rome, convinced as he was that as soon as he set foot in Europe, Interpol would arrest him for escaping from jail or, worse still, the Polish intelligence service would make him do their bidding. No way, he told the Poles. They begged they pleaded they threatened they offered more money.

CSIS too wanted him to go. They saw it as a golden opportunity to do a favour for a "friendly foreign intelligence service" by handing Paszkowski over to the Italians, he says. But he would have none of it. Doing a little spying for CSIS in Edmonton on the side was one thing, but being sold off in Europe to play double agent and infiltrate some of the world's most vicious, barbaric gangs was something else entirely.

"You are putting me in the fire," he complained to his handler Maduck in one two-hour meeting. There were five meetings with CSIS in all to convince him to leave Canada. The service too begged, wheedled, pleaded, offered money until he agreed.

CSIS told him to demand that the Polish embassy find him a passport. The Poles said they couldn't and insisted he find his own travel document. Paszkowski was afraid that if he produced a travel document too readily, the Poles would become suspicious, but Nick Maduck wrote out by hand Paszkowski's application for a special Certificate of Identity that would allow him to travel to Europe for CSIS for two years. Although by law CSIS intelligence officers are not supposed to travel abroad on missions, the agency does use a number of undercover agents who work outside the country, but Maduck now denies this is why he helped Paszkowski with his application.

Finally, in July 1986, Paszkowski obtained from External Affairs a Certificate of Identity. The application form, filled out by hand by Maduck, remains one of the solid pieces of evidence that CSIS played an active role in helping him out of the country on August 16, 1986, bound for Rome. James Kelleher, who was solicitor general at the time, would say later that CSIS only found out who he was after he had left Canada. And Maduck will say that CSIS never sent Paszkowski overseas, and that he only filled out the application form in case Paszkowski would have to go abroad.

Maduck would eventually testify at Paszkowski's refugee determination hearing that he only found out in June 1986 that Robert Fisher was really Ryszard Paszkowski, convicted hijacker and wanted man. This does not explain why Maduck did not turn him over to the RCMP and notify Interpol, instead of filling out an application form for a wanted criminal to help him get out of the country.

Paszkowski says the Poles should have been suspicious that he might be a double agent when he produced a Certificate of Identity so easily. They weren't, and he arrived in Rome on August 17, went straight to his hotel and made contact immediately with an Italian intelligence agent, a Captain Di Marco, whom CSIS had lined up for him. The plan CSIS had laid down called for him to be handed over to Italian intelligence authorities who would then monitor his activities.

On August 18, he went to the East German embassy for a meeting with four or five people who were not introduced to him. He didn't know anyone, but he studied their faces so he would remember them. Six months later he would realize from wanted posters he saw in Germany that one of the people at that meeting had been Udo Oborecht, a prominent West German terrorist. They talked in general terms about staging terrorist activities, but he says they said one thing that made his skin crawl: they were planning to put a bomb on an Air India airplane in one of the major cities of Western Europe. They didn't say when, where or how, but he assumes that somehow they wanted the Sikhs to be blamed — this is one part of his story that doesn't make much sense. Why would European terrorists want to discredit Sikhs? In any case, he says he realized he could be getting himself in a lot deeper than he had expected, and a West German prison might be the safest place for him after all. So before he went back to his hotel where Captain Di Marco and other intelligence officers were waiting, he called Interpol, told them anonymously in which hotel they could find the elusive, still-wanted Ryszard Paszkowski and then went upstairs for the official ceremony handing him over to the Italian intelligence service. The meeting in his hotel room with his new handler had barely begun when the door crashed open and four Italian policemen charged in, one of them holding his photograph. They said Interpol wanted him for charges of escaping custody in West Germany.

"You're not Fisher, you're Paszkowski!" they shouted. A big row erupted between the policemen and Di Marco and his intelligence officers. Paszkowski was sitting quietly on the bed, in the middle of it all, watching.

He says he knew that if he got involved in the heavy terrorist business, he couldn't be sure of his safety. There were too many people now at CSIS who knew his real identity. His Italian intelligence officer friends told him they'd have him out in no time but he knew otherwise. The Italian police won that battle. In October, he was back in Bernau prison, where he served the rest of his sentence without escaping and was let out on parole as a model prisoner in late 1987. Thinking that Canada would be glad to have him back, he began negotiating with the Canadian embassy in Bonn to be allowed back into the country. He was given the cold shoulder, which shocked him because he figured as an ex-CSIS undercover agent, Canada owed him something. CSIS evidently figured it owed him nothing.

When he saw his efforts were to no avail, he took his case to the Canadian news media. He contacted Rick Gibbons, who was working at the time for the Canadian Press in London, England. Gibbons flew over to Germany, and using prearranged passwords, the two met on a dark, rainy night in a dimly lit street in Cologne.

Today, Gibbons recalls it was like something out of a spy novel. Over the next two days Paszkowski spun out his incredible story and Gibbons had a blockbuster scoop which appeared in Canadian newspapers on January 22, 1988. CSIS was unmoved. However, the agency finally admitted that it had hired Paszkowski and sent him into the Polish embassy but added that he had been fired before he left for Italy and that he had gone there of his own free will.

Paszkowski's campaign to get back to Canada by going to the news media didn't work. CSIS was doing its best to keep him out of the country. Strangely, while he had been away serving the rest of his sentence in the West German jail, somebody had paid all the unpaid credit card, telephone, power and apartment rent bills he had left behind in Edmonton when he was arrested in Rome. Paszkowski has no doubt that his generous benefactor was in fact CSIS, which didn't want somebody using the unpaid bills as a legal excuse to force him to return to Canada.

"So who paid my bills?" he says. "Probably the Canadian taxpayers. I came back and I didn't owe anybody a cent."

He arrived back in Canada with his pregnant Polish girlfriend, Elzbieta Perlinska, at Edmonton airport on October 4, 1989, as much as declaring, "Here I am, boys, I want to tell my story in open court." Once again he had managed to slip in past CSIS, the RCMP and Immigration Canada. "Every airline in Europe had instructions to refuse me if they saw me arriving to buy a ticket to Canada," he says. But it didn't matter. With what the KGB had taught him, it was a cinch. "Canada is the easiest country to get into," he says. He flew Canadian International Airlines from Amsterdam with a false passport in the name of Krystjan Niaradzik. He and Elzbieta immediately claimed refugee status and the RCMP promptly clapped them into jail. They manacled and shackled him, lest he run away. Little chance, he thought: all he wanted to do was plead his case in open court. CSIS was furious. CSIS spokesman Gerry Cummings said he found it "frustrating that the news media would spend so much time listening to this guy." The service issued a denial which wasn't one. It said it had not brought him into the country to be a double agent, which was strictly speaking true — the Mounties had sent him over.

Immigration officials said he should be released from jail, but CSIS opposed his bail in criminal court and managed to keep him behind bars. The agency knew if he was allowed out he would promptly marry the pregnant Elzbieta, which would strengthen his case on humanitarian grounds. He tried to marry Elzbieta while in jail, but again CSIS intervened, he says, and prevented it. When, after hiring a new lawyer, he was finally released from jail in January 1990, he married Elzbieta within a few days.

Paszkowski got his day in court, a refugee adjudication hearing spread out over seven days between November 1989 and March 1990. Finally on June 6, 1990 he was rejected as a refugee in Canada on the grounds that he had already been granted permanent refugee status in West Germany after his 1982 hijacking. Canada does not offer refugee protection to people who already have refugee protection in a safe country such as West Germany. But Elzbieta, who was kicked, punched and threatened in Cologne last October when she refused to pressure her friend Ryszard into going back to work for the Polish intelligence service, was granted full refugee status in Canada. She reciprocated on March 2 by producing Patrick, a beautiful Canadian baby boy, who was baptized in a big ceremony at a Polish church in Edmonton on July 21. Because Patrick Paszkowski is a

Canadian, he strengthens the case of his father who has found work as a manager at Acoustical Ceiling and Building Maintenance Ltd. in Edmonton.

"I'm pushing paper around now and my feet are on the desk," Paszkowski says in mock-capitalist style. He is responsible for thirty-seven workers and he is earning a good salary, "and paying lots of taxes," he adds. Unexpectedly, on August 2, 1990, West German authorities informed him he had lost his refugee status because he had spent too much time outside the country. Now Canada was free to accept Paszkowski as a refugee.

He says it is really too bad that CSIS never understood him. All he wanted to do was to live in Canada, he says, in return for doing a little spying for CSIS around Edmonton now and again. If the agency had understood that, instead of trying to sell him off to Italian intelligence, he might still be with them, as pleased as ever to be their deepest, most reliable undercover agent in the Polish community.

He made sure he taped CSIS agents talking to him on some occasions, he says, in case the service ever tried to double-cross him. The tapes are well-hidden in a black bag somewhere in Canada.

There is an additional problem for CSIS, he says. He knows some things about the Air India crash that he picked up while working for CSIS. "CSIS knows what I know, and how I know, and that is a problem for them right now."

It is still almost impossible to figure out whose version of events, Paszkowski's or CSIS's, is true. Parts of his story, such as the faked "Sikh" Air India bombing, seem implausible, and yet it is also obvious that CSIS has been, at least, selective in its rendering of the story. At worst, it has allowed itself to be involved in an extremely embarrassing incident that has no doubt been noticed by intelligence services all around the world.

# CHANGING OF THE GUARD

**T**HE PASZKOWSKI AFFAIR WAS UNUSUAL in more ways than one, in that this time it appears the RCMP and CSIS were careful not to infringe upon each other's territory. However, that wasn't always the case. For the first five years after CSIS was set up, the agency was engaged in a nasty little turf war with the RCMP which raged on unabated, usually in secret, until 1989. Nothing illustrates this as well as the possibly tragic ramifications of the Great Libyan Bomb Scare of 1986.

On the morning of Friday, January 17, 1986, Canadians woke up to newspaper headlines screaming that police were braced for a terrorist bomb attack at a major Canadian airport that weekend. A man in Ottawa had told police about six weeks earlier that an unidentified Libyan had shown him a suitcase containing $80,000, and said he was trying to find someone to put a bomb aboard a U.S.-bound aircraft leaving Ottawa International Airport on the weekend of January 18 and 19. Police scoured the city and the surrounding Gatineau hills, but they never turned up the Libyan — although they did turn up another Libyan who had a suitcase with $31,000 in it (that money, however, was for drugs).

On January 16, the government decided to play it safe. It warned travellers and increased security at major airports. Prime Minister Brian Mulroney pleaded with Canadians to stay calm.

165

They could still use all the airports, he said, thanks to the extra security measures. Deputy Prime Minister Erik Nielsen, a former Mountie, praised the RCMP for its fine efforts and criticized the news media for alarming people. As usual, Nielsen was a bit premature. What he and Mulroney did not say was that behind the scenes CSIS and the RCMP were at each other's throats and their petty jealousies and pouting had already compromised the investigation.

The Mounties had picked up a suspect in early December 1985, and immediately closeted him in a downtown hotel where they tried to get him to confess that the Libyan bomb threat was a hoax. They deliberately did not tell CSIS about their suspect. Six days, later CSIS found out on its own. The Mounties refused to let CSIS anywhere near him while they continued to hold him, even though CSIS knew the individual and could have helped the Mounties in the case. This infuriated CSIS officials who in retaliation, refused to allow CSIS's watcher service to take part in an RCMP surveillance operation in connection with the bomb threat.

January 18 and 19 went by and no bomb went off. Ottawa returned to normal, and a few days later, on January 22, the Mounties finally extracted a confession out of their hotel guest, but it was obtained under such duress that it would never have stood up in a court of law. The suspect was never charged. The case had been royally botched, from start to finish. In fact, the RCMP and CSIS were very lucky that there was no terrorist attack and no lives were lost. Otherwise an ensuing commission of inquiry probing the tragedy might not have been as understanding about the agencies' petty little disagreements as the politicians and the Security Intelligence Review Committee were.

SIRC knew about the turf war almost from the start. It had been discovered quite by accident in April 1985, while the committee was going through CSIS reports on the Armenian terrorist attack against the Turkish embassy in March of that year. From that point until they finally made up and shook hands in mid-October 1989, SIRC would constantly harangue the two agencies to end these childish games.

It's true that from time to time a solicitor general would gently chide both services, telling them that they really should try to solve their differences and make an effort to get along. The politicians feared being any more critical: they did not want to have to admit publicly their inability to control the activities of Canada's two major intelligence agencies. Nor did they want to incur the wrath of both the RCMP and CSIS. Few politicians are so invulnerable that they can risk angering both the police and the intelligence service. So by and large nobody dared interfere in the fighting. Year after year SIRC exposed a few details of the latest battles raging behind the scenes, but generally the committee preferred to pretend the fighting was nothing very serious and instead went on praising both agencies for their close co-operation with each other.

It took SIRC several months to learn of the foul-ups in the Great Libyan Bomb Scare investigation. In its 1986-87 annual report, it noted that "turf battles and distrust" had prevented CSIS from taking part in the Bomb Scare investigation. Both CSIS Director, Ted Finn and RCMP Commissioner Robert Simmonds publicly endorsed the notion that the turf war was nothing more than the result of "healthy tensions." SIRC chairman Ron Atkey countered that the situation would be even healthier if it were a little less tense.

CSIS and the RCMP just couldn't resist tripping each other up no matter who got hurt. Two CSIS agents had banged in on the RCMP at Lester B. Pearson International Airport, Toronto in 1988 when the RCMP and Immigration Canada were trying to spirit Mahmoud Mohammad Issa Mohammad out of the country. The former terrorist's lawyers still hold CSIS responsible for the collapse of the operation.

Two years earlier, in 1986, a couple of CSIS intelligence officers on the West Coast withheld from the RCMP crucial wiretap conversations which could have prevented the shooting of visiting Punjabi cabinet minister Malkiat Singh Sidhu by four Sikh separatists on a lonely logging road on Vancouver Island. After the bombing of Air India Flight 182 in 1985, CSIS had obtained sweeping warrants to bug the homes, cars and phones of suspected Sikh terrorists in Canada. Eight days before Sidhu's shooting, two agents had overheard Harjit Singh Atwal, a Surrey, B.C. construction contractor, discuss on the phone with a friend that the Punjabi minister might get a "rough reception." The agents should immediately have alerted the RCMP, who could have given the minister protection, but they didn't. A SIRC investigation later proved they had not even bothered transcribing the wiretaps in time to prevent the attack.

Luckily, the Punjabi minister lived through the hail of bullets to return home to India and tell them all about his terrible welcome in Canada. Charges of conspiracy against Atwal were later dropped, but the four men were caught and each sentenced to twenty years. As for the CSIS officers who had done nothing to stop the shootings, they were merely reprimanded and were soon back at their desks.

(In June 1986, Atkey told a Commons Justice and Solicitor General Committee that the RCMP and CSIS were "bumping into each other" until they could sort out their respective roles in security and intelligence work.)

Nothing illustrates more clearly the continuing nature of the turf war than the RCMP's systematic refusal year after year to allow CSIS full and direct access to the Canadian Police Information Centre (CPIC) computer. Denying CSIS access to this vital tool for security and intelligence work was the supreme insult, and it had a most demoralizing impact on the new civilian recruits at a time when they needed reassurance that they had joined the right organization.

CPIC is a computerized, radio-linked network that gives officers of the RCMP and provincial and municipal police forces across the country instant access to information in three data banks held by the RCMP covering:

- vehicle registrations, stolen vehicles, driver's licences;
- known criminals, their criminal records, any outstanding warrants against them and details of bail and parole conditions;

- other relevant information about convicted criminals, such as where they hang out, who their friends are, where their parents live and where they work.

A twenty-five-member Canadian Police Information Centre Advisory Committee decides who is allowed to use the CPIC files. The committee is, of course, dominated by members of the RCMP — the keeper of the records. The RCMP had decided even before CSIS was set up that the new service would be denied direct access to the CPIC computer. The day that CSIS was created — July 16, 1984, while CSIS still occupied space at RCMP headquarters — workers came and took away CPIC computer terminals from the desks of Mounties who had transferred to the new civilian service.

The RCMP argued that since CSIS was not a law enforcement agency, it should not have access to the tools of a law enforcement agency. If CSIS was proud to be part of the bureaucracy, and considered itself smarter and brighter and more sophisticated than a mere police force — and that was the bumph government hacks were pouring out — then it wouldn't need all this criminal information. After all, the agency wasn't investigating *crime*. Crimes are investigated by police officers.

So CSIS was told by the Mounties that, like any other government department or agency, it would have to make a written request whenever it wanted a name checked. The RCMP would consider the request and respond. Ex-RCMP security service CSIS intelligence officers would no longer have immediate, ready and private access to CPIC files simply by entering a name on the computer terminal screen in front of them, as they had done when they were still part of the RCMP. Overnight, CSIS gained the dubious distinction of being the only national intelligence agency in the world that has restrictions placed on its access to its own country's criminal computer records.

One irony was that the FBI's National Information Center in Washington had access to the CPIC files, while CSIS did not. In other words, CSIS could have telephoned Washington to obtain information about Canadian vehicle registrations that it could not easily obtain from the computer terminal down the hall at RCMP headquarters.

Then the RCMP really rubbed CSIS's nose in it, by giving CPIC access to all sorts of quasi-police forces. CN Police got access on the grounds that it enforces the Railway Act (that's the law that bans spitting, gambling, playing cards for money and using coarse language in railway cars, as well as that most famous of all railway crimes — flushing the toilet while the train is in the station). CPIC access was given to Ontario Hydro security guards because they are responsible for enforcing some laws dealing with nuclear installations. And the officials of the Securities Exchange Commission got access because they enforce federal laws dealing with securities. But CSIS, which looked after national security, did not rate.

The agency tried to argue that it too was a law enforcement body because it enforced the CSIS Act and worked with the Official Secrets Act, but the RCMP laughed and said CSIS did not enforce these laws, but merely worked under them.

When Solicitor General Elmer MacKay heard about this in October 1984, he couldn't believe it. "That can't be allowed to continue," he said. "It doesn't make sense. I'm going to make inquiries right away." He was right; it didn't make sense. But it happened anyway. MacKay made his inquiries but was powerless against the might of the Mounties. Nor could two of his successors do much better. RCMP Commissioner Robert Simmonds was determined that CSIS not get total direct access to CPIC. Finally, in late 1985, the RCMP relented slightly and said CSIS could have four CPIC computer terminals. Even then there were restrictions: the terminals would be linked only to motor vehicle registration files, the least useful ones, and they would have to be physically located at RCMP Headquarters. Finn and his five deputy directors would not be allowed to have any CPIC-linked computers in their offices at CSIS Headquarters in the East Memorial Building. That way CSIS would still need to rely on the Mounties whenever it conducted a serious surveillance operation. After all, the Horsemen could access the central CPIC computer from the comfort of their own cars via the terminals mounted under their dashboards. So CSIS had to continue using at least a couple of Mounties on every major operation it staged. In this way, the RCMP was able to know at all times what the CSIS people were watching, who they were seeking information on and what sort of information they were obtaining. In short, the Mounties had ensured they would still be No. 1 in the Canadian security and intelligence business.

Curiously, this didn't bother CSIS Director Finn. Sure, he admitted, it would be "desirable" to have a computer terminal in his office, but "the lack of direct access is not hampering or inhibiting our operations in the slightest. In terms of record checks, we are in constant communications with other police forces, and our requests are granted speedily. We are not peace officers. We weren't expecting to have direct access." In a recent interview, Finn, who has been out of CSIS for three years now, recalls that being denied direct access "was not of great concern to me, but for reasons that I don't understand, it was of great interest to the service." He says today that the whole issue was "overblown."

The only problem, Finn remembers, was that it was difficult to check the huge volume of public-service security-clearance records by writing to the RCMP. "As for the computer terminal, I never had one at my desk; I didn't need one," Finn says. Today he is director of the federal Emergency Preparedness Canada. He has a bright, shiny computer right at his desk.

Ted Finn may not have been upset by the RCMP snub, but being shut out of CPIC had a devastating effect on the morale of CSIS staff. However, it did force some CSIS intelligence officers to use their imagination. They set up their own informal system to get direct personal access to the computer. Some knew people who were still in the Mounties, others had friends in the Ontario Provincial Police. In some offices, while the lone RCMP officer was out, a CSIS staffer would sneak over to his terminal and check out a name. One CSIS officer even purloined a CPIC computer terminal and used it at will. Very few CSIS employees had to actually sit down and write out a request, mail it in to the Mounties and wait for a reply. But playing these games to get around what the RCMP was doing was no way to run a security service.

In the summer of 1987, the RCMP finally gave in and supplied CSIS with four working terminals at CSIS headquarters, linked to the lowest level of files in the CPIC computer. The service could have used 400 terminals, but never mind, CSIS intelligence officers crowded around the four terminals and used them night and day. They were grateful for small mercies.

All the cajoling and complaining in three successive SIRC annual reports, all the criticism of the RCMP in the news media and the public, all the pointed questions from the Opposition parties in the House of Commons, all the entreaties from various solicitors general had failed to move Simmonds — even pleading the interests of national security.

The four terminals could access all the motor vehicles files in Level I, the lowest level, as well as the counter-terrorism files in levels II and III. Everything else, all the heavy duty counter-intelligence files, still had to be applied for in writing. Clearly, the Mounties knew whom they trusted, and whom they did not. The RCMP was playing cat-and-mouse with national security, passing out little bits of cheese one piece at a time. In the intelligence game, knowledge is power and the RCMP was protecting its power base.

SIRC Chairman Ron Atkey was upset. "When CSIS wants any other CPIC information it must go to the RCMP, which punches in the request and passes back the read-out." This entails unnecessary delay, and it fosters an unwarranted notion that CSIS is a junior partner to the RCMP." The RCMP didn't mind that at all.

Atkey continued: "Meanwhile thousands of police officers in quiet suburbs have CPIC terminals mounted under the dashboard of their cruisers, letting them check out teenagers loitering in a parking lot as easily as they could check out the getaway car in a bank robbery. But no CSIS surveillant in hot pursuit of a suspected terrorist has a similar opportunity to get an instant reading on his quarry." One more reason for CSIS to advise the RCMP ahead of time of every major operation it was undertaking, the Mounties would reply.

In a recent interview, Archie Barr, former deputy director of CSIS, was blunt, "That whole, issue about the CPIC terminals was political. It was called 'Screw CSIS.'"

"This is a classic example of institutions charged with great responsibilities giving priority instead to parochial turf concerns," said Atkey. But after Norman Inkster was appointed the new RCMP commissioner replacing Simmonds in September 1987, things began to change. Inkster was much more tolerant of CSIS. He did not view the civilian agency's existence as a personal affront to him as a policeman. He was prepared to allow CSIS more access to the CPIC computer.

Five years later, CSIS has gone from no direct access at all to CPIC files, to direct access in all regions to two of the three CPIC data banks, those dealing with motor vehicle registration and criminal identification records, descriptions of stolen vehicles, wanted lists and last known addresses.

Only the third and highest level, the one containing background police information about the names, character traits and hangouts of known and suspected criminals, and their friends — and, of course, about ordinary Canadians — are withheld from CSIS on a direct access basis.

In its 1985-86 annual report, SIRC concluded that part of the turf war problem derived from a secret directive which the outgoing Liberal solicitor general Robert Kaplan had issued on July 29, 1984, setting down the principles on which the respective security responsibilities of the RCMP and CSIS should be based. The directive, which was never made public, left unclear which agency had primary responsibility for counterterrorism and resulted in "both organizations working at crosspurposes particularly in [this] field."

CSIS was having what Finn called "teething pains." It wasn't always the RCMP that was to blame. CSIS — courtesy of the McDonald Commission — still had an inflated view of itself as better than the RCMP. It believed its own public relations about how different it was from the Mounties, and this was not lost on the Horsemen. Many times CSIS refused to take part in an RCMP investigation on the grounds that it wasn't part of its mandate. This would infuriate the Mounties, who were still working on the premise that when something big happens everybody should pitch in, and what's the use of collecting information if it doesn't lead to something concrete like arresting somebody, or punishing criminals, or preventing crime. Collecting information just to find out what is happening, rather than for some specific investigation leading to charges, seemed like a waste of time to the older Mounties.

It may be hard to believe, but there were occasional indications during the five war years that peace might break out at any time. The two agencies signed several memorandums of co-operation, although they never got around to the issue of CPIC and information sharing. They agreed to share equipment, personnel and some facilities. The Mounties allowed CSIS to use their aircraft and special vehicles with fancy electronic monitoring and listening equipment, as well as the Force's photographic services, its translation facilities, the payroll administration and accommodations in RCMP posts across the country, not to mention the use of special secure telephones and electronic data processing. It wasn't as if the RCMP were out to destroy CSIS; it merely wanted to control the agency and make sure CSIS knew who was boss.

To cut down on the friction in counter-terrorism, where the worst "bumping" (as the two services referred to their battles in public) occurred, they set up liaison officers within each other's counter-terrorism branches in the latter part of 1986. This was a very important development, because during the previous two years many of the conflicts had been in the area of counter-terrorism. All they needed for a major scandal would be an incident in which someone was killed during a terrorist attack because the two services had been bickering over access to computer files or something equally trivial.

CSIS had done the best it could to provide information during the Armenian terrorist attack on the Turkish embassy in March 1985. Four years later everyone saw the advantages of co-operation, when CSIS and the RCMP worked together during a bus hijacking. Charles Yacoub, a Lebanese-Canadian, commandeered a Greyhound bus and drove it onto the green in front of the Parliament buildings in Ottawa to draw attention to the slaughter of people in his homeland.

On that occasion, CSIS was able to provide the RCMP and Ottawa police with hijacker Yacoub's identity and a background profile while he was still on the bus with his hostages. The accurate information provided by the agency helped convince the police authorities that no lives were in danger, so there was never any impulse to charge the bus with guns blazing. As a result, every single hostage was freed unharmed and Yacoub lived to stand trial.

One area where no trouble at all was ever reported publicly was in Canadian embassies and consulates abroad, where CSIS has thirty-one security liaison officers and the RCMP has seventeen officers. In some missions they have to work alongside each other in crowded, overworked and often difficult conditions. They never seem to be fighting. It may be because they're so busy — doing hundreds of thousands of visa and passport security checks — or perhaps because they depend on each other so much in those postings where one agency is represented but not the other.

The turf war between CSIS and the RCMP was really rather a small conflagration compared to the double-crossings, back-stabbings, deals and botched investigations that had gone on south of the border as a result of the CIA-FBI tussle, when FBI Director J. Edgar Hoover was trying to prevent the CIA from being set up after the Second World War.

In fact, even using the word "war" to describe CSIS's early

relationship with the RCMP is inappropriate. This wasn't an all-out battle, but a series of petty skirmishes, small victories and pinprick wounds. There were thousands of different little ways that the Mounties let CSIS employees know what they thought of them. At RCMP headquarters it was standard practice for some Mounties to refuse to ride on the same elevators as CSIS people. They would actually stand and wait for another elevator. CSIS staff rode by themselves.

CSIS did not have its own officers' mess, a sort of private drinking club in the military tradition where clubby old men stand around nursing mugs of beer and talking about things that might have been. Finn said it was the sort of thing that his civilian organization could do without. The RCMP welcomed some CSIS employees to join its officers' mess, but not others. For the Mounties, it was a way of building a bridge with their ex-colleagues who had transferred over to the civilian service. In this way the mess was positive. But the talk at the mess frequently turned to what a lousy job the civilian management at CSIS was doing and how the new civilian recruits didn't know anything. In the long run, this talk proved destructive to CSIS.

Even within CSIS itself, distinctions continued to exist between civilian recruits and ex-Mounties. The Mounties have their own sections in a number of cemeteries for members who wish to be buried with "the Force" rather than with their families or beside close friends. The Mounties showed who rated and who didn't by refusing Mountie burial plots to all civilian (i.e., non ex-Mountie security service) members of CSIS.

Distrust of CSIS went far beyond grave matters. RCMP Commissioner Robert Simmonds, the man they called "the cop's cop," had quietly set up an anti-terrorism intelligence shadow unit in 1983, even before CSIS was set up, which was doing discreetly many of the same things that CSIS would be doing. It was nothing disloyal that Simmonds had in mind. He had opposed splitting off the security service from the RCMP in the first place. To him, when the players are no good, you fire the players; you don't move the team out of town and change the name. He simply didn't believe that the new civilian agency could do the job when it came to watching terrorists, so he had taken discretionary measures of his own. The RCMP already had responsibility for catching terrorists, so it was difficult to pin down the fact that the group Simmonds had set up had wandered into the world of CSIS.

The Mounties' shadow unit was discovered when people began reporting with increasing frequency to CSIS investigators that the RCMP had been there just before them, asking the same questions CSIS was asking, even though it was obvious no crime had been committed.

CSIS did not want to complain publicly. Instead it went to Solicitor General James Kelleher. He finally admitted outside the Commons in September 1987 that the Mounties had indeed infringed a number of times on CSIS's turf. He had discovered that when CSIS was set up in 1984, the RCMP also set up a series of "National Security Enforcement Units" across the country, with a total of fifty-seven Mounties in eleven major centres. By 1988 there were ninety-two people involved and the NSEU had become a full-fledged directorate, the highest headquarters designation in the RCMP, known as the National Security Investigations Directorate. Today there are 133 Mounties attached to NSID.

Out in the field, in the various RCMP divisions, the members of the directorate are grouped in regional "sections" and identify themselves on their business cards as members of a National Security Investigations Section or "NSIS." The acronym makes a nice counterbalance to the other intelligence agency.

Since its formation in 1989, the parent body, NSID, has been headed by Chief Superintendent Pat Cummins, a bilingual Western Canadian who is often touted as the next RCMP commissioner. The Mounties have come back into the security and intelligence field in a big way since they lost the security service to CSIS in 1984. But Commissioner Inkster explained to a Commons committee in December 1989 that NSID seeks out only criminal intelligence of a national security nature and does not collect regular security intelligence. That responsibility belongs to CSIS.

Earlier that year, on May 26, 1989 in Vancouver, two RCMP constables bearing NSIS business cards, John A. McRae and Laurie J. Macdonnell of B.C. regional headquarters, dropped in on the El Salvador Information Office, a small co-operative which works closely with the Farabundo Marti National Liberation Army in El Salvador. The group raises money for the rebels, organizing dances and speaking tours and staging an occasional anti-American protest outside the U.S. consulate in Vancouver.

Office manager Brent Anderson, who is used to being interviewed by policemen and CSIS agents, says that the trouble with the two RCMP constables who came to see him was that none of their questions had very much to do with a permit for an upcoming demonstration which they were supposedly coming around to talk about. Anderson believes they were just collecting information, doing the sort of work that CSIS officers usually do.

The questions were about the number of FMLN fighters in Canada, how the group raises money and where its funds go. One of the RCMP constables, McRae, was very interested in an open file drawer behind Anderson. He could see files beginning with the letter "C" and expressed surprise they had a file on the *Christian Science Monitor.* Anderson replied that the office receives the newspaper, which has good coverage of Latin American politics.

Then McRae spotted a file entitled "CSIS" and really became interested. He wanted to see what was in it. Anderson, who kept thinking how far McRae had wandered from the original purpose of the visit, declined politely. Eventually the Mounties tired of asking general questions about security and intelligence matters and left. Inkster later told reporters the pair had been reprimanded for going beyond the Mounties' mandate.

The turf war ended with a whimper on a dreary fall day in early October 1989 in Ottawa. CSIS and the RCMP signed a secret peace treaty called a "Memorandum of Understanding" in the offices of then-Solicitor General Pierre Blais. RCMP Commissioner Norman Inkster and CSIS Director Reid Morden both signed it, formally bringing hostilities to a close. The document spelled out in detail the duties and responsibilities of each agency in the areas of security and intelligence.

Blais could not publicly rejoice. Most interested Canadians had suspected there had been a rivalry going on, which they assumed was only natural, but they did not know the full extent of the conflict. It would not have been in the interests of the Conservative government or SIRC to publicize how serious the war had been, since they had been unable to do much about it for the previous five years. Had the public been fully informed about the extent of the turf war, it might have demanded some answers. Had national security suffered as a result of the turf war? Why had the government allowed the conflict to go on so long?

Blais announced the signing of the secret agreement on October 31, 1989 at a meeting of the Special Commons Committee reviewing the CSIS Act. He described the memorandum as "an agreement between the Canadian Security Intelligence Service and the Royal Canadian Mounted Police to coordinate the respective mandate of the two agencies, so that Canadians have the best possible assurance of national security." And he added that the agreement made CSIS Director Reid Morden and RCMP Commissioner Norman Inkster "personally accountable to me for effective co-operation between their two agencies." He said he hoped it would show off "the positive spirit that now exists" between the RCMP and CSIS. The parliamentarians were relieved. That was the announcement they had been waiting to hear for five years.

The agreement spelled out that the security system is divided into "three pillars," as Blais said. The Mounties would get two of them, enforcement and protection. CSIS would get the third, intelligence. "The CSIS role is to provide forewarning and security intelligence on threats. The RCMP's role is to investigate apprehended or actual crimes and to prevent crime or prosecute offences."

In addition, the agreement reaffirmed that the RCMP is "the primary recipient of security intelligence on national security offences." There was a feeling among some observers of the service that because it had repeatedly been stiffed by the Mounties, CSIS was moving too close to its American cousins, the FBI and the CIA, and bypassing the men in red altogether whenever it could.

It also set out procedures that have to be followed to "protect" information that is passed on by one agency to the other. The Mounties had a feeling that almost everything CSIS knew sooner or later ended up in the U.S. And CSIS in return didn't know what the Mounties did with the information it passed on.

The agreement confirmed the role of the liaison officer system, which began in 1986 with exchanges in counter-terrorism. The two agencies exchange officers at both the national and regional levels. Two CSIS men sit in every morning at the daily Top Secret operations and administration briefing at RCMP headquarters. Meanwhile, several more CSIS officials are attending similar meetings at RCMP divisions across the country in Vancouver, Edmonton, Toronto, Montreal and the Ottawa regional "A" Division. And a single RCMP officer sits in on meetings of the CSIS counter-terrorism branch in the East Memorial Building on Wellington Street in Ottawa. A new wrinkle was added in late 1989, taking the process a step further. The CSIS deputy director of operations meets daily with his counterpart, the deputy commissioner of operations of the RCMP, to discuss what information should be exchanged. A special committee of senior officials also discusses this. If they are unable to agree, the matter goes to Morden and Inkster. If they can't agree, then both of them trot off to the solicitor general and he decides. That way everybody knows what everybody else is doing, nobody feels bullied, and and nobody feels left out.

The turf war was only one of several serious problems that plagued CSIS throughout the eighties, sapping it of time and energy. By the summer of 1987, the service was in worse shape than ever, beset by morale, management and financial problems, ripe for dismantling — an agency far removed from the dreams of those who had set it up three years earlier.

For the second year in a row, the Security and Intelligence Review Committee had produced evidence that CSIS had been picking on left-wing and peace groups because it still could not distinguish between subversion and dissent. It was the same old problem that had always plagued the Mounties — how to differentiate between the bomber and the loud-mouth.

SIRC also accused CSIS of being too quick to endorse American foreign policy while failing to pay enough attention to Canadian foreign policy. The committee had discovered that CSIS kept around 30,000 files on Canadian "subversives" that it really didn't need; in many cases they were files on harmless old labour leaders from the fifties who hadn't been active for years. SIRC said that CSIS needed at the most only about 3,000 files on active troublemakers. CSIS's excuse was that it was holding on to the files while the government decided what should be done with them.

To make matters worse, Director Ted Finn's appearances before a parliamentary committee on Official Languages had left MPs with the impression that CSIS was not really committed to bilingualism. Finn had managed to appoint only one Franco-phone among his five deputy directors after three years at the helm. And Pierre Choquette, the recently appointed deputy director of administration, was not an "operations" man, but what the rank and file called "a bean-counter."

The previous year, a new government security policy had doubled the workload for security clearances in the public sector without doubling the budget for them. CSIS's resources were more pressed than ever, even though the agency was getting the biggest annual budget increase of any major government agency — averaging almost twenty percent a year. They could hardly ask for even more. The counter espionage branch suffered as its resources were funnelled into the underfinanced counter-terrorism branch. The government was now eager to make counter-terrorism a priority and was demanding massive security screenings in preparation for the Commonwealth Conference in Vancouver later that year, where Indian Prime Minister Rajiv Gandhi was expected to attend. They wanted even more massive security measures in preparation for the 1988 Calgary Winter Olympics. But very little extra money was being budgeted for all the extra work.

CSIS morale was at rock bottom. The agency still did not have the new headquarters it had been promised three years earlier, and the rank and file had lost confidence in the people at the top. Then there were the investigations. Everybody, it seemed, was having a crack at CSIS. There were four separate investigations: an internal investigation by the solicitor general; another investigation by the inspector general for the solicitor general; a SIRC investigation into labour union infiltration; and the most important investigation of all — a task force set up earlier in the year headed by former Clerk of the Privy Council Gordon Osbaldeston to examine CSIS's management practices. Some days headquarters spent more time answering critics and providing information to investigators than it did looking after security and intelligence matters.

The SIRC investigation into the infiltration of major Quebec labour unions by CSIS probed the possibility that the security service was using paid professional agitators to damage the union cause in Quebec. It arose out of evidence that for fifteen years Marc-André Boivin, a prominent, fiery Quebec strike leader with the Confederation of National Trade Unions, had been a paid informer for the RCMP and then CSIS. Boivin had pleaded guilty to conspiracy to bomb four hotels involved in a labour dispute in Quebec while he had been on the CSIS payroll — shades of the old RCMP security service. The unions were convinced that there was more infiltration of the labour movement than CSIS had admitted. Despite denials, this was confirmed two weeks later, when Svend Robinson produced a document showing CSIS had actually held a job competition to hire someone to report on the Quebec labour movement.

SIRC investigated and found that Boivin had been hired by the Mounties in 1973 to monitor "subversive activities" in the CNTU. By 1984, CSIS had assigned him to hunt for communists and "foreign influenced agents" in the labour movement. SIRC concluded that CSIS had not directed Boivin against any union leaders in their union capacities. However, in conducting its investigation, SIRC had neglected to mention that Boivin had been overseas attending a peace conference in Copenhagen and a second conference in a Soviet bloc country while he was an undercover agent for CSIS.

Boivin was angry that SIRC conducted an investigation without bothering to interview him. He filed a legal action against SIRC for more than $500,000 for damage to his reputation. The case is still before the courts.

In the Commons, restive MPs were demanding to know what CSIS was doing about the Air India bombing two years earlier. Why hadn't the case been solved? The MPs felt that the crash had been CSIS's first major challenge and that the agency had flubbed it. It was easier to blame CSIS than the RCMP, which, at that moment, had the better image. The same attitude applied to the foul-up between the Mounties and CSIS during the Great Libyan Bomb Scare in Ottawa in 1986: here again it was CSIS that was blamed, not the RCMP, although both organizations were about equally responsible for the fiasco.

And there were the administrative problems too. Three of Finn's five deputy directors had already quit: William MacIver, the deputy director, administration; John Venner, the deputy director in charge of services, including the "bugging" side of operations, which had gone so badly; and Archie Barr, the deputy director and second in command, who had retired a month earlier. Two more deputy directors, Harry Brandes, deputy director, intelligence production, and Ray Lees, deputy director, regional liaison, were still around but about to leave.

The staff of the service was still eighty-three percent ex-RCMP despite Finn's promise to make it a truly civilian service. The old Mountie mentality pervaded everything the service did, and some MPs who had never liked the idea of CSIS were openly calling for repatriation back into the RCMP. The organization was under fire from all sides. Svend Robinson called for a parliamentary inquiry. "We have an agency that is not doing the work it should be doing and bungling what it should be doing in the area of counter-terrorism because it is too busy targeting people it has no business targeting," he said. Solicitor General James Kelleher, who had a gift for understatement, said: "I think the agency is alive and well. There are some minor problems."

At the height of the crisis, in the summer of 1987, Ted Finn wrote a nasty letter to Ron Atkey, chairman of SIRC, whose annual report two weeks earlier had ripped into CSIS for being too loaded with ex-Mounties, fighting with the RCMP, being too quick to back U.S. foreign policy and failing to distinguish between subversion and dissent. Finn was furious. His letter of July 14, 1987 to Atkey reflected his anger. He wrote that the SIRC report had "distorted reality, was full of half-truths, and outright errors and misrepresentations." He said SIRC had done CSIS and the nation a disservice and suggested it might even have compromised national security by undermining the confidence of public officials in the security service, "leaving the service unable to carry out its very important responsibilities" to protect national security.

"The image of a venomously dangerous reptile is not likely to foster public trust and confidence," Finn wrote, "and the characterization of former policemen as insensitive and disrespectful of individual rights has attacked morale and generated a dangerous inner turmoil within the service."

But Ted Finn was in trouble, and worse was yet to come when an old ghost materialized and finally brought down CSIS's first director.

Canadian Press reporter Jim Brown remembers the day vividly. On the morning of September 11, 1987, Brown went to the Federal Court of Appeal expecting just another dull day in a case involving the legality of wiretap warrants obtained by CSIS as part of its investigation into the 1985 Air India bombing. A month earlier, on August 12, 1987, the Federal Court of Appeal, better known for long, boring decisions on arcane federal regulations, had ruled that CSIS had to release affidavits it had used in court two years earlier to obtain a wiretap authorization from the Federal Court of Canada. Affidavits at CSIS start with a request from an officer and are approved by senior officials, including the director and the solicitor general. Judge J. P. Mahoney had ruled that documents presented by the agency to a court of law to obtain wiretap warrants cannot be above public scrutiny. It was a reasonable judgement. No one else's affidavits are secret. Why should CSIS's be any different?

The people who were asking for the ruling were the lawyers for none other than Harjit Singh Atwal, the Surrey, B.C. contractor who two years earlier had been charged with conspiracy in the attack on visiting Punjabi cabinet minister Malkiat Singh Sidhu on Vancouver Island in 1986. Atwal was the man CSIS had listened in on and overheard telling a friend about the "rough reception" awaiting the visitor.

That day in court Atwal's lawyers and reporter Brown fully expected CSIS lawyer John Sims to invoke Section 39 of the Canada Evidence Act, the controversial clause that CSIS always uses in court cases to plead "national security" when it doesn't want something to become public.

Brown recalls the scene in the elegant, high-ceilinged, art deco, brass and wood-panelled courtroom in the Supreme Court building: "Sims stands up and starts off, 'Well, my Lord . . . ' and all of a sudden here is Sims telling the judge that CSIS bungled; that there were all sorts of mistakes in CSIS's affidavit and CSIS is really sorry and it wasn't really done on purpose, and well, if Ted Finn had known, he wants the judge to know, he would have never signed that affidavit."

Sims went on to ask the judge if the court would please accept CSIS's apology and overlook the mistakes that were made in the affidavit. But he knew that, because of the mistakes, neither the affidavit nor the wiretap warrant were worth the paper they were written on.

Brown couldn't believe his ears. Neither could Atwal's lawyer, Michael Code of Toronto. Code knew that it was only a matter of procedure before the evidence from the wiretap was thrown out, and then his client, who had spent nine months in prison awaiting trial on conspiracy charges, would go free because that was all the evidence that CSIS had against him — one wiretapped conversation.

CSIS Special Investigator, Frank Saunders, told Judge Darrel Heald that unfortunately CSIS had used the allegations of a discredited informant to get the application for a warrant approved and that CSIS officials, who were supposed to have checked out the information, had let the application go through. Saunders tried to explain to the judge how it had happened by suggesting that the service was under a lot of pressure on account of the 1985 Air India bombing, as if that were going to impress a judge.

"The heavy workload and the pressurized and fatiguing environment, together with the urgency attached to the investigation, led to the by-passing of established politics and procedures and eroded the effective supervisory control of the process," said Saunders. He was arguing just *pro forma* at this point. The case was lost. He knew it; everyone knew it.

Michael Code, the lawyer, was jubilant and Brown raced off to file his story, knowing that the fur was going to fly in the Commons on this one. What Brown *didn't* know was that behind the scenes the whole thing had been worked out ahead of time. CSIS had known for the last three weeks about the fraudulent affidavit. The government had been told and Ted Finn had already been persuaded to resign. All they were waiting for was the court appearance that morning so Finn could leave in the afternoon.

Finn had learned of the monstrous foul-up on August 26. The following day he sent for his top CSIS special investigator, Frank Saunders, who took only four days to confirm that the affidavit was a bunch of rubbish which would have never stood up in any court of law. Even a law school flunk-out could have done better. There were at least eight errors. The days, even the years, of meetings as listed on the form were wrong. Somebody had then written an erroneous observation based on a wrong year that someone else had entered. The informant who had supplied the false information had been fired by another branch of CSIS in Vancouver. In short, it was a mess.

This document that was so important because it had given CSIS virtually carte blanche to do what it wanted with Atwal's life for a year, and spy on anything or any place connected with him, had been signed and approved by half a dozen people, all the way from the unreliable informant in the field to middle-level and senior CSIS officials in Vancouver, (who had failed to spot even the most obvious mistakes) to Archie Barr, the deputy director in Ottawa, and finally to the CSIS Director Ted Finn himself, and yes, even the solicitor general. Everybody was looking bad.

The government needed a fall-guy. And they didn't want it to be the minister. The Conservatives had lost enough cabinet ministers to scandals as it was. And Archie Barr had retired a month earlier; he couldn't be fired posthumously, so to speak. So it had to be Ted Finn, the director of CSIS. Prime Minister Brian Mulroney gave his approval and Solicitor General James Kelleher called in Finn and fired him — actually he gave him a chance to resign gracefully. Finn had known for more than a week that he would be gone as of September 11.

"It was the hardest decision of my life," he said sadly, reflecting on his decision to resign, in the first interview he has given since he stepped down three years ago. He had wanted the director's job very badly and had been preparing for it even before CSIS was set up. It would have been the culmination of his career in the public service. Ted Finn had never failed at anything important before. Now, after barely three years in the job, he was leaving in disgrace, his organization in tatters. "I had tried very hard to do something worthwhile," he said in the interview. "It took me a long time to get over it. I was lost for six months."

Looking back, he says he had no choice but to leave. Nobody in CSIS had done anything criminal. It wasn't as if they had burned a barn, or even as if they had deliberately lied in the affidavit application. No, it was simply a mistake, rather eight mistakes, one after another, page after page — sloppy mistakes, which could not be tolerated or explained away when the outcome of the warrant application had such an enormous impact on a man's life — in this case that of Harjit Singh Atwal.

The irony was that SIRC had warned CSIS in its latest annual report, the one issued only two months earlier, that the agency had better revise its system of applying for wiretap warrants. Finn blames himself: "I read the affidavit. Nothing jumped out at me. People have to take responsibility for their mistakes. I felt I had let people down." His own organization had been sloppy with somebody's civil rights, and Finn, the former crown prosecutor, with all his years in law and his respect for civil liberties, just couldn't let it go.

The end came painfully that final Friday afternoon. After the announcement from Mulroney's office, Finn took a call or two and cleared out his desk and left. There was no farewell party, no handshakes all around. He gave no press conference. He made no public statement.

CSIS's first director had been a good man — too good a man, perhaps. His management skills had let him down. "The fault was not Ted's," says Archie Barr, Finn's first deputy director. "There was a heavy dose of paranoia, and far too much power in the hands of the deputy directors. When the service had been set up, we had been obsessed with diluting power. We weren't doing Ted any favours by staying around.

"I spoke to Ted in the fall of '85. I said I want to get out of here. Not only do you need some more Francophones, you need more people who are fluently bilingual. You need fewer Mounted Policemen. I left July 1, 1987. I had six weeks of holidays and I never came back."

Barr later went to work for Erik Nielsen at the National

Transportation Agency, but soon became bored with railway crossing problems. He quit and went into partnership in a firm, International Media Analysis, Inc., which provides overnight news summaries to business and government executives. Barr was upset with the CSIS agents on the West Coast who had initially fouled up the affidavit. "Somebody out there must have taken a course in creative writing," he said. He would have fired them. Actually none were fired and attempts to reprimand them met with resistance. Some were promoted and the unreliable informant was eventually rehired after promising not to tell any more stories. And today CSIS is a lot more careful about what it puts in its affidavits.

Within a year after Finn resigned, the top five people under him had all quit as well. The government was kind to the ex-director; it let him sit on a shelf as a "consultant" for the government for six months, and then reassigned him to a position as executive director of Emergency Preparedness Canada, where Finn has remained to this day. Ironically, his offices are located in a building that is used by CSIS, so he sees many of his former employees every day. They say hello to him and he waves back. Nobody ever said Ted Finn wasn't a nice guy.

Finn was gone and the job as Canada's chief spymaster was open. Out of the Privy Council Office and into the breach marched J. Reid Morden, a pudgy, forty-six-year-old career diplomat turned bureaucrat who had never failed at anything major in his professional life. He had been tracked down in an Ottawa restaurant by Prime Minister Brian Mulroney's people a week before Finn had quit and told the job would be his as soon as Finn was gone.

Morden had come out of the Privy Council Office, where Finn had come from originally, but he had been on the military and external affairs side whereas Finn had been with security and intelligence.

Morden had begun his career twenty-four years earlier as a diplomat, and most of his External Affairs postings involved mainly international trade matters. But more recently it was as a bureaucrat in Ottawa that he had made his mark, helping to settle Native land claims for the Department of Indian Affairs and Northern Development in 1984-85. The following year he was back in External Affairs in the Economic and Trade Policy Branch. And the year after that, he was in PCO advising on foreign policy. Although he pretended that all he knew about spying was what he had read in Len Deighton and John le Carre novels, actually, for the previous two years as assistant cabinet secretary for foreign and defence policy, part of his job had been to deal with the ultra-secret Communications Security Establishment, the $100-million-a-year telecommunications monitoring network that Canada operates largely on behalf of the National Security Agency in Fort Meade, Virginia.

Morden caught Mulroney's attention when he prepared a trade and aid package for the Caribbean that made Mulroney a big hit down at the Commonwealth conference in Nassau in 1985. The pact opened Canadian liquor store shelves to Caribbean rum in a big way, as well as Canadian markets to winter fruits and vegetables from the islands. Mulroney has always noticed people who make him look good — or bad.

More recently Morden had helped bring the French and other Europeans to the bargaining table for a round of negotiations on North Atlantic fish stocks — no mean feat at the time. His principal skills had been negotiation and smart political analysis, not management or organization, but his political skills told him the latter were the qualities the government would be wanting to parade in its new CSIS director.

Morden was born in Hamilton but grew up in Montreal, where his father was a bank inspector. Despite growing up in a French-speaking milieu, Morden still speaks French with an English accent. He took his first year of undergraduate studies at McGill University and then transferred to Dalhousie University in Halifax where he finished his bachelor's degree in history and political science. Brian Mulroney was there in first-year law at the time. They met, but did not chum around. Morden was president of the Conservative campus club but Mulroney was not active in campus politics there. Morden did spend time with Joe Clark, his future boss at External Affairs. And Joe was interested in Tory politics — too much, perhaps, for his studies. They both went into first-year law and both dropped out after a year. At twenty-two, Morden tried writing the External Affairs exams, some of the most difficult in the country. He aced them and was on his way to becoming a career diplomat and senior public servant — one of the rare mandarins in Ottawa with few academic credentials. What Morden achieved in the public service, he did out of hard work and sheer ability.

He attended arms control talks with the Russians in Geneva in the sixties and learned something there that has stayed with him since: "With the Russians, everything's on the table, everything is negotiable." Although he learned to respect the Soviets then, and later as a diplomat, he has remained a Cold Warrior at heart. He still talks about "Russia" instead of the "the Soviet Union" and feels a strong attachment to New York, acquired during his postings there.

Morden is a hard worker, but not a workaholic, say several people who have worked with him. Unlike most Ottawa mandarins, he does not reach for the newspapers first thing in the morning. As he says, "Hey, I had two postings in New York so I don't read things in the morning. I flip channels. Listen, every New Yorker in the world stumbles out of bed, eyes half-closed — boom — he gets the Tube on. I wake up at 6:30 a.m., do the cablevision thing, then do 'Canada A.M.' and then flip over to the American stuff."

Later he will look at the newspapers after he has paid sufficient attention to the electronic media. He usually drives himself to work. Apart from a special RCMP VIP alarm inside his car and in his home, Morden is under no special security protection. At work there is a limousine parked outside the office door, often right on the sidewalk, in violation of local traffic regulations, idling and waiting to take him wherever he goes for top-level briefings.

Morden's modest, modern, low-ceilinged office in the East

Memorial Building at 284 Wellington Street is a study in eclecticism. On his desk are the usual pens, papers, photos of family, but on a credenza behind his desk is a huge, bloated stuffed piranha fish with plastic worry beads dangling nonchalantly from its razor-sharp teeth. Morden insists the fish has no special meaning. He calls it Fred, after his children's pet goldfish. But CSIS insiders say it represents Morden himself, deceptively overweight and quiet, but with very sharp teeth and plenty to worry about. In a glass case nearby there is a mug with the KGB crest on it, the fake kind that can be bought through mail order in the U.S. But next to it there is an authentic West German border guard's hat. Some CSIS insiders say it had to do with a secret diplomatic mission into East Germany, but Morden denies he was ever a spy for anybody, and won't say how he came by the hat.

He seems to have a quiet domestic life. He and his wife Marg were married in 1964. (Joe Clark served as an usher at the wedding.) They live in Ottawa's Glebe neighbourhood, with two teenage children and a small terrier. Morden enjoys classical recordings and owns a collection of rare World War I books.

What Morden walked into that day, back in September 1987 when he accepted the directorship of CSIS, was no bed of roses. Morale was at a low point, investigations were still going on, and the whole agency was leaking classified information from every pore. And the leaks did not stop just because a new director had been appointed.

In late September, hard-working New Democrat MP Svend Robinson, CSIS's *bête noire*, released Top Secret CSIS documents showing that, despite its pious claims to the contrary, CSIS still had four people monitoring peace groups — a remnant of the notorious "peace desk" of the RCMP security service days, which had pulled off so many dirty tricks against "peaceniks" in the sixties. Apparently it had never been broken up.

Two days later Robinson came back again, this time with CSIS documents showing the service had been watching the Communist Party of Canada and the Quebec Communist Party. The leaks had the desired effect. CSIS looked like an an old-fashioned, unsophisticated organization, still rooting around for Commies under the bed.

Solicitor General Kelleher was furious. He had been burned often enough by CSIS in the past. This time, on the advice of his staff, he put the already overly secretive agency on an even tighter leash. CSIS would no longer be allowed to talk to reporters, not even to issue its usual non-denials. Gerry Cummings, the service's official spokesman, said he had been told to transfer all calls to Kelleher's office. The minister's press spokesperson Ghislaine Delorme, a genuinely kind and helpful woman, took reporters' calls, telephoned CSIS to obtain the information, and relayed it back to reporters. If the topic was the slightest bit complicated, it might require several telephone calls to reply adequately to one reporter. An exasperated Delorme confided to frustrated reporters that it wasn't her idea and that she didn't know how much longer she could take it. Within a few months she was gone and CSIS was back to issuing its own bland non-denials.

The gag order was a deliberate slap at the service, and had the new director been a manager of less foresight, he might easily have made a big thing out of it, challenging the minister to a public showdown over the agency's right to speak for itself — with most of the news media on CSIS's side. But there was never any public showdown. Morden the consummate public servant kept his cool demeanour and did not openly challenge his minister. Within a year Kelleher would be gone but Morden is still there.

Morden's problems continued; there may have been a new tillerman on board, but all they saw in Winnipeg was the same old service in a stage of crisis. In Manitoba, the NDP provincial government refused once again in the fall of 1987 to allow CSIS access to provincial government files. All the other Canadian provinces except Quebec had given in. Manitoba's Acting Solicitor General Roland Penner said that as long as CSIS was "running amok like a loose cannon," the agency would not have access to files. CSIS was seeking access to the files of the nineteen provincial departments, including welfare files, the provincial child abuse registry, provincial tax statements, birth and death records, medical and mental health records, communicable disease records, and tourism, industry and business records. "We don't want to sign that agreement until we're satisfied the situation is under control," said Penner.

Several provincial governments had held out initially in 1984 against giving CSIS full access to information of a private nature about its citizens. Civil libertarian groups had led the fight against granting full access, arguing that some things are too personal for even the security service to have access to. CSIS argued back that if it was so secret, why were the provinces collecting the information in the first place? But eventually the civil libertarian groups had to admit defeat, and one by one the provinces began signing agreements with CSIS in the late 1980s. Even Manitoba finally opened its files after the New Democrats were swept out and the Conservatives came to power. Eventually all the provinces except Quebec gave in. To this day, the Province of Quebec refuses to let CSIS have access to the files it holds on Quebeckers, and even restricts somewhat access to Quebec motor vehicle files: if CSIS wants to know who owns a car with Quebec licence plates it must make a special request to the Sûreté du Québec.

In fall 1987, the Independent Advisory Team, appointed by the cabinet in July 1987 and headed by former Clerk of the Privy Council Gordon Osbaldeston, handed in its report. The task force had been charged with examining management problems at CSIS, looking into the adverse effects of the Counter-Subversion Branch and developing a plan of action for the agency.

It had been a rescue bid. Most task forces in the federal bureaucracy use up a lot of time and money and end up producing very little. And then, occasionally, a task force such as Osbaldeston's comes along and in two months draws up a remarkable blueprint for the recovery of an ailing government agency. Osbaldeston made thirty-four recommendations dealing with effective leadership, better human resources management, an improved recruitment and career training program and what he called "remodelling the corporate culture," which meant getting some old-fashioned team spirit going and changing the old Mountie mindset.

The task force had discovered that CSIS was driven by whatever events happened to be occurring, that the agency really had no long-term plan of attack, and not even a committee to produce annual threat assessments. It made many good suggestions.

First of all, the director would have to be more visible. There would have to be major changes in administration and planning, including the dissolution of the Counter-Subversion Branch, which was more trouble than it was worth. The service should also work more closely with the solicitor general to get him on its side promoting the agency, and providing better services for CSIS employees.

On November 30, Kelleher announced sweeping changes to CSIS based on the findings of the Osbaldeston Task Force. First he announced the disbanding of the Counter-Subversion Branch. Six months earlier, Finn had said that subversion was "a most important concern" of CSIS; Kelleher now said it was a "low-level threat."

The "C.S.", as it was called, was the poor side of the family. It amounted to no more than ten percent of the personnel or about five percent of the budget . . . and drew about fifty percent of the criticism levelled at CSIS by civil libertarians, because it was always targeting people who had nothing to do with either terrorism or foreign espionage but were simply dissenters and protesters advocating a different kind of Canada, usually through entirely legal means. Left-wing activists in Montreal, a few old Commies playing chess outside the Labour Temple in Winnipeg, housewives for Latin America, farmers helping out in Nicaragua — they didn't seem like much of a threat. Little wonder that counter-subversion soon became known as the dead end shop at CSIS, the one that everybody avoided, the place where no one wanted to go.

Actually, it wasn't the absolute worst place. That distinction belonged to the Security Clearance Branch, which examined reports of security clearance interviews of public servants turned in by ex-Mounties working on contract for CSIS. What could be more exciting than having to read through the transcript of a two-hour interview about the personal life and daily work habits of a middle-aged Ottawa public servant whose idea of a wild time is going to Eaton's St. Laurent on a Friday night and trying on a pair of gloves. At least counter-subversion got to investigate an occasional crackpot, which livened things up around the office.

But Osbaldeston had been right. It was time to wrap up counter-subversion. Whatever it had been watching could just as easily be taken care of by the two big branches, counter-intelligence and counter-terrorism. The files that had a foreign tinge to them were given to counter-intelligence. The ones that dealt with something that could develop into violence were turned over to counter-terrorism. In the end, it turned out that there had been over 54,000 files in counter-subversion. When the two bigger branches went through them they found that ninety-five percent were not worth keeping.

Kelleher also didn't want any more wiretap affidavit scandals. Neither did Morden. So CSIS tightened up the use of intrusive techniques. From now on they would only be used when there was a demonstrated and clear threat to national security.

Morden took over one committee after another and set himself up as chairman. He took over chairmanship of the Target Approval and Review Committee, the powerful "targeting" committee that decides which groups or individuals will become official targets of CSIS, subject to intrusions into their private lives. Targeting a group or an individual is very serious business at CSIS, and is not supposed to be done for a trivial reason. There is an elaborate committee procedure leading up to a person or an individual being declared an official target of CSIS in Canada, something like the intelligence equivalent of being put on the RCMP's most wanted list.

The word "targeting" is well-chosen. A group or individual that has been declared a target is just that — a target for whatever surveillance, intelligence gathering or wiretapping that CSIS can get authorization for from a judge. Less than 100 people a year are targeted by CSIS for the full treatment, the most extreme use of "intrusive techniques," which must be approved by a judge from the Federal Court of Canada in every case. The procedure is now complex, with careful checks and balances at every step.

A new system with twenty-one safeguards was set up to ensure that no more falsified affidavits would ever be filed by CSIS in a court of law. Each warrant application had to be approved by the committee. One of the safeguards featured a CSIS lawyer who would act as a "devil's advocate" at these meetings, arguing why no warrant should be sought. It was a sophisticated public-service style of management applied to security and intelligence. Morden again insisted on chairing each committee meeting himself, making good on his promise to bring a hands-on approach to CSIS management.

Within a few months, Morden had also made plans to bolster morale. He was well aware of what Osbaldeston had said about developing a corporate culture at the agency. It had to be more than just another bureaucratic mill. There had to be a new spirit. And he made immediate plans to get the new headquarters project going again, despite the financial squeeze. The organization was still spread out in five different buildings around Ottawa.

The new director made major administrative changes as well. He brought in new people, such as Joanne Sulzenko-Cohen, whom he had known at the PCO ten years earlier. He created a new position, director general of the secretariat, through which all committees would have to report. She in turn would report to Morden, who would effectively control everything. That was the way he had said it would be done, and it was.

Finn's approach had been to delegate the work to his five

deputy directors, who all ended up fighting because their responsibilities overlapped. There was no danger of that after Morden took over. He would have all the power. The responsibilities of each deputy director were clearly spelled out and did not overlap at all. And woe betide any deputy director who strayed off into somebody else's backyard.

And one by one the old Mountie guard at the top was leaving. The last deputy director from the previous administration, Ray Lees, in charge of operations, would be gone within a year. The bureaucrats and people from External Affairs and the PCO had taken over. Robert Clarke, the former ambassador to Pakistan, would be brought in to help with human resources management.

Within three months after taking over, with the help of the Osbaldeston Report and Kelleher's blessing, Morden had completely demolished the existing top management structure at CSIS and set up a completely new structure with himself as the undisputed boss.

The politicians had wanted CSIS to do something concrete to show it was committed to bilingualism. Morden promptly elevated Official Languages to the rank of a full deputy directorship, right up there alongside management, services administration, operations and the other senior functions of the organization. The politicians were impressed. It didn't end there. Morden began promoting Francophones up from the ranks, and providing time off for unilinguals to pick up the second official language. No more moratoriums on language capabilities. And two new deputy directorships were created, one for personnel and another for general management.

Morden also set up a new orientation program for all CSIS employees to familiarize them with the objectives of a civilian intelligence agency. New operation manuals, training manuals, targeting manuals and security clearance manuals were ordered to replace the old RCMP manuals that the agency had been using. It would be two years, however, before the new manuals would be ready, translated and printed.

Not all of this sat well with the rank and file at CSIS. From the vantage point of his desk in the farthest reaches of the Security Clearance Branch, Stephen Beatty, the young intelligence officer, watched what was happening at the top.

Like most of his colleagues he was glad to see the last of Finn and his crowd, and he was impressed right away with Morden's "political skills" and his ability "to control and contain situations" as they arose.

"But I was not impressed with his organizational skills," says Beatty. "When we had the problem with Finn, it was because operations were taking place that he didn't know about. Morden put down an elaborate set of mechanisms which just handcuffed operations. It was as if Morden had said, 'And by God, nothing's going to happen unless it's crystal clear that we are 100-percent sure of what we are doing,' so that by God, it no longer becomes intelligence. 'Okay, I read it in the newspaper, so now I can go out and investigate it.' "

Beatty had little respect for running an intelligence service in this way. To him it amounted to doing no more than "harmless things that won't rock the boat." He says that a lot of the changes were cosmetic or things the politicians cared about, such as more bilingualism, more women in management and the abolition of counter-subversion, but that down in the trenches, when it came to operations and the way the agency operated, not much had changed.

The filing system was just as chaotic as ever; CSIS didn't have a computerized personnel list; the abuses of the security clearance process were not eliminated; CSIS was still leaving up to individual intelligence officers what material should go into the computer files, which were still not modernized to make retrieval and cross-referencing more efficient. According to Beatty, nobody raised a fuss because these are failings that do not attract public attention — and in this case he may be right.

After Ray Lees retired in 1988, Morden left the position of deputy director of operations vacant for more than a year, in effect becoming the DDO himself. Since the position is not publicized much, the vacancy passed almost unnoticed.

Even James Kelleher began to trust the new director and went to bat for him, hitting the road with a series of speeches he announced would "demystify" CSIS. It was simply a public relations exercise, but it made excellent news copy. For instance, Kelleher announced in Toronto that CSIS had uncovered three terrorist plots during the Commonwealth Conference in Vancouver that year and that authorities had been able to take steps to thwart the conspiracies. Unfortunately he left it at that, so nobody really knew how serious the threats had been. Later he announced at another speech in Kitchener, Ontario that 100 persons — including a number of diplomats who had been refused accreditation to Canada because they might be spies — had been turned back at the border since CSIS was formed in 1984. But again, he never gave any more details. Still, it produced interesting headlines such as "CSIS Nabs 100 Spies", which did wonders for morale at the agency.

As 1987 drew to a close, the government heaved a sigh of relief; it appeared at long last that the crisis of the past year might finally be over. It had been a terrible year, and with a federal election looming in 1988, the Conservative government was keeping its fingers crossed that this new man Morden could do the job and keep the lid on things — at least until the election was over.

There were a few setbacks during the winter. The Mounties still did not trust CSIS, and RCMP Commissioner Norman Inkster went ahead with his plans to set up the new National Security Investigations Directorate. It was obvious that if CSIS went haywire again, the Mounties would be in a good position to step into the breach and demand that security and intelligence be reintegrated into the RCMP. Then, in February, the Mohammad Affair erupted, and people were quick to say, "Same old CSIS," but in fact the operation had started a year earlier, long before Morden had come on board. However, he ended up taking the blame for it.

By April 1988, Morden was ready to launch a major program of personnel changes to get the old ex-Mounties out of the organization. He offered them a lucrative incentive — fifteen months of salary for quitting if they had twenty-four years of combined RCMP and CSIS service. Many jumped at the chance, leaving room for new civilian recruits. And in the same month, the Sir William Stephenson Academy reopened in Ottawa. Its first class numbered only twelve students. However, the balance was excellent. There were eight women, and the class was fifty percent Francophone. In addition, three of the twelve students were former surveillants who were being allowed to move up into the intelligence officer class. And every single one was bilingual. Things were indeed looking up.

# OF MOLES AND MEN

**O**RGANIZATION AND MORALE AT CSIS may have improved under Reid Morden's leadership, but there were still problems, and a major worry at the agency was the continuing leakage of information to the media. The leaks were more embarrassing than dangerous, but any leak is regarded very seriously by a security service. Immediate steps must be taken to find and silence the person responsible — and sometimes the methods that a service uses are unacceptable to outsiders who don't realize that an information drain, or the presence of a mole, can absolutely destroy an entire intelligence network.

CSIS has had its share of seepage (such as those of angry Francophone staff in Montreal) which sent waves of shock and paranoia through the organization. The following case is interesting partly because it involved a very senior level of government, but also because it shows to what extremes CSIS will go when tracing a leak.

Whatever it was that the mysterious Mr. Chang had done, the prime minister's office wanted him out of the country very quickly. In 1986, Pei Chi Chang, or Patrick Chang, as he liked to be called, was the highest ranking Taiwanese government official in Canada. He had arrived here three years earlier to represent the government of Taiwan, but since Canada had broken off relations with Taiwan in 1970 when it recognized the "other" China, Chang could no longer go around as a Taiwanese diplomat. Some way had to be found around the problem because Canada was doing $1.7 billion worth of trade a year with the Asian nation.

So Chang was allowed into Canada officially on an immigration minister's permit, as the representative of the General Chamber of Commerce of the Republic of China, sponsored by the Chamber of Commerce of Cornwall, Ontario. That took care of the diplomatic niceties. He had an office at 123 Edward Street in Toronto, and did what they do at most other consulates or embassies. He promoted various business interests, handled immigration matters, and took care of visiting delegations. He even handed out passports and issued visas to Taiwan. It saved people having to go to New York, the next closest Taiwanese government office.

Chang had registered the name of his operation as the Chamber of Commerce of Chung-Hwa — which meant China — something he perhaps shouldn't have done, but at least it impressed the big boys in the Foreign Affairs Department back in Taipei.

The other Chinese knew about him, but they didn't mind. As long as Chang didn't make too much noise, they weren't going to say anything about it. Chang worked hard at bettering relations and promoting trade between Canada and Taiwan. By all accounts he was a delightful man, married to a charming wife, with two lovely children. In short, he was the perfect diplomat.

He was also very friendly with Conservative MPs, particularly the right-wing claque that had gravitated around Brian Mulroney in 1981 and worked to dump his predecessor, Joe Clark, in 1983. Chang liked to invite his Tory friends on freebie junkets to Taiwan and the occasional little side trip to South Korea. He seemed to have a way with Taiwanese foundations and institutes, always finding one eager to pay the way of a Canadian MP travelling over to see the beauties and marvels of Taiwan.

One day, quite unexpectedly, Chang received a letter from Patrick Donovan, an immigration officer in Toronto. The letter asked him to show up for a meeting on January 30, 1986. Chang did not know it, but Donovan was with the expulsions unit of the immigration department.

At the meeting, Chang was handed another letter written by no less than the executive director of immigration for Canada, J. B. Bissett, which said that he and his family were being deported in two weeks time. The Canadian taxpayers had even graciously bought one-way tickets for them, worth almost $4,000. There was no explanation, no reason given, no opportunity to defend himself.

Chang wanted to know what he'd done. No one from Immigration had ever come to see him, no one from CSIS, or from the RCMP. True, he had once unfurled a Taiwanese flag at a reception in Chinatown, but he didn't think that was enough to get him thrown out of the country. The precipitous action could not have come at a worse time. Chang was on the verge of closing a number of lucrative business deals involving Canadian and Taiwanese businessmen, including an automotive deal that he claims would have brought a multi-million-dollar auto plant to the country, similar to the Canada-Korea deal that brought Hyundai to Ontario.

Chang had no shortage of friends in high places. He was very close to former defence minister Robert Coates, who had resigned the previous year. In fact, Coates' former executive assistant, Richard (Rick) Logan, was the clerk of the Canada-Taiwan Friendship Committee that Chang had set up with his Tory MP friends in Ottawa. Four months earlier, Chang had organized a ten-day junket to Taipei to coincide with Taiwan's national holiday, October 11; he had arranged for the trip to be paid for by the Asia and World Institute, a Taiwanese business lobby group seeking better diplomatic and business relations with Canada. One of the Tories on the jaunt was backbencher Pierre-H. Cadieux, who later became solicitor general. As well, fiery Liberal MP and ex-rat-packer Don Boudria went along. Brian Mulroney had a good laugh when he heard about it. But Mulroney wasn't laughing when Chang turned to his high-powered friends in the Tory caucus in early February 1986 to try to rescind the deportation order.

Toronto lawyer Richard Boraks, a former Conservative candidate and long-time party organizer, was brought in to co-ordinate a political campaign within the Tory caucus, while immigration lawyer Mendel Green was hired to fight the legal case. He was able to get a court injunction to hold off the deportation for at least a week, until he could find out what had happened, and perhaps have a chance to defend Chang in court.

Chang had entered Canada on a permit good for one year that had been automatically renewed every three months for two years after that. Absolutely no conditions had been imposed on him when the permit was issued. It was a most bizarre case, recalls Boraks. He doesn't believe the deportation order could have had anything to do with the trip to Taiwan four months earlier. There had been several similar trips before that one. In fact, Boraks himself had organized a trip for the Taiwanese, and sent Elmer MacKay and John McDermid over to Taiwan on a freebie in 1982, the year before Chang arrived.

Boraks's job was to get key members in the Tory caucus worked up over the deportation order against Chang, so it would turn into a big political issue, and the government would have to back down. The help of the Canadian Chinese-nationalist community was enlisted. They were quick to see the sinister hand of Beijing behind the decision, and letters of support poured in from the Chinese-Canadian community to Immigration, the PMO and MPs' offices.

Boraks doesn't think that the People's Republic of China had anything to do with it. "This was strictly a fight within the Tory caucus," he says. "The orders had come from very high, from the office of the big guy himself probably, to get this guy out, and quick. No reason given, just get him out."

Apparently, a group of Chang's Tory MP friends, many of whom had been on freebie trips before and were now cabinet ministers, created a big row over the deportation order. According to Boraks, "There was screaming and yelling at one caucus meeting." Tory MPs John Oostrom and Andrew Witer both spoke in favour of Chang.

Rick Logan, the clerk of the Canada-Taiwan Friendship Committee, says Chang was innocent. "This guy was no more a spy than any other diplomat would be a spy," says Logan. "I don't know what CSIS had on him. I think it was just a big ball-up, a big screw-up by someone, somewhere. I should know. I went on enough trips with them. I was clerk of that committee." Otto Jelinek was president of the committee at one time, says Logan, and, according to Richard Boraks, Jelinek was one of the people helping Chang.

Immigration spokesman Les Westerberg told reporters he could not reveal the reasons for the deportation order "because it's a sensitive matter."

Chang was distraught. His sixteen-year-old son and his nine-year-old daughter, both honour students, would certainly lose their academic year if they had to leave and go back to Taiwan. His daughter had a piano recital coming that Wednesday. Could the order please be delayed for a while, he pleaded. Boraks says it was shameful the way the Conservatives were treating Chang after having happily gone on the trips he arranged.

*Globe and Mail* reporter Victor Malarek found an immigration official who told him that whatever immigration violations Chang had allegedly committed, they were "really minor" and they were not the reason that he was being deported. Chang said he was baffled. "I cannot figure it out, and I cannot get immigration to answer my questions," he told reporters. Eight telex queries from his lawyer to immigration officials had failed to produce a single reply. There was a good reason for their silence. Immigration officials had been told to mind their own business, that the orders were coming from the PMO and they were not to get involved, so that was why they did not reply to Chang.

In fact, Chang had been the subject of a major CSIS investigation. Boraks remembers some time earlier a couple of CSIS intelligence officers came to interview him. They took him out to lunch at a military club on University Avenue in Toronto. He remembers that they mainly warned him about a business deal he was working on with the Polish consulate that might have resulted in his being entrapped in something, "but they may have asked some questions about Patrick too."

The subsequent CSIS report that was prepared went directly to the PMO where the decision was taken to expel Chang as soon as possible. Six months later, Ron Atkey, appearing before the Commons Justice and Solicitor General Committee on June 3, 1986, said that a special report had been sent by CSIS to the prime minister, bypassing the solicitor general to whom CSIS normally reports.

On February 25, 1986, *Toronto Star* reporter Bill Schiller quoted reliable but unnamed Ottawa sources as saying that Chang had been working for Taiwanese intelligence services and that CSIS had run "checks" on him and even had copies of "coded communications" that the service had decoded.

Meanwhile, three more Conservative MPs who had taken an all-expenses paid trip to Taiwan the previous summer — Murray Cardiff, Don Blenkarn and Felix Holtmann — all went to bat for Chang. Blenkarn said, "He operates what amounts to a consulate. He expedited my visa. It has your photo on it and his signature authorizing you to go." In July 1985, the trio had attended a World Anti-Communist League rally in Taipei paid for by the WACL.

A new date, March 4, was set for Chang's deportation hearing. CSIS vowed that if it were asked to say what it knew about Chang, it would invoke a "Section 39" — the national security clause of the Canada Evidence Act which the service uses frequently to keep secret whatever it wants to keep secret.

Caucus sources were telling reporters that if Chang decided to talk, there would be plenty he could say about the Tory caucus. A showdown loomed. But on March 3, Chang changed his mind and abruptly flew out of the country. Taiwan had ordered him home. He explained in a letter he left with Green, his lawyer, that "it would serve no purpose to stay and try to fight or delay the deportation order." Departure was judged the better part of diplomacy in Chang's case. He was promptly replaced by another Taiwanese Chamber of Commerce representative, who was more careful what sort of business he conducted with Tory caucus members. As for Chang, he reappeared in West Germany a year later and is now running a Taiwanese Chamber of Commerce out of Frankfurt.

It appeared to all the world that CSIS had caught a spy and had him tossed out of the country, without having to reveal its evidence publicly. Match point for CSIS. However, the story of Patrick Chang had some very peculiar ramifications — and involved at least one very surprised young entrepreneur.

Dan Donovan became involved in the Chang affair a lot more deeply than he ever wanted. When he began poking around the Chang file in 1986, he never suspected he would soon find himself caught up in a major CSIS mole hunt.

Donovan, who later became an executive assistant to Toronto Broadview-Greenwood Liberal MP Dennis Mills, is also in his off-hours an accomplished nightclub comedian. But he has nothing funny to say about his brief brush with CSIS over the Chang Affair. Donovan and his partners, Maureen Kennedy and Donald Lanouette, had set up a small firm, Access Information Consultants, Inc., which operated by obtaining government information under the Access to Information law and then selling it to a number of clients, usually the news media or private firms. Donovan had scored some early media successes by obtaining the names of firms illegally selling arms to Chile, which Southam News Service bought and used in an article, exposing the arms shipments and giving credit in print to Donovan. This helped business immensely.

Soon afterwards, Donovan sold information on a series of government public-relations contracts awarded to Roger Nantel, an old and dear friend of Prime Minister Brian Mulroney. The *Ottawa Herald* used the material and also gave Donovan credit. He was quickly making his name in the business. Then one day, somebody Donovan refuses to identify, whom he says he had met only once before, contacted him and gave him some documents and information about Patrick Chang — and his relations with Conservative cabinet ministers. Some of the documents contained information so sensitive that Donovan had trouble believing they were authentic.

According to Donovan, they showed Chang had close ties with the Tory caucus. "I had access to some documents that I probably shouldn't have had," he recalls. Possibly the most sensitive of all, he says, was one "pertaining to a meeting" between CSIS and Prime Minister Brian Mulroney two days before Chang was asked to leave the country. In addition to the notes from that meeting, he says, he also had the times of certain meetings in the days prior to the order to deport Chang, as well as information involving Conservative cabinet ministers.

"I had the briefing notes that went to the prime minister," says Donovan. In Canada there are not many documents more secret than CSIS's briefing notes for the prime minister. If what Donovan had was authentic, there had been a major leak at the highest levels of either CSIS or the PMO. The documents clearly showed, Donovan said, that "people in the highest levels of government" knew "what the hell was going on."

"My total thrust at this point was to find out what had happened," he recalls. The trail of the long-gone Mr. Chang was already almost a year old at that time. He began teleph'oning around.

"The first persons I looked up were the Conservatives who went to Taiwan in 1985," says Donovan. That was the junket Chang had organized. He also called people who had been close to Chang and helped promote his activities while he had been in Canada. Through Chang's ex-lawyer in Toronto, Mendel Green, Donovan obtained Chang's telephone number in Taiwan and was able to reach him right away. "I told him who I was," Donovan recalls. "I told him I was with an information service in Ottawa and was trying to put together a story." Donovan asked him why he had been deported when there was no indication of wrongdoing, and he had close relations with Conservative members. Chang was upset that he had been thrown out of the country. "He told me he had helped Canada and the Canadian government, but they had treated him unfairly. It became very evident that there was something really wrong and that in fact something had happened."

When Donovan called back the following day to find out more, another man answered and told him there was no Mr. Chang at that number. Suddenly it was as if Chang had never existed; and Donovan was not able to go to Taiwan or even to pursue the investigation. "We were trying to run a business. I was searching stuff during the week and waiting on tables on the weekend to make it go. I didn't have the resources at my disposal but I wanted to do something. I thought it was just, like . . . brutal," he says.

That was when he decided that maybe he should talk to the people at CSIS. "I just put in a call to the front desk. I said that I had some stuff we should talk about." Soon afterwards someone at CSIS called him back and asked him to come down to the office at 400 Cooper Street in Ottawa. Donovan arrived there alone shortly before 8:00 p.m. and was ushered into a room where two CSIS men were waiting.

"At first I thought they knew absolutely nothing of what I was talking about," he remembers. The two agents sat motionless and just listened to his story. Donovan explained that he had been given "some information" about Chang, the Taiwanese lobby and Conservative cabinet ministers and was in the process of establishing more facts. He explained that there must have been something going on other than immigration irregularities, and perhaps CSIS should look into it. He did not say that he had been given what appeared to be CSIS's briefing notes to the prime minister. He kept using the term "information" instead.

The two CSIS investigators said nothing and let him talk on. The conversation was all one way. Finally, after about half an hour, Donovan tired of this and decided to wrap it up and go home. He told them, "That's all I have to say" and got ready to leave. That was when one of the agents asked him about the calls he had made to Taiwan. And Donovan, who had made no mention of these calls at all, was shocked. He asked them, calmly, what calls they were talking about. Just as calmly, they replied with numbers and dates. Donovan explained that he had called Chang because he was trying to "piece everything together." But the two agents were not interested in helping to piece together the evidence Donovan had. They wanted one thing, and one thing only. "Where did you get this information?" they asked. Donovan refused to tell them, and he wouldn't describe the documents he had in his possession. But he did tell them he had information about a meeting before Chang was asked to leave Canada. "I told them I had information on who was there," recalls Donovan. "I told them there were seven people. That's when they really flipped out on me."

"At one point they said, 'We're concerned because some of the things you are saying . . . are true, and we're concerned about how you got that information because very few people have that information.' "

They continued to press him for his source. By now it was 12:30 Saturday morning. They had been talking since 8:00 Friday night. Finally, the two CSIS agents tried a different tack. They asked Donovan to find out whether the source would be willing to meet them. He agreed to contact his source, but insisted they should let him do it on his own time, and there was to be no following him. The two agents agreed. "Had I been more experienced I would have gone to the RCMP instead of CSIS," he says. The Mounties would have been concerned about the information he had, and wouldn't have spent their time trying to find out how he got it. He had gone to CSIS because the agency was mentioned in the documents he had seen.

Donovan was shaking as he left the RCMP building in the middle of the night. When he got home, he called his partner, Maureen, and then his father in Winnipeg to ask his advice. His father told him to stay put, and a friend of the family who had experience in these matters would come to see him in the morning.

The friend showed up early and immediately recognized the voice of the CSIS agent on Donovan's answering machine as that of Frank Pratt, head of internal security for CSIS at the time and one of the greatest investigators Canada had ever produced. It was Pratt who broke the famous case of Hugh Hambleton, the quiet Laval professor who had spied for the Soviet Union and was finally found out, put on trial in Great Britain and convicted.

Pratt is both respected and hated, and yet he is a quiet, unassuming man in his mid-forties, not particularly listinguishable from any number of men his age who go around in business suits. He is considered one of the leading experts on Israeli and American spy networks in Canada. As head of internal security for CSIS at the time, Pratt handled only the toughest and potentially most damaging cases, the ones that occurred within CSIS. If there was a mole or a leak inside CSIS, it was Pratt's job to ferret it out.

Pratt is an unlikely looking man for internal security. He does not even have a good poker face, say his colleagues. He sometimes blushes when he gets excited about something he is told, and may even quickly whip out a pad and pen and begin making notes, to cover his nervousness. He seldom makes mistakes, but he did make one at the Hambleton trial in London. He wasn't watching, and a news photographer caught him unawares and took his picture, which ran in the Ottawa *Citizen*. For Pratt, that was a major breach in security and his colleagues still tease him about it.

Pratt has one skill that has made him one of the best there is at what he does. He never lets go. He is persistent. Donovan's friend knew the Chang affair was a serious matter if Pratt had been assigned to crack the case. "Whatever it is, you have something here that these guys are after," he said. "Don't be worried if in the next couple of days, there's surveillance on you," he added. Donovan thought he was joking.

Since he was working that night, as he did Saturdays and Sundays, at the Café Bohemian off the By Ward Market in Ottawa's Lower Town, Donovan decided to take Maureen

Kennedy to the movies at the Rideau Centre that afternoon. "That's when it happened," he recalls. "We go into the theatre. Maureen goes to the washroom before the movie starts, while I go take my seat. When she comes out of the washroom, she hears this guy on the telephone next to the door to the ladies' washroom. There's a telephone right there. It's a guy in a blue ski jacket. He's saying, 'Should I stay here or follow them? What do you want me to do?' "

Kennedy headed past him to join Donovan, and told him she thought they were being followed. He refused to believe her, but the man in the blue ski jacket came in and took a seat at the rear of the theatre. He was still there when the movie ended. And he was still following Donovan hours later when he dropped by Pat and Mario's, a restaurant in downtown Ottawa. By now there was a full-scale stake-out operation going on. Down the street in front of the Chateau Lafayette Hotel, Donovan could see two men with "bug pieces" to their ears. And across the street there were two other men in suits, also with listening devices to their ears.

Frightened, but trying to remain calm, Donovan headed for the Café Bohemian down the street, where he was expected shortly after 5:00 p.m. for the start of his evening shift. He had called his friend Claude, who was a photographer, after he left the theatre and told him to grab his camera and meet him at the café so that if he was being followed, Claude could capture it on film.

Claude was at the cafe already, camera in hand. Donovan quickly explained to manager Tom Bimpson what was going on. He also told waitress, Jennifer Kennedy, Maureen's sister.

"What happens next is wild," says Donovan. "These guys with short hair and flannel pants come in." One of them was wearing a black-and-grey herringbone tweed sports jacket and carrying a copy of the *Vancouver Sun* under his arm. He sat down alone and ordered a glass of milk. His order was somewhat out of place at the Café Bohemian, a popular hang out for the artistic community in Ottawa. On a Saturday night the place throbbed with loud music. Nobody, but nobody, went into the Café Bohemian on a Saturday night for a glass of milk.

After a while, the staff telephone rang. It was Frank Pratt. He wanted to meet Donovan at the Four Seasons Hotel later that evening. (CSIS agents often use hotel rooms for meetings. They like the better hotels. Since it is their room, because they have registered and paid for it, they don't need a warrant from a judge to install a listening device as long as one of the people taking part in the conversation is from CSIS. After the meeting is over, they simply remove the bug and leave with it. Because the room is sometimes registered in a false name, this is a useful cover should the service have to deny later that the meeting ever took place.)

That night Donovan wasn't up to any nocturnal get-togethers at the Four Seasons. He was scared and angry, and they were bothering him at work. He told Pratt he had nothing more to say to anyone at CSIS.

But Frank Pratt would not be Frank Pratt if he gave up this easily. He called back twice more during the evening. Tom Bimpson, the manager, wanted to be understanding, but this was getting to be a bit much. Employees, even friends such as Donovan, had work to do. Meanwhile, every time Pratt called, Jennifer listened in on the line in the kitchen, so Donovan would have a witness if this ever went to court. And Claude, to his credit, was knocking off a few good photographs. He would stay the whole evening to accomplish his assignment.

Donovan knew Pratt would be waiting for him when his shift was over. He was beginning to feel like a tracked animal. He was also wondering why he should be subjected to this. He had done nothing wrong. He had gone to CSIS on his own. There was no police investigation, and he suspected there never would be. As he left the restaurant, a CSIS car, a large, unmarked North American model, pulled up, and the agent in the back seat rolled down the back seat window in the darkness and said, "Psst, come here" — just like in the spy movies.

"It's the guy who was taking the notes for Pratt the night

before," recalls Donovan. "They asked me to get in the car. I said 'No.' "

They asked again and Donovan refused again. All this time, he kept on walking, trying to get away from the car, which followed him slowly down the street, the agent in the back imploring him to get in. Meanwhile, Claude was trying to take a photo of all this, but he was having mechanical problems with his camera and had to keep making adjustments to it and then running to catch up to the others.

The car followed Donovan up the street, around the corner and most of the way down the block until he got to Daphne and Victor's restaurant and went in. Finally, the CSIS agents gave up and drove off. But Pratt was not through. He continued to apply pressure in the days that followed. From then on, Donovan refused to speak directly to Pratt, but "discussions" were set up through a "friend" he won't identify. For reasons he also won't reveal, Donovan thought it best some weeks later that he finally co-operate with Pratt.

"This is the way it was solved," he says. "Basically we had agreed I'd give initials. I had to agree to give information. I was getting tired of all this stuff."

The deal was that Pratt would throw initials at Donovan, until he happened to hit the right ones and then Donovan would say "Yes." That way, Donovan explains, he would not be breaking his promise not reveal his source's name.

Any journalist caught playing such a game with a source's name would be summarily fired, and any CSIS agent who treated the confidentiality of an informer's identity this loosely would be called up on the carpet right away. But Donovan was not a journalist, and certainly not a CSIS agent. He was a waiter trying to become a professional researcher, and he was tired of CSIS's unrelenting pressure. Besides, he never intended to tell CSIS the real initials of his source.

Pratt offered him all kinds of initials. They also asked him if his source was Ottawa Citizen reporter Neil MacDonald. An absurd question: had MacDonald had the information, he would not have taken it to Donovan. In all, CSIS offered four names and numerous sets of initials. Finally Donovan settled on a set of two initials. "What I did was I just agreed on one of them."

That was the end of it, for a few months. And then, out of the blue, CBC television reporter Der Hoi Yin called up. Donovan recalls that she had obtained some information on her own, and was "aggressive" about finding out his source. Donovan wondered whether it was ever going to end. So he arranged a meeting with his source and handed back the documents, and was pleased to be able to tell him not to worry — that he had not, as promised, photocopied the documents.

After that he could tell anyone who called, including author John Sawatsky, who pressed him as well, that he no longer had the cursed documents and the whole thing was over for him. Or at least he thought it was over.

"About six months later, Pratt calls me up and asks me if I want to go for a beer with him," says Donovan, who declined. "I had gone to CSIS for all the right reasons. I wasn't doing anything wrong. And they treated me like this. They had given me this song and dance about Canada and tried to make me feel like I was unpatriotic. It was almost like being in the Boy Scouts. In the end I just reconciled myself that I went to the wrong people. I should have gone to the RCMP.

"I was never able to prove what I had, which is why I dropped the whole thing. I had information that obviously there were people in the government, in CSIS, who knew what had gone on. So the question becomes, if they knew, what were they doing worrying about me?"

But CSIS wasn't just worrying about Donovan. Nor was he the only information broker to come to some grief over the mysterious Mr. Chang.

Richard McNeely is a Native Canadian who now has a very lucrative business buying and selling tobacco on behalf of Natives. He is one of the big wholesale suppliers of tax-free tobacco sold on reserves in Ontario and Quebec. But in the summer of 1986, he was involved in something completely different. He was in the information business, collecting commercial and political information on behalf of about a dozen very wealthy offshore Canadian clients.

In the course of his information collection, he came across something on Patrick Chang. He did not get documents, just information. Whatever he had, CSIS heard that he had it. And so did a couple of other people. He began getting messages that reporter Neil MacDonald was trying to reach him, and so was a researcher by the name of Dan Donovan.

Then one day there was a call on McNeely's answering machine from a man identifying himself as Frank Pratt, who said he wanted to see him. McNeely called back and Pratt identified himself as being from CSIS. They arranged to meet at Coasters restaurant in the By Ward Market. "He used an old friend's name as a reference," recalls McNeely. "The old friend was a former member of the RCMP." So after he hung up McNeely telephoned his old friend and asked who Pratt was. The friend had never heard of the guy, but he made some inquiries and called McNeely back. "He told me, 'I don't know what the hell is going on, but it doesn't bode well for anybody. It'll never end if you open the door.'" McNeely wanted to take his friend's advice, but he didn't want CSIS to be angry at him. So he went to meet Pratt at Coasters.

Pratt arrived at the bar with a tough-looking young man called Ken Ross. He ordered a glass of wine, and settled down for a chat. McNeeley asked him pointblank what he was after; in fact, he assumed Pratt wanted information on activities in the Native community, but he was wrong. Pratt wanted to talk about Patrick Chang.

Pratt told McNeely that he knew he had an "interest" in Patrick Chang. "We have reason to believe," Pratt said, "that some of this information may have come from our files. And the security agency . . . this is devastating to have people inside giving out information that we don't know about." Pratt mentioned Dan Donovan's name, and suggested that McNeely had had something to do with him. The CSIS official seemed particularly keen to know whether McNeely had any copies of cheques or information on his activities. They also hinted at payments. They never said what kind of payments, or to whom. Pratt gave McNeely a card that said he was director general of internal security.

McNeely was eager to convince Pratt that anything he knew about Patrick Chang, he had come by honestly. He did not have a source inside the intelligence agency. However, he agreed to meet Pratt again a few weeks later at CSIS headquarters in the East Memorial Building. At that meeting, McNeely again did his best to convince Pratt that he had no source inside the agency, but he didn't seem to succeed. A number of other topics came up about which he had peripheral information, that they apparently thought could only come from somebody on the inside.

In fact, McNeely's pastime is collecting embarrassing scandals about the Conservative government which he picks up from reporters he occasionally calls into his office. He then spins this information off to other reporters, who leave thinking that he knows a great deal. During the course of their investigation into the Chang leak, CSIS officials were obviously under the same impression, because they held a couple more meetings with McNeely over the next few months. Finally, however, they came to the conclusion that McNeely couldn't help them, and they left him alone.

Pratt probably never did find out who leaked the information on Patrick Chang, and we may never find out what Chang had actually done, although he clearly had links to the highest levels of the Tory caucus. And there wasn't even any real evidence to suggest that the leak emanated from within CSIS; it could just as easily have come from a disgruntled Tory in the PMO. But mole-paranoia was rampant then at CSIS, so the Great Mole Hunt continued.

If CSIS was upset about the putative mole within the agency, that is entirely understandable. The fear of finding a mole burrowing away in the undergrowth can almost destroy any intelligence agency. The RCMP security service ripped itself apart in 1972 in a hunt for a mole and, in the process, ruined the career of security service chief Leslie James Bennett. The CIA conducted a futile, damaging mole hunt of its own at about the same time. The KGB, of course, purged itself every time Stalin was constipated. By comparison, CSIS's behaviour appears almost restrained. What was troubling and embarrassing about the leaks at CSIS was that they were so public. Whoever did the leaking went not to a hostile foreign government, but straight to the Canadian news media. The intent was to damage not the country, but the agency.

An embarrassing series of leaks occurred within CSIS in the summer of 1987 and again in the summer of 1988. They may have been linked to the feeling of alienation in the agency's Montreal offices, although there is evidence that at least some of the leaks might have originated in Ottawa. The two major leaks in 1987 were most damaging to Ted Finn, the then-director of the service, whose administration was on its last legs.

There had been a leak to Radio-Canada reporter Normand Lester who revealed on June 12, 1987 that Marc-André Boivin, the Quebec labour-union strike organizer on trial in Quebec for conspiracy to bomb four motels in a labour dispute, was also a paid CSIS undercover agent inside the Confederation of National Trade Unions and a possible *agent provocateur*. This was very embarrassing to CSIS because it evoked images of the Mountie dirty-tricks-squad era.

There was another leak to Normand Lester that month, and this time he broke a story on a major CSIS coup. On June 23, 1987, Radio-Canada reported that CSIS had diverted twenty truckloads of debris from the Soviet consulate in Montreal, which had burned down five months earlier. The Soviets had been lax when they ordered a Montreal contractor to haul the debris from the fire to the gaping Miron quarry dumpsite in the north end of the city. The trucks were all easily diverted by police to a privately owned dump located on the Kanawake Mohawk reserve south of Montreal. There CSIS, RCMP and forensic science specialists sifted through the material and came up with enough choice pieces to fill an entire dumpster, which was hauled off to the RCMP science laboratory in Ottawa. British and American forensic specialists were invited and joined RCMP experts who went through the material over the next several months.

It was a treasure of technical information on how the Soviets build their embassies and consulates, because the entire interior of the consulate had been sent over from the Soviet Union. There were lots of useless pieces of burned wood, chunks from outer stone walls, electrical wiring and plaster debris, but there were also very valuable things such as smashed-up filing cabinets complete with the original locks. Expert locksmiths examined the locking mechanisms, photographed them and made drawings so they could be rebuilt or copied and used in Western spy missions against the Soviets elsewhere in the world.

The investigators also found bits of documents and papers that had not been completely burned, and analysed them to determine the kind of paper and ink, and what kind of typewriter had been used.

There were electromagnetic sensors still imbedded in chunks of wall, and the Mounties were able to see places where the Soviets had detected old RCMP listening devices and ripped them out of the walls. Radio-Canada reported that for the first time Western experts were able to analyse what materials the Soviets used to construct their spy-proof isolated code rooms in missions abroad.

It had been so sloppy of the Soviets not to make sure the material was well and truly buried that CSIS debated for a while whether it might be a set-up, a deliberate plant of misleading material, to fool Western counter-intelligence experts. But since most of the consulate ended up in the trucks, that theory was eventually dismissed.

When CSIS headquarters heard the Radio-Canada news report, there was hysteria. They had hoped to keep their coup quiet. The Americans found out and demanded to know what was happening up in Canada. This didn't look like the work of a mole — who would have been more likely to tip off the Soviets directly. But the news report had accomplished the same thing, and now the Soviets were aware that the Canadians cared — and now knew — about the construction of their embassies and consulates abroad. A major investigation was ordered by CSIS headquarters to find and plug the leak.

Lester had another story four months later. He found out that CSIS offices in Montreal had seen a résumé of the Osbaldeston Task Force report on CSIS before it was made public. In fact, Lester had seen a copy of the advance information CSIS had on itself. It begged the question, "Was CSIS spying on the task force set up to investigate CSIS?" An affirmative answer would not have pleased Osbaldeston at all.

The search for the leaks continued, all through the winter and into the spring of 1988, without success. By the early summer of 1988, CSIS still didn't know where the leaks were coming from.

If Reid Morden, who had taken over as director, thought the earlier leaks had been directed against the previous Finn administration, he was in for a nasty surprise. In June 1988, CSIS was congratulating itself on all the favourable publicity it was receiving over the expulsion of a pack of Soviet diplomats who had been spying on Canadair and Paramax Industries in Montreal and on the American naval base at Argentia, Newfoundland.

At the end of the month, however, Normand Lester and Pierre Beauregard, the highly respected Canadian Press reporter in Montreal, struck again. They put out a story that caused another stir in the senior management at the agency. Beauregard and Lester had obtained a copy of an internal letter, dated May 12, 1988, from thirty CSIS employees in the Communication Intelligence Production Unit in Montreal to Eric Boulet, the president of the CSIS Employees Association.

This was a major administration leak. The CIPU group, mostly Francophone women, complained about staff cuts and transfers to Toronto. They identified themselves as the people at CSIS in Montreal who monitored telephone calls and telecommunications going in and out of the Soviet, Czechoslovak and Cuban consulates and trade offices. They also monitored communications and bugs in the homes and offices of Eastern bloc diplomats and members of Eastern bloc delegations to the International Civil Aviation Organization and the Soviet, Czech and Cuban airline offices in Montreal. The letter complained that six new jobs were being created in the CSIS offices in Toronto, and four jobs being cut in Montreal, when there was really a lot more work to do in Montreal because CSIS had identified 122 Soviet spies operating out of Montreal, but only fifty out of Toronto.

The letter's publication was a major embarrassment to Morden, who had not been faced with any major leak before. It must have been of interest to the Soviets to find out how many spies the Canadians thought the Soviets had in the two cities, and how many people the Canadians had listening to them. To the Canadian public, it revealed that all the CSIS listening unit cared about were Soviets and Eastern bloc operations in Montreal. Wasn't anybody listening to any other intelligence networks there? It again confirmed the suspicion that CSIS was still locked in a Cold War mentality, as SIRC had complained so often. Just to confuse CSIS investigators, the same letter had been leaked to Jean-Denis Girouard of *Le Journal de Montréal.*

The next leak came only three days later, from Beauregard, who reported on July 2 that a week earlier a senior CSIS official in Montreal had seriously compromised the life and safety of a recent Soviet defector who was being transferred from Montreal to a safe house elsewhere in Canada by way of a flight to Ottawa.

Yuri Smurov, who had defected June 20, 1988 from his job as a translator with the Soviet delegation at the International Civil Aviation Organization in Montreal, was being moved with his family out of Montreal the following week. He was hardly a big-time spy, merely a minor Russian bureaucrat who had stayed in Canada too long and become too Canadianized. He didn't want to go back home. Still, because he was a defector, he had a right to some protection from CSIS for himself and his family.

A regular Air Canada flight to Ottawa was waiting to board passengers at 3:00 p.m. on Tuesday, June 28, 1988. Three seats had been reserved for the Smurov family: Yuri, his wife Margarita and their twelve-year-old, Canadian-born daughter Christina. A CSIS car was to drive onto the tarmac and go right up to the aircraft and they were to board just before take-off.

But Beauregard revealed that at the last minute a senior CSIS official insisted on driving the Smurovs to Ottawa in his private car, a 1981 Black Cougar. It turned out that he wanted to claim that twelve-cents-per-kilometre mileage — and at the same time pick up his wife, who had been shopping in Ottawa. The Cougar sped along Highway 417 without police escort. The only back-up was a second CSIS car carrying four men, all unarmed. Smurov was unaware how unprotected he was on the trip. Beauregard described how one senior official was physically sick when he had heard what had just happened at the airport. A few CSIS officials suspected that it was part of a plot to assassinate the Smurovs along the way, and police cars were quickly dispatched to intercept the Cougar, but everybody arrived safely and happily at Ottawa airport two hours later.

The implications of this story were major. Potential Soviet defectors discovered what kind of protection they might expect should they choose to defect to Canada, and it made the service look like a bunch of fools whose venality was so great they couldn't move a defector from Montreal to Ottawa without trying to make a buck on the side. CSIS headquarters wanted to know who was doing the leaking and how it could be stopped, but they also needed to know what other secrets were headed the way of the media. Headquarters huffed and puffed and threatened jail terms if they ever caught the source of the leak, which put an end to it. But they still could not find the culprit, though they searched up and down all summer. Finally, they had to swallow their embarrassment and call in the Mounties for a criminal investigation.

On August 2, detectives of the RCMP Commercial Crimes Squad swooped down on the Radio-Canada offices. They located Normand Lester's desk and made off with a three-foot-high stack of notes, files and clippings. Their search warrant stated that they were looking for the May 12 letter from the women employees in Montreal. The detectives said they wanted to take fingerprints, which made Lester laugh. What fingerprints would they get from a letter passed around the office for the past six months? And besides, he never had the original letter, only a photocopy which he had made himself, and it was no longer on his desk. He says they were really after the names of his sources and, in the process, aimed to frighten off any more CSIS sources he might have.

Meanwhile, another team of Mounties had raided Beauregard's Canadian Press office in Montreal that same day. They didn't come up with anything either. Beauregard, a hard-working reporter, responded by telling anyone who asked that he knew about 200 of the 400 CSIS employees in Montreal and considered every one of them a source. If nothing else, these reporters knew how to protect their informants. Both raids produced the usual denunciations by news organizations and comparisons with the old RCMP dirty tricks squad by editorial writers, but, also as usual, CSIS ignored everything. It was locked in a headlong search for what management was by now convinced was someone so well and deeply buried that there had to be a conspiracy. There had to be a mole. If it wasn't a Soviet mole, then at least it was a media mole, because that appeared to be the name of this game. The mole seemed determined to embarrass CSIS, whether it compromised national security or not.

Reid Morden was becoming desperate; the mole could strike again at any time. So he resorted to a tactic he should not have. He tried to get a journalist to do CSIS's work.

"You can't go to a journalist and say to the journalist, 'How did you get this document?' It's just not done," says Ted Finn. "As a practical reality, it is not advisable. It'll get you more trouble than it will solve. You can't talk to a reporter because of what the next story will be."

Either Morden had never heard Finn's sound advice, or else he thought it was worth taking the risk if it meant finding the leak. He authorized two CSIS agents to meet with Ottawa CJOH television reporter Charlie Greenwell, who had been trying for months to line up an interview with Frank Pratt.

Soon after Beauregard's story about Smurov appeared, somebody at CSIS telephoned Greenwell and told him Pratt was willing to meet him. A meeting was arranged for a late-night encounter at the Talisman Hotel in Ottawa in mid-August. Pratt arrived with another CSIS investigator.

Greenwell said later that this other agent suggested that Pratt could offer him some inside information in return for the name of the person who was feeding Lester and Beauregard their information. Greenwell refused. He could hardly spy on Lester and Beauregard, two reporters who helped him out on stories occasionally. Greenwell went on the air with CSIS's attempt to recruit him as a spy.

At first CSIS denied any of its officials had met Greenwell. But Greenwell, who makes extensive use of a tape recorder, insisted the meeting had taken place, and that seemed to jog CSIS's collective memory. Then the service denied it had tried to recruit Greenwell to spy on his colleagues. Finally Morden admitted that CSIS had tried to enlist him. Morden said that Greenwell had called with information that had "operational implications." CSIS is always careful with words. Morden insisted that they had not asked Greenwell to spy on his friends. "We wouldn't say 'spying,'" Morden said. "We would say 'collect some more information.'" He refused to apologize. CSIS communications director Gerry Cummings defended the recruitment attempt and explained: "We've had a tough time in the last year and a half." He also made it clear that not all reporters are as reticent as Greenwell, Lester and Beauregard. "Some reporters do realize the threat from East bloc countries and have no compunction about passing along information," said Cummings, although he refused to identify his sources within the media.

CSIS is still searching for the mole, but less enthusiastically. And the leaks seem to have stopped — for now.

# CLEARING HOUSE

SECURITY CLEARANCE IS THE ONE AREA where CSIS and the Great Canadian Public meet face to face. In 1984, CSIS took over from the RCMP responsibility for security screening of all immigrants and refugees, all visa and citizenship applicants, as well as all federal public servants and private industry workers doing classified or secret work on contract for the government. Only the Mounties and the Department of National Defence were allowed to continue screening their own employees.

Currently, CSIS conducts about 300,000 security clearances a year. The majority involve immigration, visa and citizenship cases, but about 70,000 public servants require security screening every year. Some are first-time applicants for public service jobs. Others are public servants seeking promotions or transferring to jobs which require a higher security rating. Others, such as diplomats and people in sensitive military jobs, have to submit to regular security reviews every year, five years or ten years, depending on the level of security clearance required by their jobs. Lately the government has decided that all 8,000 airline pilots in Canada will have to be screened.

Security clearances soak up eleven percent of the service's personnel, but that is a misleading figure because so much of the work, especially in the field interview section, is done on contract for CSIS by retired RCMP officers.

A security clearance starts with the subject answering a long questionnaire on family background — father, mother, brothers, sisters, grandfathers, grandmothers, etc. At this point, CSIS is trying to establish if a person is who he or she says, and not an illegal alien. The service will also want to see employment records and previous addresses going back one, five or ten years, depending on the level of security required. In addition, subjects are often asked about political views and leisure-time activities. This is to establish if there is anything in the person's background that would make it risky to grant access to official secrets. As well, CSIS requires the names of a number of people who can give character references. Here, the service is trying to find out whether the subject has any political associations that might put loyalty to Canada in question, or if there are any "character weaknesses" that might make him or her a target for blackmail. The most important of these include indebtedness and the use of drugs; the agency also cares about sexual proclivities, and will want to know if the subject talks too much to the wrong people.

The first part of a security clearance is not very different — only more detailed — than the type of questioning that applicants for jobs in large corporations undergo. However, since 1987, public servants have not been tested on their lifestyle, only on their loyalty to Canada. Nor, as we have seen, are they asked to submit to a polygraph test. This delightful pastime is reserved for CSIS employees.

For security reasons, CSIS never says what it will or won't check out. The extent of the investigation varies depending on the applicant, the nature of the desired job or visa, and how much time the investigation has. Investigators have been known to visit landlords and ask about the young man who lived nine years ago in apartment 1302.

Some landlords have a remarkable memory for detail and can give CSIS a most intimate graphic decription of their former tenants' private lives. Neighbours are also a source of information, as are former work colleagues. CSIS investigators who go out "in the field" to do security clearance interviews are skilled veterans at getting information out of people. They have been trained to be as low-key, as gentle, sweet and casual as possible. A security clearance is not a drug-bust investigation; it is a mission to collect information. Invesitgators cannot browbeat or threaten the people they talk to. All interviewers have to say, if they don't like the approach the investigator is taking, is "I don't remember" and there is nothing the investigator can do.

Some people make quite innocent but thoroughly horrendous mistakes on their questionnaires, which are never picked up, but some get one digit wrong in the birthday of their maternal grandmother, and the CSIS investigator comes back to check it out. It never pays to lie in these questionnaires, because a lie, once detected, sets off all sorts of alarms at agency headquarters. The investigator's superior gets involved. People begin speculating as to why the subject has lied, whether there have been other lies, and if so, what else may be hidden.

Conducting these interviews can be mind-numbing, often insulting work for the investigator — asking people over and over, day after day, what their friend is like, whether he or she drinks too much, sleeps around too much, is secretly a Communist, acts strangely sometimes, has debts, lies a lot, can be trusted, etc. When CSIS security clearance investigators say, "Believe me, I like this less than you do," they usually mean it.

The RCMP used to employ very young Mounties to do this sort of work. Later they began using older men from the lower ranks of the Force who were about to retire. CSIS mostly hires ex-Mounties who do the field interviews on contract for the service. Experience counts most of all in spotting a phony story, which is basically what security clearance checks are about. Former CSIS Deputy Director Archie Barr, who has more than three decades of experience in counter-espionage, says a very good field investigator will beat a polygraph any day. The investigator will know when a wrong answer is important, and when it is not. The machine won't differentiate.

Security clearance investigators sometimes have to interview the people who are undergoing the security screening. They have to ask some very personal questions — whether they use drugs, have financial debts, partake in weird sexual practices, cheat on their spouses or have anything else in their background that could leave them open to blackmail or cause them to betray their federal oath of secrecy. Some people lie about the most innocuous things in their past and are never found out. Others get caught out on some small fib they have told, for no apparent reason, which in turn forces a major, time-wasting review of their other answers. And some people are brutally honest about their private lives, and will volunteer much more than they are asked.

One young, college-educated aspirant to a job which required a personal interview came prepared for his security clearance with a neatly typed list of every woman he had slept with in the past five years, along with addresses and phone numbers. The security clearance officer managed to keep a straight face but said he wished the young man had been as scrupulous about listing his own addresses. Still, he duly noted the names and addresses of all the women named, and discreetly checked out some of them later on. As well, he checked with some other sources who knew the young man, to find out if he might have been deliberately trying to hide someone by appearing to be so meticulous.

Whenever a security clearance subject does something unusual, perhaps equivocating over apparently straightforward questions, or trying to provide too much information on questions most people *would* be trying to evade, it is usually worth a second check.

When CSIS was set up in July 1984, the structure and resources available for security screening were totally inadequate to meet the need. A huge backlog began building up of public servants waiting to undergo their clearances. Since the government could not always wait around for CSIS security clearance officers to show up, it went ahead and hired people for sensitive security jobs who had not been cleared. Some public servants were in their jobs up to six months, a year, or even two years before they went through a security check. Occasionally a CSIS agent would show up to do a check on someone who had left the department several months earlier. This created hilarity around the office. He would be greeted with remarks like, "Sorry, she's gone back to Russia." The security clearance process became a joke, and few people respected it. This only made things more difficult for investigators who liked to believe that what they were doing was worthwhile.

The backlog became so bad that security clearance investigators could not even get around to clearing the staff members of the Security Intelligence Review Committee. It didn't take long for SIRC to launch a full investigation into the delays. CSIS security clearance investigators were showing up six months or a year late in ministers' offices where aides change every two to three months. If there were a better way for the agency to convince the politicians that CSIS was running around in circles, it had not been invented.

Former Public Works Minister Roch La Salle had two aides with serious criminal records for violence and reputed underworld connections working on his staff for almost a year without a security check ever being done on them until *Maclean's* exposed the matter. La Salle may have been in no hurry to call in CSIS, but the story underlined the fact that security clearance investigators had not yet come around to his office. In September 1985, the federal government promised a major overhaul of security clearances. It took a full year and still didn't speed things up.

One problem is that in the federal public service, one's security clearance level is a status symbol. (So is the size of the rug in one's office, the rug's colour and whether the office is located in a corner. There is an elaborate manual in the federal public service that spells out in precise terms which categories in the public service can have a rug, a white rug, a corner office, a washstand or full in-office bathroom.)

As a result, public service managers always want the highest security clearance ratings for the employees under them. Obviously, the more employees they have who have been cleared to the "Top Secret" level, the more important must be the work that they are doing and, therefore, the more important they must be. And only public servants with a "Secret" security clearance can handle "Secret" documents — of which there are an abundance, since many documents are so stamped when there is no real need to keep them "Secret."

CSIS, therefore, which too often displays an obsession for secrecy that far exceeds the requirements of the situation, goes in the opposite direction when it comes to public service clearances. The agency is always trying to convince the public service to lower the level of its security clearances.

There is an important cost factor at work here. The two lower security levels involve mainly a quick credit check done by a private firm at $13.62 per check, plus a look through the police computer for a criminal record of some sort. The Top Secret clearance requires a full background investigation going back ten years, numerous interviews, telephone checks, and extensive paper documentation. The average cost was estimated in 1985 at $1,425 per security clearance. The Top Secret – Special Activities designation requires an even more rigorous check going back twenty years instead of ten.

In 1985, CSIS had requests for 69,647 security clearances in the public sector alone. More than two-thirds, about 48,000 requests, were for the bottom two levels, Confidential and Secret. The rest were for the Top Secret variety. But CSIS was so badly organized and understaffed that it managed to complete only 2,898 of the 4,438 full field investigations required that year. More than 1,000 cases were delayed simply because papers had not been completed by the typing pool at CSIS headquarters.

In a memo entitled *Personnel Deficiencies* the director-general of security clearances, Ian MacEwan, an old Featherbed man, wrote to Finn and others, "I trust the gravity of this situation is clear." His people had just wracked up 251 hours of overtime in one month and still not made a dent in the blossoming backlog.

On June 18, 1986, the government finally brought out its long-awaited Government Security Policy (GSP), replacing an old 1956 PCO policy and a secret cabinet document, CD 35 of 1963, both of which were worded in such a way that they gave preferences for security clearances to people who were white and heterosexual and with ethnic origins in Northern Europe.

The new policy spelled out that deputy ministers would be responsible for security in their departments, that documents could only be stamped "secret" for very well-defined reasons. It was no longer enough to stamp something "secret" so the fellow at the next desk couldn't see it. Departments had to draw up a list of exactly who should get what level of clearance, and to reduce the total number of Top Secret documents as much as possible.

Unfortunately, the new policy had just the opposite effect. Public servants became more security conscious and put more people than ever on the Top Secret list. Requests for clearances shot up at CSIS, which had been hoping to see the backlog reduced. Instead it simply increased. Now people were waiting up to a year.

By November 1986, the number of requests for clearance had shot up to 74,500, an increase of seven percent over the year before, despite a last-minute campaign earlier to force deputy ministers to trim back their security clearance levels. In addition, an extra 600 Top Secret clearances were required for the 1986 Commonwealth meeting in Vancouver.

By 1987, the backlog was so serious MacEwan was writing to External Affairs that he didn't have the staff to run summer students through security checks. He told the Treasury Board to forget any hope of having part-time secretaries checked out.

By 1988 it was taking a full year to complete a Top Secret clearance, and seven months to complete lower level clearances. CSIS was swamped. In the 1987-88 fiscal year it conducted 90,000 clearances on immigrants, another 90,000 on citizenship applicants and 46,000 public service checks, but the government insisted on CSIS doing another 14,000 checks on airport workers because it was afraid of a repetition of the Air India tragedy. In addition there were another 7,000 checks on private industry workers. And the numbers kept on rising. In 1989, the government announced that 38,000 other transportation and airport workers, including 8,000 pilots — for what reason? — will have to undergo security clearance. As well, status-conscious public servants want their clearances increased to as as high a level as possible.

"Everybody wants to be Top Secret," says one exasperated CSIS security clearance investigator. "But nobody wants to answer the questions."

Security clearances have little to do with classification or salary. For instance, at the bottom end of the scale, a file clerk may require a very high Top Secret security clearance if that clerk happens to be filing cabinet documents, or security information, or next year's budget plans. One of the first things they did at the Government Printing Bureau in Hull after Finance Minister Michael Wilson's famous budget leak was to upgrade to Top Secret the security clearance requirement for everyone who so much as went near the area where they print the budget. Previously, they had forgotten about the fellow who swept up in the garbage room. He did not have any security requirement at all. He was the one who left with the copy of the budget summary that eventually ended up in Global Television reporter Doug Small's hands.

Sometimes the level of security clearance required has nothing to do with the nature of the work, but simply the proximity to someone important. The gardeners who plant tulip bulbs for the National Capital Commission don't require a very high security rating. But the two gardeners who work for Prime Minister Brian Mulroney at 24 Sussex Drive require the highest security clearance because of their proximity to the national leader and his family as well as to visiting foreign dignitaries.

Two years ago there was a minor public controversy when news leaked out that it cost Canadian taxpayers more than $10,000 to conduct a full Top Secret security clearance on each gardener. CSIS stood by its decision, which was a good one. The last thing Canadians would want to hear about was that some gardener came charging out of the bushes during a photo opportunity at 24 Sussex Drive and attacked a visiting Soviet leader with a scythe.

Guards at Rideau Hall, the governor general's residence, also have to undergo security clearance checks, less to protect the governor general than to ensure the safety of visiting foreign dignitaries.

Security clearances are required because there are secrets to keep and people to protect. Some of the information to be protected can be of a financial nature. The weekly Bank of Canada interest rate is issued on Thursdays. A leak to a broker-age house even a few minutes ahead of time could result in damages to Canada in the billions of dollars. Other clearances are there to protect us — the guard with unusual political beliefs who lets a terrorist past the metal detector has just signed the death warrant of an entire planeload of people.

Still, what is perhaps more troubling than the backlog of clearances, or how to decide who needs to be screened, is the question of what is done with the results. Take the case of André Henrie, a young public servant whose only crime was that in Ottawa, Canada in 1984 he happened to believe in the political doctrines of Marx and Lenin, and he occasionally hung around with other Canadians who felt as he did, some of whom voted for the Communist Party of Canada candidate at election time.

When CSIS got through with him, Henrie's life was a shambles and he could kiss off any hope he might have had of further advancement in the federal public service. What happened to him when he appealed to SIRC is such a bizarre and perverse tale that it could easily come straight out of a Kafka novel. The story shows the immense power that CSIS can exercise as the thought Police of the federal public service, and how little SIRC can do to provide luckless public servants with a fair hearing.

Henrie, who came from a well-established, French-speaking public-service family, had worked seven years for the federal government in Ottawa. Since 1977 he had held a Secret security classification which he had obtained when he began working for the federal Employment and Immigration department. Life might have continued happily enough for the mild-mannered young man, who did his work well and cheerfully, had it not been for a secondment to the Department of Energy, Mines and Resources in 1984. His new job required only a lower Confidential security clearance. Nowadays, he would automatically be given the lower level without any review. But in 1984, CSIS seemed to be looking for work to do, and so two agents were sent out to interview Henrie.

He admitted freely and openly that he hung around with "Commies." "So what?" he said. That wasn't a crime. The CSIS Act of 1984 made it clear that "lawful advocacy, protest or dissent" were not threats to the security of Canada. But CSIS, as we have seen, does not interpret "lawful advocacy, protest or dissent" to mean "You can be a Commie and it's OK." Henrie, however, did not know that, nor did he know that the two CSIS agents would be surreptitiously recording their interview with him. The recording would be used as evidence when CSIS defended its decision to deny Henrie a security clearance at a subsequent SIRC hearing.

The two agents would be allowed to erase portions of that taped interview and it was admitted in its expurgated version as "evidence" at Henrie's hearing. The agents would claim they had erased part of the tape because it contained things Henrie had told them which might have jeopardized national security. Henrie's attorney, Craig Paterson, a noted Vancouver human-rights lawyer, says that the erased portions would have shown that the two CSIS agents were trying to annoy Henrie by making crude remarks about homosexuals. The lawyer would later say that this portion of the tape would have made the agents sound like "Neanderthals" in court, and so would have hurt their case.

During his interview, which was more like an interrogation, Henrie admitted that he had been a member of several left-wing study groups in the Ottawa-Hull area. He had also been an active member of the Quebec section of the Workers Communist Party and occasionally attended their meetings, which were not secret. The group openly recruited members. Later, after the WCP group broke up, Henrie became a member of the Groupe marxiste-leniniste liberation (GMLL).

The two CSIS agents asked Henrie whether he was a homosexual. He told them his sex life was none of their business.

Then they began asking Henrie questions about the other people in his Marxist group. They wanted him to name names. He refused. At that point, it was all over, SIRC hearing or not. Henrie might as well have quit the public service and gone to sell shoes on the Sparks Street Mall.

CSIS labelled him a "security risk" and sent a report to his employer which stripped him of the Secret security clearance he already had. Without a security clearance Henrie could still work for the federal government, but the job he wanted, and the job he had, were no longer available to him. The irony of course, is that both jobs were later re-classified as not requiring any special security clearance at all.

Henrie appealed to the SIRC panel, as provided for by the CSIS Act. He thought he would get a reversal of the CSIS decision. In a departure from normal procedure, two SIRC commissioners sat on the panel. (Usually only one member of SIRC does.) One panel member was Jean-Jacques Blais and the other was Paule Gauthier.

The Henrie case brought to light details of SIRC's legal procedures. Typically, the complainant gets only a short summary of what evidence CSIS has against him or her, a summary that usually says so little that the complainant seldom knows what the charges are about. The procedure does not leave much for the complainant's lawyer to go on. SIRC may also decide to exclude one or more of the parties from the hearing while evidence is given or representations are made by another party. And what this generally means is that the complainant gets the boot while CSIS makes its case to SIRC. Not even the complainant's lawyer is allowed to remain in the room, even if the lawyer holds the highest Top Secret CSIS security clearance, happens to be a former cabinet minister and is willing to swear an oath never to reveal to his or her client the nature of the evidence CSIS has against the complainant.

SIRC sets its own rules and at its hearing, the principle of natural justice, that one has the right to face one's accuser, goes out the window. The hearings, which are always held behind closed doors, turn into a strange drama. They feature long pleas, repeated over and over, by complainants demanding in vain from the SIRC panel to be told exactly what it is that CSIS has against them, or that they be given the chance to confront their accusers, while CSIS lawyers repeat over and over that the service refuses to give out any information about the evidence it has.

This amounts to CSIS saying: "Trust us, we know you're a security risk."

"But please tell me how I'm a security risk, so I can know too."

"No, that would create a security risk. Trust us, you're a security risk."

If the complainant does manage to score a point, or pick a hole in the CSIS charges, the CSIS lawyer can ask for the hearing to be adjourned, so that new evidence can be presented *in camera*, contradicting what the complainant has just said. But the complainant has to leave the room while this evidence is presented, and so is unable to refute it. Occasionally, the complainant is given access to a highly censored précis, but that's it. No other court of law in the Western world would operate by SIRC's rules, which were drawn up six years ago when CSIS was created and have never been amended or challenged. CSIS has no objection to the rules and has expressed no interest in having them changed.

In March 1990, Craig Paterson told a Commons Committee reviewing CSIS and SIRC hearing procedures that the SIRC hearing at which he had represented Henrie lacked fairness.

"I acted as counsel for Mr. Henrie and went through a complaint procedure under the statute," Paterson testified. "When evidence is put forward before SIRC that is judged to be confidential, and I can tell you that I objected, my objections meant no more than a passing breeze. There was no argument allowed on whether or not the objection was properly taken. The chairman of the committee simply pounded his gavel and said: 'CSIS has spoken; therefore it must confidential.' "

Paterson explained that he and Henrie had been excluded from the room when evidence was presented against Henrie. When it was over, they were allowed to return and handed a summary so brief that it was impossible to make any submission or argument based upon the material it contained.

In an interview afterwards Paterson said that he had never seen as unfair a legal process as he witnessed in the Henrie hearing. "Whatever CSIS said, Blais just went along with it," says Paterson. "No discussion, no debate. Every principle of natural justice was violated. It was extraordinary."

There were some comic-relief moments, however. According to Paterson, his client, who had known SIRC member Jean-Jacques Blais, a fellow Franco-Ontarian, for a number of years, lectured Blais on Stalin's famous writings on the rights of national minorities. Blais, in his turn, couldn't believe somebody could be a Communist and still believe in Franco-Ontarian rights.

Reg Whitaker, a professor of political science at York University who attended one of the four days of hearings in the Henrie case, describes what he saw.

"Relations between Paterson and Blais were strained, to say the least. At a session which I attended, Blais belligerently and continually interrupted Paterson. The atmosphere was anything but that of an impartial quasi-judicial body, which the SIRC is supposed to be when it hears appeals.

"It also became apparent the CSIS had no intention of making the real nature of its case against Henrie available to him.

"Henrie was denied access to at least fifteen or sixteen documents furnished to SIRC by CSIS as part of the case against

Henrie. And in most of these cases, he was not even allowed to know what kind of documents they were, or who wrote them, or when."

Henrie was able to call witnesses, but CSIS witnesses cited "national security" as their reason to refuse to answer questions put to them by Paterson. "Their objections were automatically upheld by Blais, with no rationale offered," writes Whitaker. "All of this makes an utter mockery of the notion that SIRC furnishes the sort of forum in which injured parties can have an opportunity to receive natural justice — a chance to understand the case being made against them, a chance to cross-examine hostile sources of information, and a reasonable opportunity to resolve the doubts."

Whitaker says that all Paterson's attempts to prove that the groups Henrie had been involved with were not staging clandestine activities designed to subvert or overthrow the Canadian state failed.

CSIS said the Groupe marxiste-leniniste liberation spoke of armed struggle. Henrie attempted to show this was just empty Marxist rhetoric, which nobody in the group listened to, and he repeatedly said that he himself didn't believe in violence. However, Clifford Pearcy, the senior CSIS analyst who testified at the hearing, said CSIS believed that although the group had not indulged in violence, there was "revolutionary violence in the minds of the members" of the group. Whitaker questions the ability of CSIS to know with certainty what is in the minds of anyone at any given time.

The SIRC panel handed down its decision in April 1986. Henrie was associated with "Communist" groups with "basic tenets unacceptable to and incompatible with our Canadian democratic system." Unable to prove that Henrie meant to commit any violence, SIRC had fallen back on that old bugbear "communist subversion" and used this to take away his security clearance.

He took his case to the Federal Court but he did not have

money to fight the government for very long. There was a small grant available under the legal challenges law, but that was soon exhausted. (The case is still before the courts, but nothing has happened for months.) Finally, Henrie had no choice but to accept the government's offer to go back to his old job as a program manager in the immigration department, which no longer required a security clearance. He figures the CSIS action cost him a loss of a promotion from a PM-2 to a PM-4, or about $4,000 a year in pay for the past five years.

Of course, Henrie could have saved himself a lot of time and expense and held on to his security clearance if he had co-operated with CSIS and named names. More than likely, he would have been told he could keep his security clearance as long as he continued to co-operate.

There is no obligation under the CSIS Act for the service to reveal annually how many of the 70,000 public servants who undergo security clearance assessments are asked to "co-operate" in this manner, and how many of them, out of fear of losing their security clearance or of losing their good government jobs, choose to become CSIS informers. There *is* a directive from the Treasury Board spelling out under what conditions CSIS can recruit public servants to spy on fellow workers, but the directive has never been made public. And most likely, if CSIS gets its way, it never will be.

Two years ago the Council of Regents of the Province of Ontario made Henrie, who is highly respected in the Franco-Ontarian community, one of the directors of the new French-language junior college being built in Ottawa. Apparently his communism didn't frighten either the Francophones in the Ottawa area or the Liberal government of David Peterson in Toronto. Henrie is still a communist, but in the meantime he has served with distinction on the college's board, helping it get started.

Recently, one of the names of prominent Franco-Ontarians being considered on the short list as president of the new college was none other than Jean-Jacques Blais. But however good he might have been in spotting security risks, Blais didn't have the educational qualifications they were looking for at the college. His name was turned down even before the interview stage.

"Too bad," says Henrie with a whimsical chuckle. "It would have been interesting grilling Blais on his loyalty to the Franco-Ontarian cause."

One interesting development over the past few years is the difference in motives for spying. The famous moles in Western intelligence — Kim Philby, Guy Burgess and even Canada's own Hugh Hambleton — spied because of their political convictions rather than because they were paid to do so. But today spies are moved much more by the almighty dollar.

U.S. military submarine secrets have recently been sold to the Soviets and Israelis for as much as $1 million by people whose political philosophy is as far from communism as could be imagined. The same thing is happening in the Soviet intelligence community. Some Soviet KGB defectors have been paid similar money for defecting to the United States. It depends on the value of the material they come over with. Some daring defectors have been known to try to negotiate the price of their defection beforehand, offering tantalizing samples of what they would bring over, provided that, first, some payment of goodwill is deposited in a Swiss bank account. In the nineties, it's money, not ideology, that counts.

CSIS still spends far too much time trying to establish whether someone is a member of the Communist Party and not nearly enough time studying his or her finances. Membership in the Communist Party of Canada soon may not mean much in any case, because under the Charter of Rights and Freedoms a person cannot be discriminated against on the grounds of membership in a registered and legitimate Canadian political party, whether it is the Conservative Party, the Liberal Party or the Communist Party. It's only a matter of time until somebody wins a case in court that makes it official.

One intelligence officer who spent two-and-a-half years working in CSIS security clearances says the agency needs a more modern approach to evaluating financial security. There are all sorts of models available in private enterprise. A number of factors could be included: the size of the salary, the size of the mortgage, credit card charges, major recent expenses, the cost of the car, a cottage, foreign trips. "Get a fix on everything and plug it into a computer," he says. "If it doesn't add up, then the light should flash on. If a guy has a $300,000 house and is making a $16,000 salary, we should want to know why. Maybe he won a lottery or inherited money. Okay. But maybe there's an outside source of income. Let's find out about it." An individual with major financial problems is much more likely today to resort to espionage to stay solvent than is somebody who sympathizes with the Soviet Union.

If anybody at CSIS should know about the lure of money, it's the old RCMP security service officers. The only Mountie ever known to betray his country to the Soviet Union did it for money. He was James Morrison, known as Long Knife, who, in 1955, sold out a Canadian double agent to the Soviets for $3,500 — about a year's wages for a Mountie at the time. Morrison had run up huge debts because of extravagant spending and gambling at the racetrack and was in trouble for having misappropriated secret RCMP payments to the local telephone company. To cover his debts, he sold the name of a double agent to the Soviets. The agent was called back to Moscow and disappeared. Morrison was anything but a Communist, but he needed the money very badly, which is why he became a traitor to Canada.

With East bloc ideology growing more like the West's every day, money is likely to become an even more common reason for espionage — and financial insecurity should become a primary target of the security clearance procedure.

As if domestic security clearances weren't enough of a headache, CSIS must also handle clearances for prospective immigrants. And since 1984, things seem to have gone from bad to worse. In the mid-eighties, people were being told they might have to wait a year or even two years in some cases before being processed for security clearances and allowed to enter Canada. Immigration officials blamed the bureaucratic delays in part on CSIS officials. They said the service was too slow doing security checks on refugees, prospective immigrants and visitors applying for visas. And no wonder — CSIS had to process and screen anywhere from 75,000 to 100,000 of them every year.

Some Canadians had ageing mothers and fathers holed up in God-forsaken refugee camps who couldn't get out because CSIS couldn't get the paperwork done on people who were too old to walk across the street by themselves, let alone plan and execute terrorist attacks or run off with Canada's state secrets. For the most part, all they wanted to do was see their grandchildren before they died, but they had to wait in line like everybody else until the harried CSIS liaison officer at the embassy could find time to get around to their security clearances.

Processing a prospective immigrant begins when the applicant fills out a personal history form, which the CSIS officer uses to decide how intense the screening will be. Then an application is made by CSIS to the local police authorities for an "indices" check that may reveal criminal activities. In addition, the applicant may be called in for an interview to provide more information or to answer remarks in the indices check. In some cases, two or three interviews are required before the officer has enough material to make a decision.

The CSIS officer will either recommend acceptance, which is what happens in the vast majority of cases, or issue a rejection brief. There is also a third category, an "information brief," in cases where the applicant is not a security threat but there are suspicions nonetheless. As a rule, immigration officials generally reject all applicants on whom an information or rejection brief has been filed. There are very few rejections for security reasons. Between 1980 and 1986 there were only twelve rejections in the most popular "family-class" category of immigrant.

By 1986 some CSIS offices abroad had begun "profiling" family-class applicants. That meant applicants who fit a certain profile — such as the eighty-year-old grandmother sponsored by her children — could be cleared without having to undergo a security check. Only those who might appear to present a problem would have to undergo the full verification process. Still, the backlog continued to grow. Within two years, the Hong Kong office alone would be swamped by 25,000 applications a year as the colonists began a massive exodus to Canada before the date of the Chinese takeover. The immigration process was in a mess, and it looked like it was going to get worse before it got better, so anything anyone could come up with to alleviate the problem would be more than welcome.

Groups of MPs headed out to visit Canadian immigration offices in Asia, Central America, South America and Europe. Toronto York-West MP Sergio Marchi, the Liberals' outspoken immigration critic, was part of one group that went to Manila, New Delhi and Hong Kong.

What Marchi found in those cities shocked and appalled him. Immigration offices were understaffed and officials were swamped with tens of thousands of people trying to get into Canada any way they could. It was especially bad in Hong Kong, recalls Marchi. "The CSIS agent there was downright hostile to the MPs. If he didn't want to tell me about money-laundering or drugs, okay, that's fine by me. But hey, immigration, I had a right to know what was going on."

The CSIS agent was supposed to be the person in charge of security screening, recalls Marchi, "but the immigration guys knew more about security screening than did the CSIS guy. I don't know what he did with his time. Maybe it was his intelligence liaison work. It certainly wasn't security clearances." And the officer was extremely reluctant to tell the MPs what he was doing and what he was finding out, even though they were there on a fact-finding mission.

Marchi says the MPs learned from Canadian immigration officials that the police in Hong Kong are so corrupt that the authorities have set up a permanent anti-corruption police commission to root out crooked practices in the regular police force. The CSIS liaison officer, however, relied mostly on the corrupt Hong Kong police for his security assessments. Immigration officers went behind his back to check out his findings with the more honest anti-corruption commission. They assigned one of their own staff members to act as their liaison with the anti-corruption commission. "They were balancing what they got from CSIS against what they were getting from the anti-corruption commission," says Marchi. "They were getting one guy on the immigration side to do it part-time, because they didn't trust the information they were getting from CSIS."

The Liberal immigration critic says he came away from Asia with the distinct feeling that CSIS was part of the problem, not part of the solution to Canada's immigration backlog. Hong Kong was the worst CSIS office in his view, Marchi says. The others were not as bad, but none that he visited was very good. None of the MPs on the committee was overly impressed with CSIS's security clearance work either.

The MPs were determined that when they got back to Canada they would write a scorching report about the pitiful CSIS performance they had discovered, so the agency would at least pull up its socks or get out of the immigration business altogether. However, when they got back to Canada, they were told that it would not be in the interest of national security to criticize CSIS publicly, nor to point out the weaknesses in the system because hostile foreign groups might be able to take advantage of them. This is an old CSIS trick; it's called "Don't criticize CSIS or you might damage national security." The MPs were told not to worry, that CSIS had heard their criticisms and would take corrective measures. "Trust us," the agency said once again, and once again it worked. The MPs toned down their criticism of CSIS to a couple of sentences in their report made public in June 1986.

" . . . The Committee has a major concern that in some countries, the information used by CSIS to evaluate immigrants on security grounds may not be trustworthy. Canadian officers rely on the good graces of the police and security agencies in the host countries, whose priorities, methods and loyalties may be quite different from Canada's.

"The Committee does not have the expertise to advise CSIS in detail on how best to assess potential immigrants but we do recommend that the service re-evaluate its methods."

Marchi regrets now that the MPs allowed themselves to be convinced to tone down their remarks about CSIS. If they had made lots of noise, the government might have done something. By playing down their concern, they ensured that the government focused its attention, time and money on other immigration problems that the MPs criticized more vehemently. So the problem at CSIS was never solved, and CSIS offices abroad continue to this day to be understaffed and ill-equipped.

Reid Morden says the answer to cutting down the backlog is to use more profiling, and CSIS has a pilot project going that will do precisely that. "We should have things referred to us by exception," says Morden. "We shouldn't be taking the burden off other people's backs in terms of decision making in a routine fashion. The burden of making most decisions on immigration cases should be with the immigration department." He's right, and for once appears to agree with critics of CSIS.

Marchi's harsh criticism of CSIS's immigration security clearance work is all the more interesting because, until recently, his wife Laureen worked there. She joined the service in 1984 when it was set up, after having worked for Ted Finn in PCO in 1980. "It was a job," she says. "I never had the heart beating for the nation and all that. I was never in operations. I was just doing a really boring administrative job, something like clerical work."

She left CSIS recently, she says, where she had been earning between "$25,000 and $35,000" a year for her clerical work, although she refuses to define what exactly it was she did at the agency. In fact, there are very few employees doing "clerical work" who earn anywhere close to $35,000 a year. Intelligence officers, considered to have the most prestigious jobs in the service, start at $28,500 a year.

Laureen Marchi says she never hid from CSIS that she was married to an MP, and she says that she was never asked to "do anything on the Hill." A source at CSIS has confirmed that she was never assigned to spy for CSIS on Parliament Hill, "but she was something more than a clerk, I can assure you." Whatever she did at the agency, Laureen managed to keep her professional life separate from her personal life. She never discussed CSIS business with her husband, nor did he tell her any Liberal caucus secrets. In Ottawa, she says, there are many happy couples whose professions might appear to conflict, but who learn never to talk shop at home.

Perhaps the strangest screenings CSIS does are those for our neighbours to the south. This sometimes makes for unlikely scenes, as when a CSIS agent recently approached CTV news show host Mike Duffy and said he wanted to ask him a few questions about his friend Tim Dunn, a U.S. diplomat stationed at the American embassy in Ottawa. Duffy was momentarily caught off-guard. The CSIS agent, an elderly ex-Mountie, assured him that Dunn was not under any suspicion. His five-year diplomatic security clearance had simply come up for review and CSIS was conducting a security check on Dunn on behalf of the U.S. State Department. He simply wanted to ask Duffy some questions about Dunn's personal habits and lifestyle.

Duffy immediately telephoned Dunn to ask him what he should do. Duffy says his friend replied, "Tell them everything you know, Mike. I gave your name as a reference."

Duffy of course gave Dunn a glowing recommendation. He told the CSIS agent that he couldn't think of a single bad thing to tell CSIS about his friend Dunn, which is probably why Dunn picked Duffy as a reference in the first place. And credibility? Well, if you can't trust Mike Duffy, who can you trust in this world?

At CSIS they see nothing wrong with Canadians clearing Americans in Ottawa for security and Americans clearing Canadians in Washington. We're all on the same side, they say, and if one of our diplomats is getting a little too friendly with the Americans, we can trust the FBI to tell us, just as the FBI can trust CSIS to tell them they've got a loose-lipped diplomat up here. The idea of Americans being allowed to intrude on the privacy of a Canadian in Washington on behalf of External Affairs doesn't trouble the folks at CSIS any more than it bothers them to have to make a decision on the reliability of an American diplomat in Ottawa.

CSIS Director Reid Morden told the Commons special committee reviewing the CSIS Act on June 5, 1990 that the service has "reciprocal screening arrangements" with "foreign governments or their institutions." None of the MPs on the committee seemed surprised by this remark, nor did any of them question the ethics or reliability of such an arrangement.

Viewed from a traditional Cold War perspective, all that counts in screening American diplomats in Ottawa is really whether they may have done anything that would make them vulnerable to KGB blackmail. However, viewed from the perspective of the new global economy in which the Cold War is diminishing in importance and global economic strategies are becoming paramount, there are a few questions that might be asked about the wisdom of entrusting security clearances to the intelligence services of any country but one's own.

An FBI agent might not, for instance, be the best person in the world to detect whether a Canadian diplomat is contemplating a career representing a major American multinational firm whose interests conflict with those of Canada. And would an FBI agent be attuned to, or even forthright about turning in a Canadian diplomat in Washington who showed signs of favouring the American-based contra movement in Nicaragua in violation of Canadian foreign policy?

Conversely, would a CSIS agent be the best person in the world to report back to the U.S. State Department that a particular American diplomat is privately quite upset about acid rain and believes the time has come to pass quickly from study to action? Would CSIS turn in an American diplomat who believes that siding with the Nicaraguan Contras is wrong and has been secretly helping Alberta farmers sending aid to Nicaragua? Or would CSIS turn in an American diplomat who believes Canadian undersized-lobsters are being kept out of the U.S. unfairly and has told a Canadian journalist where evidence of that might be found in Washington?

Canada prides itself on its good relationship with the U.S., its closest ally and biggest trading partner, and keeps very few military secrets from the Americans. But there are some very important trade secrets in this country, some that involve hundreds of millions of dollars — even billions of dollars in the case of the recent Canada-U.S. free trade pact — ranging all the way from softwood lumber and limousines to lobsters and carnations. For Canada it is most important that these secrets be kept from the Americans, and it will be even more important in the nineties as economic and industrial secrets surpass military and political secrets in importance.

In Mike Duffy's case, his friend Dunn was being screened at about the same time as acid rain and free trade were hot issues between the two countries. And yet the CSIS agent did not ask him if he knew Dunn's position on free trade or acid rain or any other major political issue of a contentious nature between the two countries. All he cared about, says Duffy, was what kind of life Dunn was living, whether he drank a lot or had any big debts or personal problems.

Ironically, although CSIS screens Americans for the State Department without any trouble, none of the ten provincial governments in Canada has asked CSIS to screen its public servants. There is a special section of the CSIS Act that allows CSIS to provide this service. But the provinces would rather screen their public servants themselves — or not at all — than allow CSIS to do it. This says something about how the provinces feel about the agency.

The problem of CSIS's relationship to the U.S. has been addressed several times by SIRC. As we have seen, SIRC has issued warnings to CSIS on a couple of occasions about getting too chummy with the U.S. and trying to impose American foreign policy on Canadians. The problem extends far beyond security clearances.

SIRC reported an incident in its 1986-87 annual report which provides an indication of the extent of American influence on the activities of CSIS. A CSIS counter-subversion investigator was trying to persuade his superiors to declare an unnamed Canadian-Latin American support group an official "target" of CSIS, thus clearing the way for all sorts of heavy-duty "intrusive measures" which could be used against it. CSIS could resort to wiretapping, round-the-clock surveillance, sending in spies, bribing informers, opening mail, digging up confidential personal, health, medical and financial reports on the membership, and questioning their familes, friends and employers. What had the Latin-American support group done to merit such attention from CSIS? What violence, terrorism, murder and mayhem was it planning? What seditious threat to Canada's national security did it pose? SIRC examined the documents prepared by the investigator and found itself "perplexed."

The reason the investigator wanted the group targeted was because it had made an "attack on the anti-communist, pro-U.S. government of El Salvador . . . in direct support . . . of policy objectives to . . . blunt American foreign policy initiatives."

SIRC does not say whether the investigator's superiors "targeted" the group or told the investigator to drop his efforts. But it concluded that the incident "lends weight to our concern that CSIS may too readily accept the foreign policy objectives of our allies as its own and neglect Canadian foreign policy."

Poking around a little further, SIRC discovered that CSIS has a double standard. For instance, while the service gets really upset about attacks on "American foreign policy" in El Salvador, "there seems to have been minimal CSIS interest in fund-raising inside Canada for the Contra rebels in Nicaragua." And this despite the fact that the CSIS Act specifically says that CSIS must keep an eye out for groups raising money to instigate "serious violence" in foreign countries.

Nobody ever heard of CSIS targeting Oliver North's Contra war fund-raisers in Canada, but several left-wing and Latin American support groups have complained about CSIS intrusion in their activities. At one point, CSIS had only four people watching ultra right-wing political groups in Canada, and more than 400 watching left-wing groups. The argument at CSIS is that there are more people worth watching on the left side of the spectrum than on the right. "For all the threat they are, we could have three guys on all the right-wingers in Canada and still have covered them well enough," said one CSIS official.

There have been other instances when CSIS's pro-American mindset has shown through in its approach to issues. Two years ago some CSIS investigators were asking questions about what they called a "Red Indian" movement.

Now, "Red Indian" is an American term. In Canada the terms used most often are "Native" or "First Nations" or "Aboriginal" or even simply "Indian." For trained Canadian ears, the use of the term "Red Indian" is as much of a giveaway as saying "ice hockey" instead of "hockey."

The CSIS agent who went looking for "Red Indians" on the warpath only drew ridicule upon himself. Everyone he interviewed in the Native community knew where CSIS was getting its information. This only served to strengthen a popular belief in Canada's Native community that CSIS is too closely linked to the FBI's campaigns against the Indian Movement in the U.S. Which brings us to the question of how well CSIS is carrying out its most important functions — surveillance and intelligence.

# WHAT CONSTITUTES A THREAT?

WHEN MOST PEOPLE THINK OF ESPIONAGE and counter-intelligence, they conjure up images of large, quiet men meeting in deserted parking lots late at night. Spies in trenchcoats pass the secret microfilm to each other while spycatchers in trenchcoats watch from a distance, waiting to pounce. In the course of these transactions, the watchers are Canadian, the watched are foreign. This, however, does not necessarily reflect the reality of CSIS. Occasionally, the objects of agency surveillance are Canadian.

The voice on the telephone in early December 1988 sounded sincere enough to Bob Bartel, a Mennonite community worker with the Innu of Goose Bay. The man who called identified himself as being with the solicitor general's office. He said he wanted to talk with Bartel. Could they meet at the Labrador Inn in Goose Bay on December 12? Bartel agreed.

Originally from Saskatchewan, Bartel had gone to the village of Sheshashit three years earlier to work among the Innu population. He had become close to them and actively involved in their protest against low-level NATO military flights over their homes in the area. British, Dutch and West German fighter planes which used the nearby Canadian Forces Base at Goose Bay for training missions had been flying as low as thirty metres off the ground, frightening children and small animals.

Bartel said that when he arrived at the Labrador Inn and went up to Room 115, the man waiting for him there identified himself as Roy Kearley from CSIS in St. John's, Newfoundland. Kearley was in fact the senior CSIS official in the province. There was a second man with him, whose name Bartel couldn't remember. That man was Constable David Dork of the RCMP "B" Division, NCIS, in Newfoundland, and a member of the Mounties' National Criminal Investigation Section. He had accompanied Kearley to the interview to observe him at work. For the next two hours, while the RCMP constable listened from the adjoining room with the door ajar, Kearley interrogated the Mennonite lay missionary about the Innu of Sheshashit.

CSIS Director Reid Morden would later explain to a Commons committee that this was part of an "awareness" process run jointly with the RCMP to show the Mounties how CSIS operates. Bartel had no idea that he was being used in any "awareness" process to improve relations beween the Mounties and CSIS. All he knew was that Kearley was pressing him for information about the Innu he worked with.

"The moment he said he was from CSIS, I was about to go out the door," recalls Bartel, "because I don't trust CSIS." But he decided to stay at least long enough to find out what the agent wanted.

Kearley began asking him questions about the Innu and their protest. Eight times they had blocked the runways at the big military airstrip where the foreign jet fighters took off and landed. The protest was attracting world attention because at the time the Conservative government was trying to convince other NATO members that they should build a big air base at Goose Bay so they could practise their low-level flights there all the time. Natives were all over the runway and forever going in and out of court with their protest. All this was certainly not helping sell NATO on the idea of a Goose Bay training site.

Kearley wanted to know about the protest. Who was involved? Who were the organizers? Bartel refused to answer. He was not going to betray his friends, he said.

The official asked him if he knew of any foreign manipulation of the Innu by Eastern bloc or Middle East countries. He replied in the negative, but thought the question about the Arabs a little strange. They don't see too many Arabs in Innu villages in Labrador. He was about to make that point, when he thought of a better answer. Yes, there was foreign influence at work in the village, Bartel said — the agent's face lit up — the British, the Dutch and the West Germans were all over the local town council. But the agent wasn't interested. This wasn't the kind of foreign influence he was after.

Kearley kept asking Bartel to name the Innu leaders organizing the protest at the airforce base, and Bartel kept refusing. If Kearley wanted to know the names of the area leaders, such as Peter Penashue, a member of the Innu Band Council, he would have to find out for himself by reading the local papers like anybody else.

By now Kearley's approach was becoming tiresome, so Bartel did what any good young Mennonite missionary would be expected to do when things drag a little. He pulled out his trusty bible and began reading Holy Scripture to Kearley. "I thought the passage about 'good justice' would be particularly appropriate in his case," he said.

Kearley didn't seem too keen on Scripture, so Bartel began explaining Mennonite beliefs to him. Kearley wasn't interested. He kept bringing the topic back to who was leading the Innu protest against the military flights. "He said he was going to give me four names. I said I didn't want to hear them," Bartel remembers.

Kearley got nowhere with Bartel, who left the hotel room after two hours without having revealed anything. He drove back home to Sheshashit and told the Innu leaders what had happened. He warned them to expect somebody "from Solicitor General" to contact them very soon. Actually there appears to have been no attempt by Kearley to contact any of the Innu leaders in the weeks that followed, Bartel says. His interrogation in the hotel room in Goose Bay appears to have been an isolated incident on Kearley's agenda.

That meeting, however, set off a series of events that have had a major political impact in Ottawa ever since. NDP MP Svend Robinson, CSIS's nemesis, heard about Kearley's visit a couple of months later, conducted his own investigation, had a chat with Kearley and came to the conclusion that what Kearley did that day in Goose Bay amounted to an unwarranted counter-subversion intrusion into a peaceful Innu protest. Robinson didn't buy for one minute the suggestion that Kearley was in Goose Bay searching for "foreign influences" among the Innu. He believed Kearley was trying to find out the names of the Innu protest leaders because they had embarrassed the government. The question Kearley asked about foreign influence had just been tucked in, Robinson believed, so that Kearley could justify his interview with Bartel as a counter-espionage operation, because he could not justify it as a counter-subversion investigation.

The visit to Goose Bay coincided with a decision two days later, on December 14, 1988, by CSIS headquarters in Ottawa to launch a massive, nation-wide low-level investigation into what it called "Native extremism" in Canada. Once again, Natives were being targeted by CSIS to receive its "special treatment" as they so often had been in the past by the Counter-Subversion Branch. In Labrador, the pretext for the visit was "foreign influence"; in the rest of the country the pretext was "terrorism." Section 2(c) of the CSIS Act gives the service the right to investigate whenever it suspects "a threat" of "serious violence" may occur "for the purpose of achieving a political objective". The act does not define "serious."

George Erasmus, the national chief of the Assembly of First Nations, had made a speech in May 1988 warning that if people didn't start paying more attention to Native concerns, there might be serious violence further down the line. The next generation of Native Canadians might not be as meek and might resort to "armed terrorism," Erasmus said. In fact, his editorial predicted quite accurately the direction that Native protest would take at Oka in the summer of 1990.

Erasmus later told a Commons committee in February 1990 that he never intended his remarks to be used as an excuse for CSIS to launch an investigation of his people. But by September he realized his comments might have been misinterpreted by the service. Often in the past the RCMP security service had used the slightest pretext to mount huge investigations into suspected Native subversion and threats of violence. They had opened the mail of Native leaders, sent spies in, wiretapped their telephone lines and paid Natives to inform on their leadership. Erasmus didn't want this happening again, so he called up CSIS. That was a terrible mistake.

"I personally contacted CSIS and I asked for a meeting. I met with an individual named Greg Savicky," said Erasmus. He didn't know it at the time, he told a Commons committee, but Savicky was one of the former RCMP security service officers who had once paid Native Canadians to inform on their leaders.

Savicky came to Erasmus's office in September 1988. The band leader tried to reassure him that the demonstrations were peaceful. The violence he worried about was in the future. Erasmus later said: "I was trying to stop a probe. Apparently I created one. It is hard to believe." In fact, his remarks that day were later used by CSIS to further justify the big investigation into Native activities. If he had known what CSIS would do, he says, he would have kept his mouth shut and let them figure out for themselves what the future might hold.

CSIS analysts clipped out the newspaper accounts of Erasmus's remark about the possibility of "armed terrorism" by future generations. They added to it news reports of the Mohawk Warrior Society blockade of the Mercier Bridge in Montreal on June 1, 1988, plus a statement in October 1988 by native leaders that there could be violence in the Lubicon Lake land dispute and another statement by some native leaders in B.C. in November 1988 that they needed native peacekeeping units to defend their lands. Finally, CSIS had enough material to hold a meeting of the Target Approval and Review Committee. This is the high-level committee of senior officials at CSIS headquarters that supposedly carries all the safeguards against abuses of civil liberties, including a devil's advocate process, plus twenty-one complicated steps, a need-to-justify approach and everything else to ensure that targeting is fair and justified. It decided in its wisdom in December of 1988 to approve the major nation-wide investigation into "Native extremism" again under Section 2 (c) (activities in support of the threat of serious violence for the purpose of achieving a political objective).

CSIS opted for a "low-level" investigation, which meant interviewing, researching, listening to Native leaders' speeches and attending public meetings, but no undercover agents, no wiretapping and no bribing of Native informants would be used.

On December 19, 1988 a Telex message went out across the country to all six CSIS regional headquarters in Ottawa, Montreal, Toronto, Vancouver, Halifax and Edmonton and to the eleven district headquarters in Sudbury, Quebec City, Hamilton, Kitchener, Windsor, Victoria, Moncton, St. John's, Winnipeg, Calgary and Regina. Investigators were told the hunt for Native extremism was on. For the next three months they spoke to hundreds of Native leaders and white support workers in Native communities in an attempt to gauge the extent of discontent and the seriousness of the threat of serious violence among Canada's Native population.

CSIS conducted its massive investigation into "Native extremism" so discreetly and so well that nobody noticed, and not a word leaked out publicly. People involved in Native organizations did not notice anything unusual about the visit of a local CSIS intelligence officer. The investigation was intended to prepare for the Government of Canada what CSIS later called "a detailed assessment of a potential threat" by Native Canadians. There is no indication of what the report might have contained, or whether it was ever read.

The investigation only leaked out because on April 26, 1989,

Svend Robinson telephoned Kearley and asked him what he had
been doing in Goose Bay back in December of 1988. That
conversation led Robinson to place another call, this time to
CSIS Headquarters, where Director of Communications Gerry
Cummings situated Kearley's visit in the context of the much
larger nation-wide "Native extremism" investigation. What big
investigation? asked Robinson. Cummings explained. And later
that day, by coincidence, Raymond Boisvert, the deputy director
of internal communications at CSIS, explained the same thing
to a news reporter.

Now the cat was out of the bag. It was only a matter of time
before Native leaders were demanding to know on what basis
CSIS had been investigating them and at what "level" the investigation had been conducted. Every Native leader whose mail
had arrived from the post office opened and resealed in a plastic
bag, or who had heard strange noises on the telephone line to
the reserve, wondered whether he had been the subject of an
investigation.

Erasmus read in the papers that his remarks had prompted
the CSIS investigation. He was furious and wrote to the Security
Intelligence Review Committee, demanding that it investigate
what had happened. But SIRC ignored Erasmus's request because he had not, according to the committee, written first to
CSIS Director Reid Morden and complained to him, waited for
his reply, and then written to SIRC. In fact, SIRC does not need
to wait for any letters of complaint to begin an investigation: the
moment Erasmus tipped off SIRC that he was upset, the committee could have swung into action instead of giving him the
run-around.

Erasmus had had enough and gave up on SIRC. He had more
important things to worry about than how CSIS interpreted his
remarks and did not pursue the matter further. SIRC finally
launched an investigation in June 1989 but only after Svend
Robinson had made a big stink about it in the Commons and
written a letter to SIRC.

Finally, more than five months later, in November 1989, SIRC was ready. Its report was entitled *Report on the Innu Interview and the Native Extremism Investigation*. But despite the months it took, the work appeared to be rushed, incomplete and poorly prepared. The government withheld the report from publication for another two months and gave censors time to obliterate large parts of it with a black felt pen. This was done in the so-called "interests of national security." The government released what was left of the report on February 5, 1990.

Solicitor General Pierre Blais trumpeted that SIRC had found no evidence of misconduct by CSIS, absolving the service of any wrongdoing. Actually what it showed Canadians was that CSIS was still very much involved in counter-subversion activity except that now it was being passed off as counter-espionage by asking about "foreign influences" or counter-terrorism, citing the "threat of serious violence" angle. The Mounties used to spy on the Natives, but at least they told them point blank it was because they were Natives. Now CSIS was spying, but with nobler motives.

Blais was hoping the issue would be resolved by the report. It wasn't.

SIRC appeared before the Commons Justice and Solicitor General Committee on April 10, 1990 to discuss their report on Native extremism. This was the first appearance of the watchdog committee with its newly-appointed chairman, television tycoon John Bassett — who was a long-time friend of the prime minister and a generous contributor to the Conservative Party. Bassett had been passed over several times for a senate appointment that would have added "P.C." (for Privy Councillor) to his name. He gained that honour with the appointment to SIRC. Although he claimed not to have any experience with intelligence work, Bassett himself was once the subject of surveillance. During the 1962 election campaign, a very personal telephone call between Bassett, on a mobile car telephone in Toronto, and Prime Minister John Diefenbaker, in his office in Ottawa, was illegally intercepted. It has been played around the country at festive gatherings ever since. When the recording was made, mobile telephone systems were primitive and it was fairly easy to monitor conversations for several minutes at a time.

In the tape recording, a copy of which fell into the hands of *Brantford Expositor* reporter David Judd years later, Diefenbaker is heard calling up Bassett and giving him hell because Bassett's newspaper *The Telegram* printed a "scandalous article" by Douglas Fisher, who was a New Democrat candidate as well as a columnist in those days.

In the recording, Diefenbaker orders Bassett to yank the Fisher column for the duration of the election campaign and Bassett agrees. Then Diefenbaker warns him not to tell anyone about his call and Bassett is heard to say, "Nobody knows you called me, except you and me. I'm sitting in an automobile on Queen Street and nobody knows that you called me at all." Bassett then promises that his newspaper will do all it can to help re-elect the Tories.

Fisher says his column was dropped for the rest of the campaign, but no one ever told him the reason. He just remembers an editor asking him if it should be dropped, and he was so busy with his own NDP campaign, he said yes. Clearly, Prime Minister John Diefenbaker knew how to give orders.

Twenty-five years later, Bassett again found himself dealing with Ottawa. This time it wasn't his newspaper they were angry at, but his committee.

Sitting at the bottom of a U-shaped table, the five SIRC members attempted to defend their report. Led by NDP Justice critic John Brewin, the Justice committee laid into SIRC. Brewin was particularly scathing about SIRC's use of the phrase "Native extremism" to describe the object of the CSIS investigation. Bassett explained that they had inherited that particular term from the agency, but he agreed that perhaps quotation marks should have been put around it. The report had even neglected to examine whether CSIS had been justified in launching the investigation.

It turned out that SIRC had not talked to Bob Bartel or any of the people involved as subjects of the CSIS investigation. In fact only a few CSIS people were interviewed. Basically, SIRC had just looked at the CSIS file, copied out the title verbatim and drawn a conclusion that CSIS was not guilty of any misconduct. They let the solicitor general's people black out about half of the report, and released what was left to the public. This did not augur well for what was supposed to be an independent body, a watchdog of the public's rights.

The Justice committee was not happy. John Brewin said that SIRC had remained "silent" in the face of what was obviously an attempt by the government to "cover up" CSIS's behaviour in its investigation of Natives. No one seemed to disagree with him.

Most of the five SIRC members were contrite. Jean-Jacques Blais admitted, "You may chastise us and you may criticize us, and we will accept that." Paule Gauthier agreed that there was some "looseness" in the report. Blais pointed out that the poor quality of the report might have had something to do with the change-over in SIRC administration, as Ron Atkey, the first SIRC chairman, was in the process of leaving while it was being prepared.

New SIRC chairman Bassett, however, wanted something firmly on the record. "Let me make it clear to you," he said, "that I had nothing to do with the report. It was before I was chairman of this committee."

The Natives aren't the only Canadians the government is spying on. Take, for instance, the following case, in which the federal government ended up spying on itself.

On January 23, 1986, External Affairs Minister Joe Clark made a speech in the Commons in response to arms control proposals announced ten days earlier by the new Soviet leader, Mikhail Gorbachev. Clark urged closer co-operation with the USSR; it was a sound move at the time. External Affairs analysts had told Clark that a major shift in Moscow's foreign policy was taking place, and they were right. What they had accurately spotted was the start of *glasnost* and the larger theme of *perestroika*. Things were warming up between the Soviets and the West.

However, back at CSIS headquarters in the East Memorial

Building on Wellington Street in Ottawa, the Cold War still maintained its icy grip. CSIS had kept up its surveillance on Soviet diplomats, and continued to warn politicians to beware of the Evil Empire. Any sign of openness, the agency said, was merely a ruse to lure the West into a false sense of security. The agency should not really be faulted for its attitude. Back then, it was by no means clear that the changes then beginning in the Soviet Union would last beyond the "Moscow Spring" of 1986.

The right-wing cabal within the government and the news media were no less distrustful of what appeared to be an easing of tensions between East and West. So it was with a certain circumspection that External Affairs Minister Joe Clark spoke that day about the need for "promoting a more active and meaningful dialogue with the countries of the Eastern bloc." He called for "the inclusion of a healthy element of people-to-people contact" between the two countries.

Clark's speech was largely ignored by the media, but there were some who were paying attention to it. At the Soviet embassy, Clark's words struck a responsive chord with a group of diplomats stuck to their television sets while a Soviet representative sat in the diplomatic gallery in the Commons to hear the speech first-hand. The Russians were particularly struck by Clark's words: "a healthy element of people-to-people contact." Being Russians, they mulled the whole thing over for a couple of months and, in the spring of 1986, decided to make the most of Clark's offer. Rather than approaching Joe straight on, which might have been the diplomatically correct thing to do, the Soviets chose another course of action.

Valeri Sofonov, the second secretary of the Soviet embassy in Ottawa, wrote a friendly letter to Robert (Bob) Corbett, a veteran New Brunswick Tory MP who has done a lot of world travelling at other people's expense and is proud of the lasting and valuable contacts he has made on these trips around the globe.

Corbett was a founding member of the Canada Arab World Parliamentary Association, and was also involved in the Canada-Korea Friendship Society. He had travelled to Europe, Asia, the

Near East, the Far East, even the Middle East — and usually not on his own nickle. Once, in the company of Montreal Liberal MP Marcel Prud'homme, he appeared beside Yasser Arafat at a big rally in Algeria. A photograph taken on that trip shows the MPs, one on either side of Arafat, each holding one of the Palestinian leader's hands above his head. It now hangs on the wall of Corbett's parliamentary office.

Corbett is by no means unique among parliamentarians in his love of foreign travel. There are about two dozen Conservative backbenchers and senators, about half a dozen Liberal MPs and senators and one or two New Democrat MPs who are members of what is known on Parliament Hill as "The Travel Club." It is an unofficial organization made up of MPs, most of whom realize that they are not ever likely to make it into a federal cabinet, who have therefore resigned themselves to a life of looking after their constituents in the best way they can and spending whatever time they have left travelling around the world.

The members of the Travel Club exchange information, in an informal way, about the latest junkets available, which countries are offering the best trips this week, which ones are the fun trips, the boring trips, the ones featuring the best hotels or the best meals, the nicest entertainment, which countries want spouses along, which do not and, most important, which countries expect something in return and which ones are only doing it for goodwill or propaganda purposes.

Canadian MPs are free to accept trips from foreign powers. There is even a special book in the Commons Clerk's office where the MPs register their junkets. The law draws the line at accepting cash donations, but airline tickets, hotel bills, meals, taxis, entertainment and incidentals are all okay.

Sofonov, the Soviet diplomat, was aware of all this and knew exactly how to make his approach to Corbett. He began his letter by quoting at length from Joe Clark's speech and then brought up the possibility of creating an exchange group, or even perhaps a Canada-USSR Association to bring the two peoples together, and improve relations between the countries. Sofonov concluded by asking Corbett to talk it over with his colleagues and get back to him.

Corbett was a little surprised at this approach, especially since he was a well-known right-wing anti-Communist. He says that he immediately called up the RCMP, and someone came over to talk to him. This officer assured Corbett that he should feel free to return Sofonov's contact. The Mounties informed CSIS, which would be in a position to watch developments from a distance, knowing that an "approach" had been made. In fact, within two years, Sofonov would be branded a spy by the Canadian government and barred from ever returning to Canada as a diplomat.

Corbett also informed Joe Clark about the approach that had been made. Clark made it clear to him that he should continue the liaison, and that indeed the government was interested in upgrading relations with the USSR. Obediently, Corbett went to work on what he called his "Russian connections." He assigned his right-hand man in such matters, Bhupinder Liddar, to get cracking on the project.

Liddar passed the word around Parliament Hill on behalf of his boss that the Russians wanted to set up a friendship society. Everybody knew what that meant — better relations between the two countries. (Translation: free trips for all.)

In June 1986, Corbett organized a lunch for Sofonov in the Parliamentary Restaurant on the Hill. There the Russian met with a few parliamentary travellers — Liberal Senator Alasdair Graham, Tory Senator Heath Macquarrie and NDP MP Derek Blackburn. The makeup of the group was ecumenical; the topic was setting up the friendship group. Corbett noted that the Canadians' response was positive. A week later Sofonov was back in Corbett's office. The ambassador wanted to have a group of MPs over for lunch; could he please arrange it? He could — Liddar looked after it.

So a few days later, a number of Canadian MPs and senators waltzed up to the Soviet ambassador's elegant residence in Rockcliffe Park for a light lunch and some banter. This time, then-Liberal MP Lucie Pépin joined the group. It was followed by a second lunch afterwards for more MPs. They were coming from all over to welcome the Soviets in from the cold.

Soon, Sofonov appeared again in Corbett's office with a pile of letters to be distributed by hand to MPs who supported the friendship club project. But he also had some bad news. Sofonov was being called back and somebody else would be taking his place within a month. Such moves are generally anounced three months ahead, so this was somewhat unusual — unless Sofonov knew all along and chose not to tell Corbett.

In July, Corbett hosted a going-away lunch for Sofonov, who brought along the No. 4 man at the Soviet embassy, Counsellor Sergei Labour. Joined by Corbett's trusted aide Liddar, they all went over to the Hungarian Village restaurant on Laurier Street West in Ottawa. In all, Corbett had had about twelve lunches with his Soviet diplomat friends within a six-month period. However, he denies that anyone made any attempt to entrap him. "At no time did [Sofonov] ask what I would consider an improper question," says the MP. And there was no offer of money or request for classified information.

Corbett and his Russian pals were getting along very well. And yet another lunch meeting was held between Sofonov, Corbett and Liddar so that Sofonov could introduce the new man at the embassy who would be taking over when he left. But Sofonov had been the No. 12 man, and this guy was the No. 21 man. Clearly the project was being downgraded by the Soviets. (There was a reason. Senate Speaker Guy Charbonneau, a long-time friend of Prime Minister Brian Mulroney, had visited the Soviet Union and, while there, had met with a number of high-profile Russians including the chairman of the Soviet Council of Nationalities and the first deputy secretary of the Praesidium of the Supreme Soviet. They had discussed the idea of a parliamentary friendship club as well. The Soviets were not putting all their eggs in one basket.)

There is very little that happens between MPs and the Soviet embassy in Ottawa that CSIS does not know about. Everybody who goes in or out of the embassy is monitored. Telephone calls are heard and recorded, though not necessarily by CSIS. The Communications Security Establishment has the right to monitor all embassy communications and the RCMP can obtain wiretaps as well. CSIS also has access to twenty-four-hour closed circuit video monitoring of all the major embassies in the city, which is carried out by a special section of the RCMP. The embassies go along with this because they are told that it protects them against terrorists.

The cameras outside the Soviet embassy were no doubt kept busy during the summer of 1986, monitoring embassy employees on their way to meet Bob Corbett and his friends. By fall of that year, the project was way beyond Corbett's control. Everybody and his brother was in on it, making their own arrangements with the Russians. A huge reception was being planned in December at the ambassador's residence, in honour of a visiting Soviet delegation which had been asked to testify before a joint session of the Commons External Affairs and the Senate Foreign Affairs committees.

On December 15, capitalizing on the appearance of the Soviet delegation, a three-page letter was circulated to all MPs formally announcing the creation of the Canada-USSR Parliamentary Association. The letter was a well-crafted document outlining a number of cogent and coherent reasons for setting up such an association, and it was signed by high-profile MPs from all parties.

Then disaster struck. Calgary Tory MP Alex Kindy, a practising psychiatrist of Ukrainian descent, and Toronto Tory MP Andrew Witer, a staunch supporter of a number of self-styled Ukrainian "Freedom Fighter" associations, attacked the idea of any kind of parliamentary rapprochement with the Russians.

Mysteriously, information travelled to a number of right-wing ethnic and emigré associations in Canada, along with the names and photocopies of the signatures of the two dozen MPs who had signed the friendship club charter. The protest letters poured in.

What happened next is shrouded in secrecy. Either Joe Clark changed his mind — it's been known to happen — or someone got to him. Perhaps it was CSIS with some highly secret information, or the Americans, or just pressure from the ethnic communities. Whatever it was, within two months the word went out from External Affairs to the MPs and senators, who by now could almost taste the caviar, that they could forget about their Canada-USSR parliamentary association for a while. It was out of the question and they shouldn't ask why. There was never anything written down on paper, it was just something that was passed around — "Hey, have you heard? The Russian thing is off, the word came down from External."

At any given time, CSIS, just like any other self-respecting intelligence agency, has perhaps a half-dozen borderline espionage cases going on. The service can continue monitoring them or turn them over to the RCMP for active criminal investigation, knowing that it could eventually lead to public exposure, which would have political ramifications. All this is usually discussed behind closed doors in secured rooms with External Affairs, the PMO and the RCMP.

CSIS could easily have said, "We've been watching Sofonov, and it's not without reason that he's left." Or the service could have said it was close to cracking another Soviet spy case that would make the USSR look very bad, and did the government really want to be seen organizing a parliamentary friendship group with a country that was spying on Canada? It may have been nothing more than CSIS being uneasy that some MPs might be entrapped by the Soviet security service. Whatever it was, the government listened, as it had to. Governments who ignore the advice of their security services do so at their own peril.

Whatever CSIS's involvement in the Sofonov case, its interest in Corbett and his staff continued. In 1987, Corbett and Halifax MP Michael Forrestall, along with Corbett's aide Bhupinder Liddar — who also worked part-time for Forrestall — were called in by the Conservative Party whip, Scott Fennell.

Fennell told them that Liddar was under investigation by CSIS for his Soviet connections, and that as a precaution he should be fired immediately from both MPs offices. Forestall fired Liddar on the spot, but Corbett demanded reasons, which Fennell was unable or unwilling to supply. Corbett, who felt that any contact that Liddar had had with the Soviets was as a result of his orders, refused to go along with this directive.

Later, Liddar testified under oath at a SIRC hearing that he had been told at this meeting that CSIS had been to see Deputy Prime Minister Donald Mazankowski about the matter of his Soviet contacts. Properly, CSIS reports to the solicitor general. So why would the agency be seeing Mazankowski? An organization such as CSIS does not make mistakes like reporting to the wrong cabinet minister. The only official reason for reporting to Mazankowski would have been in his capacity as deputy chairman of the committee on security and intelligence, where only the most secret of security and intelligence problems are discussed. Officially, this committee is chaired by the prime minister, but in practice, it is normally Mazankowski who is in charge.

This would mean that the question of Liddar and the Soviets had gone for discussion to the highest level of all in the government, a committee that normally wouldn't concern itself with discussing how many lunches a backbencher MP's aide had had with a Soviet diplomat. Indeed, how would Tory whip Fennell even know that CSIS had been to see Mazankowski? And if he did, why would he pass that information on to a man he suspected of being an information conduit to the Soviet embassy?

Yet more pressure was soon put upon Corbett. Then Solicitor General James Kelleher asked the MP if Liddar worked for him. Corbett replied that he did. Kelleher told Corbett that there was "an investigation" going on and that there were some "concerns" about Liddar's "Russian connections." Corbett was scared. So was Liddar.

Liddar wrote to Jamie Burns, then chief of staff to Mazankowski, listing all his contacts with the Soviets — where he went to lunch, with whom and when. He outlined everything that was discussed and assured him that nothing improper had taken place at any time. Meanwhile, Kelleher asked Corbett to write down everything he knew had happened with the Soviets, which the MP was delighted to do. Later on he said, "I felt that [Liddar] was being unjustly accused and I felt responsible because he had been acting on my instructions to establish and assist in contacts with the Russian embassy."

Corbett finally did get his free trip to the USSR. He went with a couple of his cronies — Halifax MP Howard Crosby and Toronto MP Robert Pennock — after a NATO parliamentarians conference held in Oslo during the fall of 1987. The three enterprising MPs telephoned the Soviet embassy in Ottawa and managed to arrange a one-week add-on trip to Moscow, Kiev, Leningrad and Minsk, after the conference was over. External Affairs was furious; Tory whip Scott Fennell was angry; the entire Conservative caucus was mad as hell. How would it look, they said, for three Canadian parliamentarians to arrive in Moscow right after a NATO conference, with their suitcases bulging with NATO documents? The MPs saw it differently. They thought of themselves as building a bridge of friendship between Canada and the USSR.

The letter Kelleher had requested from Corbett ended up in a CSIS file that was used by the agency two years later to deny Liddar — a British subject — his Canadian citizenship. Corbett thought he was doing the right thing by co-operating with the solicitor general, but what he did in fact, was unwittingly condemn his own friend. CSIS couldn't get to Corbett because he was an MP, so they got the next-best guy they could, his trusted aide Liddar.

The case of Bob Bartel and the Innu and the unfortunate events surrounding the attempt to establish a Canada-USSR friendship club show how CSIS spies on Canadians. But far more of the agency's time is spent spying on spies — real spies, the kind you see in the movies.

At the height of the Cold War, life was very simple: we had to spy on the Commies and fellow-travellers, to keep the world safe for democracy. It's more complicated now. There are a lot more players in the game; they are playing for very high stakes; and they come from some unexpected places.

No country would ever admit to spying in Canada. Even caught red-handed, they will stick to the first rule of spying: "Admit nothing, deny everything and launch counter-accusations." And finally, when confronted with all of the evidence, they will protest that they were merely trying to foster closer political, cultural, scientific and commercial relationships with ordinary Canadians. Or else they will deny any connection with the individual who was caught. And if they can't do that with any degree of credibility, they will claim that they were set up in a conspiracy.

The Security Intelligence Review Committee said in its last annual report that there are at least two dozen foreign countries spying in Canada. Very few of these countries, which SIRC was careful not to name, would agree that what they are doing here should be called spying. As Director Reid Morden said in 1988, when his agency was caught trying to persuade television journalist Charlie Greenwell to spy on two other reporters: "We wouldn't say 'spying.' We would say 'collect some more information.' "

In the sixties, spies were after computers; in the seventies, lasers; in the eighties, microchips; and in the nineties they may be after computer economic models. As late as 1973 the Soviets were using discarded cigarette packages and hollows in tree trunks off the Gatineau Parkway north of Ottawa as secret hiding places for microfilms. It was all documented in court evidence with hand-drawn Soviet maps giving directions in broken English, including how agents should leave a *Maclean's* magazine in the rear window of a car if the coast was clear and place an orange on the side of the road if it was not. Then came the eighties and the trend towards spying more for industrial and technological secrets, that had begun in the sixties and seventies, intensified. With it came a new kind of spy, the "technobandits," who wore three-piece business suits, read the *Wall Street Journal*, were fluent in seven languages and could handle any kind of computer ever invented.

The Soviet bloc countries and Third World countries developed an insatiable appetite for modern technology. They wanted it all, quickly and, where possible, for free. Canada is one of the world's leading nations in technological and scientific research in a number of areas, including plant breeding, food production and processing, computer research, transportation, hydro-electrical production and high-voltage transmission. As well, Canada has access to most of the latest American technology. There is plenty for anybody to steal in Canada and Canadian firms are among the least guarded and the most proud to show off their discoveries and techniques.

The job of watching spies in Canada belongs to the Counter-Intelligence Branch of CSIS, which, along with counter-terrorism, is the agency's most important section. In most major countries counter-intelligence would be more important, but after the Air India Flight 182 bombing in 1985, the Conservative government ordered CSIS to make counter-terrorism its No. 1 priority. The Conservative goverment is not nearly as concerned about Soviet spies lurking about as it is eager for CSIS and the RCMP to solve the Air India bombing. And at this point, the government is probably right.

SIRC says that some supposedly "friendly" countries have been spreading "disinformation" in Canada to shape policies and turn events to their own purpose. SIRC has not named them but, as we shall see, India is one country often reported in the news media as engaging in disinformation in Canada.

"Some ethnic communities are the targets of foreign agents who want to undermine enemies of the regime in the homelands," says SIRC. The Soviet Union, the Philippines under Ferdinand Marcos, the Indian government, Chile, China, Korea, Romania under Nicolae Ceausescu, Libya, Iran and South Africa have all been cited in the courts or named in the news media in this context.

But immigrants don't figure much in the plans of countries spying in Canada: if caught and convicted, they must serve their sentences in Canadian prisons, whereas foreign nationals can be swapped for spies of Canada's allies. The vast majority of CSIS's attention is focused on "diplomats," visiting professors and businessmen and other foreign nationals who are constantly coming and going. A study conducted by SIRC in 1989 showed that eighty-four percent of the people CSIS had under surveillance as suspected spies were foreigners. Only sixteen percent were Canadians.

All this foreign activity keeps CSIS busy. The Counter-Intelligence Branch has several options for dealing with these threats. First it can respond by merely watching developments, using human sources and electronic surveillance, and keeping the government informed about any developments as they occur.

The second option consists of casually talking to the government official or private individual who has been approached by a suspect foreign power and explaining the potential threat. Toronto lawyer Richard Boraks says he was warned once by a couple of CSIS agents that a deal he was working on with the Polish consulate in Toronto could compromise him. He re-examined the deal, realized what they were talking about, and was thankful they had tipped him off. Actually, there is nothing in the CSIS Act that says CSIS agents have to go around warning people about potential threats, but they do it all the time anyway. This kind of measure is useful because it often neutralizes a security threat without making a costly public scene or an ugly diplomatic incident.

The third option is the full active operation, with all the surveillance and invasion of privacy CSIS can manage. Again, CSIS has no official powers at all to swing into action; it cannot arrest or charge anyone. It must turn over its information to the government and let the RCMP, which still has responsibility for the criminal investigation side of espionage in this country, conduct the investigation.

The government can lay charges against spies or expel diplomats as it did with seventeen Soviet diplomats in 1988, or it can refuse to extend visas, as it did in the case of Patrick Chang in 1986.

Unofficially, (there is nothing in the CSIS Act about it), the service has another "active" option it can use to counter an espionage threat. It can try to "turn" a spy to act on behalf of Canada, in effect making him a double agent for Canada.

For a relatively small international power, Canada has had a remarkably high rate of success in turning spies, because so many of them realize that when they finally come out of the cold, the prize is a set of Canadian citizenship papers; Canada is considered a nice place in which to live the rest of one's life in peace. It is not without reason that so many international fugitives have fled here, including a number of Nazi war criminals who live very pleasant, undisturbed lives. SIRC reported that two Soviets, who remain unnamed, defected as recently as 1989.

Not all investigations require elaborate technology. One way of detecting which diplomats posted to Ottawa might be involved in intelligence gathering is to have Canadian diplomats abroad establish which accredited Ottawa embassy personnel of a particular country are on that country's foreign affairs personnel list. The ones who aren't on the list are probably from another department. Guess which one? This is actually an old trick that an enterprising Canadian journalist pulled off in Washington a number of years ago. He obtained the State Department's list of personnel posted to Ottawa, and compared it with the list of U.S. embassy personnel issued in Ottawa. After that it was a simple process of elimination until he had correctly identified the CIA bureau chief in Ottawa.

CSIS has also begun assigning former Security Liaison Officers returning from abroad to work in the Production and Analysis Branch, using what they know from the foreign side with what the CSIS investigators are picking up on the street. Again, it's a wonder it wasn't done earlier.

Most countries begin the year by setting intelligence priorities. For one country it may be nuclear technology. Another may be seeking computer technology. Still another may seek telecommunications. It depends on factors back home as well as political and economic considerations abroad. If a country can get something for free from a friendly superpower, or buy it at a reasonable cost, or manufacture it at home, why spy to obtain it? When none of those options is possible, the message goes out to a country's foreign missions around the world, and to whatever other intelligence system it may have.

Targets for this kind of approach may include the emigré communities in the host countries, exchange professors, business people lined up through foreign friendship societies or simply old foreign business friends. Intelligence services are skilled at spotting a Canadian company in financial trouble and offering to bail it out — provided a few export control corners are cut and the right product is shipped over. It is often painful for a business person to have to refuse.

Several countries actually send a shopping list to their embassy in Ottawa once a year, listing the information and material they want sent back in the coming year. If it's equipment they want, most countries specify brand name, model and the price they are willing to pay for each particular item. The Soviets, for instance, are fond of Digital Equipment Corp. (DEC) computers because the product is reliable, because it is available with European electrical specifications, and because DEC has many offices in Europe, making it easy to service.

A Frenchman, Joseph Lousky, was nailed in Montreal four years ago, following a two-year-long watch-and-wait operation by CSIS. Lousky, a thirty-eight-year-old engineer, who had done the same sort of thing before in the U.S., was shipping mainframe parts and computers to the Soviet Union through Belgium using a series of intermediary companies and cash payments. They were DEC computers, suitable for a missile guidance system. Lousky knew CSIS and the Mounties would be watching any DEC shipments going out of Canada, so he stuck Hitachi labels on the huge computers and called them medical machines on his bills of lading.

An eagle-eyed member of Canada Customs at Mirabel Airport took one look at a shipment and said: "Hey, Joe, come here. Hitachi doesn't make big medical machines like this, eh?" So they peeled off the sticker.

Lousky pleaded guilty and was placed on probation for a year and fined $75,000 which he paid on the spot. He had been making about $300,000 every six months. His only complaint — the Russians who claimed they'd never heard of him, still owed him $500,000 on the last shipment.

Much that would be highly secret in some foreign countries is quite public in Canada. You have only to ask. Sometimes it is even given out free-of-charge at trade fairs or lectures. On many Canadian government contracts, almost anyone is allowed to examine the specifications. A lot of private firms also open their doors to visitors or allow their executives or scientists to write long dissertations on their discoveries. Many developing countries, some of which harbour the most despotic and oppressive regimes on the face of the earth, are encouraged to send students over to Canada. In quite a few cases, their tuition and expenses are even paid for by Canadian taxpayers. Canada does not take into account a country's human rights record when it accepts foreign students.

Occasionally, someone who is something other than a legitimate student gets into Canada on a foreign-student visa. The pseudo-student will attend classes for a while and then gradually drop out of school and move to a new location. Everyone suspects the student has either fallen in love or found a job and decided to try to stay in Canada, and most often that is what has happened. But sometimes it is something more sinister. It can sometimes take months to locate missing students after they have stopped attending classes and turned their attention to more profitable "assignments."

Paradoxes and ironies abound. Canada decries Libya's construction of a nuclear reactor in the desert for fear that it could be used to build a nuclear bomb, but at the same time Canada encourages Libyan students, who have jobs waiting for them at that very same nuclear installation in the desert, to come over to the University of Manitoba and other schools of higher learning to study science and nuclear physics and chemistry. The students say the nuclear reactor they will be working on will produce electricity which their desert nation needs desperately — if the oil supplies ever run out.

Much of the foreign intelligence gathering done in Canada is conducted through embassies, trade missions, trading companies and large multinational companies. When it is done through embassies, it is called collecting information. This is the protocol that we shall respect too as we examine a few of the countries "collecting information" in Canada.

Recent events in Eastern Europe may change its activities of countries' "information collecting" quite radically. But until a very short time ago, most of the Eastern bloc nations were extensively involved in acquiring Canadian technology. The Romanians had an ill-conceived plan to steal Canada's heavy-water manufacturing process but were never able to profit from it and are still buying heavy water while their unfinished Candu reactors lie idle. And five years ago, the Bulgarian attaché in Toronto, Raikov Ivan Delibaltov, was booted out for spying after trying to get unspecified high-tech material in the Toronto area.

Czechoslovakia implemented "technology transfers" until Vaclav Havel came to power. CSIS ran a big counter-intelligence operation against the Czechslovakian spy network two years ago, interviewing hundreds of Czechoslovak Canadians. We know for sure that the agency was monitoring consulate and airline communications in Montreal three years ago. Now CSIS is waiting for developments before disbanding its Czechoslovak desk. The East Germans did not have an embassy in Canada (and now never will) but ran huge spy operations, using business contacts and sailors as couriers, out of Montreal and Toronto.

The Hungarians were traditionally considered to be the "numbers" people in the Eastern bloc, collecting information on anything that involved specialized knowledge in mathematics. Now the numbers don't add up any more. The Hungarians also used to lend people to the Soviets. CSIS Director Reid Morden says Hungarian-Canadian spy Stephen Ratkai was on loan to the

Russians: "What does Hungary care about submarine signatures? The last time I looked, Hungary was land-locked."

China remains a monolithic bastion of old-school Communism. The Chinese have a huge embassy operation, thirty-five people in Ottawa, seven in Toronto, fifteen in Vancouver. They have an extensive intelligence network in the Chinese-Canadian community which they use to advantage. Joe Clark served notice on the Chinese government after the Tienanmen Square slaughter to stop hounding Chinese students in Canada. The Chinese watch activities of nationalists in Toronto and Vancouver very closely, and in return the nationalists watch them closely too. This is great for CSIS, who is able to use one group to monitor the activities of the other.

China is obsessed with Taiwanese arms purchases in Canada and keeps a close eye on Hong Kong financial transfers and real estate purchases. It is especially interested in several recent mergers of Chinese financial empires linked to Canada. China uses a number of large state trading companies to conduct monitoring activities. Much use is made of immigration to obtain favours and information. China is always careful not to jeopardize its heavy economic reliance on Canadian financial aid and industrial development.

The Cubans use their Montreal consulate and their huge trade mission offices in the north end of the city to spy on the Americans because they have no base in the U.S. The consulate or the trade mission has mysteriously caught fire regularly every few years, and the Mounties have always arrived quickly to help fire fighters. The last fire was at the consulate in 1988. Three people died, and onlookers viewing the fire from Pierre Trudeau's home across the street ruined his lawn. The Cubans rely heavily on Canada for trade goods they can't get from the U.S. and for indirect Canadian foreign aid, so they are very careful not to hurt this country in any way that might jeopardize their privileged trade position or hurt the big Canadian tourism market that compensates for the American trade embargo.

Almost all of the Middle Eastern nations who have an intelligence presence in Canada are here to keep an eye on their own nationals or on each other. One of the biggest intelligence operations of all in Canada belongs to Israel. Mossad agents are located in every major city, working closely with CSIS, protecting El Al aircraft and airline installations and watching PLO political activities, especially those of Arab and Iranian students. Israelis are CSIS's prime source of information on a number of suspected terrorists and spies, but often the information is laundered through Washington. The Israelis have several additional intelligence networks linked to Israeli military and Israeli national organizations. The Israelis monitor very closely the Lebanese, Syrian, Iraqi and Libyan political influence in Canada but do very little military or economic spying here, although they do try hard to influence Canadian foreign policy. They have an extensive political lobby and work very closely with the Canadian Jewish community. Their propaganda effort is considerable and highly people-intensive. Israel spends plenty on image and is the country's biggest supplier of free junkets for MPs. It lays on extremely effective security for its political visitors to Canada.

Libya has no embassy here but has one of the most extensive intelligence operations, using businessmen and members of other Arab communities. Moussa Hawamda ran the Manara Travel Agency at 55 Metcalfe Street in Ottawa in 1987 as a front for Libyan intelligence activities. Hawamda distributed hundreds of thousands of dollars to extreme right and extreme left groups that opposed Israel, anti-semitic groups and fringe groups of all kinds. He funded free travel to Libya for politicians, labour leaders and journalists and looked after the travel plans of Libyan students in Canada. CSIS and the RCMP both had him under surveillance for an entire year but were unable to prove he did anything illegal. Finally the FBI charged him with money laundering in the U.S. in 1988. He jumped bail and made his way back to Libya.

Ottawa businessman Ahmed Murad organizes free trips for politicians on behalf of Libya. He has also had English versions of Moammar Gadhaffi's *Green Book* printed in Canada. Murad occasionally talks to CSIS and says he has nothing bad to say about the service.

The Lebanese government is too weak to do anything organized, but the various factions of the large Lebanese community spend their time spying on each other. CSIS plays each group off against the other to find out what is happening. Jumbalists in Montreal have attracted special attention from CSIS for unspecified reasons. The agency is closer to the Lebanese Christian and Muslim factions than to the Iranian Hezbollah or Syrian groups for ideological reasons. Much of CSIS surveillance is concerned with possible terrorist threats and trading information with friendly foreign intelligence services such as American or Israeli.

Iran and Iraq were busy in Canada trying to buy everything that even looked like a weapon during their long and bloody war against each other. Both of them use their intelligence services to try to track down dissidents and student activists. The Canadian Iranian community is helpful to CSIS because it is so opposed to the reign of the mullahs. Now that the Iran-Iraq war is over, and Iraq has become Canada's enemy, CSIS will be keeping an even closer watch on Iraqui diplomats and other nationals to ensure that Canada is taking an effective part in the world economic and trade boycott.

CSIS works closely with Turkish intelligence to protect Turkish diplomats from Armenian terrorist groups — there have been several attacks over here, including an attempt by Armenian-Canadian terrorists to take over the Turkish embassy in March 1985. CSIS stays out of "local" quarrels between Turkey and Greece over Cyprus and the Aegean islands.

The Egyptians and the Pakistanis have old, long-established community links in Canada to help them collect technological information and maintain links with Muslim countries, but they attract very little attention from the agency.

The Chilean Secret Service (DINA) allows opponents of the regime to come to Canada and then follows them around, thus identifying dissidents for future reference. Surprisingly,

Chilean intelligence has supplied information to CSIS for use against refugee Chilean refugee claimants.

India has an extensive intelligence operations in Canada and its activities have attracted attention from External Affairs. India sees Canada as a haven for Sikh terrorists and still blames Canada for lax airport security which may have led to the bombing of Air India Flight 182. The Indian government believes this could happen again at any time and feels obligated to infiltrate the Sikh community in Canada to make sure it doesn't.

Three former Indian diplomats left Canada in 1987: Brij Mohan Lal, Gurinder Singh and M.K. Dhar. Joe Clark said last year he would check to see if they had left because they had been caught spying; as of this writing, he was still checking. The Sikh-Canadians say Indian government agents have infiltrated their community to provoke violence in Canada in order to discredit them and undermine their peaceful campaign for an independent Sikh homeland. They accuse India of deliberately misleading Canadian intelligence officials with phony tips. The Indian High Commission is very unhappy with a book, *Soft Target*, which substantially carried that message. The Indians are close to Clark, who views India as a major trading partner and an ally of Canada. Clark got into a lot of trouble three years ago when he counselled provincial premiers to stay away from a major Sikh group.

CSIS still has massive electronic surveillance operations against the Sikh community in an attempt to crack the Air India terrorist bombing. The agency is trying to make up for its inability to penetrate the Sikh community by using electronic surveillance instead. It bungled the only useful bit of information that came its way — the 1987 wiretap that disclosed a possible plan to attack a Punjabi cabinet minister. This, as we have already seen, cost the first CSIS director his job.

When the Air India tragedy struck, CSIS did not have a single Sikh-Canadian on staff. The situation is no better now. In Ottawa, a CSIS intelligence officer believes he has recruited two valuable contacts in the Sikh community. He meets the pair, both taxi drivers, once or twice a month over lunch in an Ottawa restaurant where they brief him on Sikh and Indian community news. He gets something he can write up in a report, and they get lunch. What he doesn't know is that they have discussed everything beforehand with fellow community members at the temple. After each meeting they report back on what he asked and what they replied. "I do not know why he would want to speak to those people," says a local Sikh community leader, with just a trace of jealousy. "One is illiterate and the other one can barely speak Punjabi. What do they know?" Actually the arrangement is working better, because lately members of the community have been striving to furnish more accurate details to the taxi drivers to pass on. A number of Sikh leaders have actually begun speaking to CSIS. Otherwise, they realize the Indian High Commission will be doing the talking to CSIS for them.

The Koreans, North and South, watch each other like foxes. The North has few intelligence resources. The South has an embassy, is allied to Taiwan and spends heavily to influence Canadian politicians by giving them trips to Seoul. CSIS is watching the pair carefully. Korea works with Taiwanese intelligence services, especially against Chinese Communists.

South Africa specializes in disinformation, propaganda and influence-buying — and the occasional illegal arms purchase. The country fights very hard to get around economic sanctions. There is a possibility that South Africa is fomenting agitation within radical Native Canadian groups, so CSIS keeps an eye on that and also investigates its possible funding of right-wing and anti-bilingualism extremist groups. The service is watching several South African business lobby groups in Toronto and Montreal. South Africa spends heavily to achieve propaganda success; it funded and distributed the powerful propaganda film *The ANC Method: Violence* narrated by Canadian journalist Peter Worthington. South Africa was caught trying to use two Canadian students as spies on church groups and pro-black groups in Manitoba last year.

They were responsible for a phony letters-to-the-editor campaign in favour of South Africa. Clark let the ambassador off with a tongue lashing after CSIS had turned the two South African agents into double agents.

British spies are allowed to come to Canada — with CSIS's permission and co-operation — to conduct covert operations against IRA terrorists and gun-runners.

There are some anomalies in the field of international espionage: though they have no operations here, the Dutch have a very efficient spy network. It grew out of their Second World War resistence movement and also their colonial strength. Every ex-colonial power has on average about double to triple what a developing country of comparable size will have. Brazil, for all the overbearing influence its military has had on its internal affairs and the fact that it is a world economic power on a par with Canada, has an intelligence network that does not even approach that of tiny Portugal, the mother country.

Japan, a major economic power, does not spy here, but it does collect a great deal of economic information in a strictly legal fashion. Saudi Arabia does not have an extensive intelligence-gathering network but depends on other poorer Arab countries who trade information in return for Saudi money.

The USSR and the U.S. remain the two big superpowers. They watch each other all the time and have lately been competing economically. The Soviets spy on everything they can get away with in Canada, but technology remains their prime interest. CSIS, of course, is completely on the American side. However, all too often the Americans come up to Canada and stage a little CIA covert activity on their own, which infuriates CSIS. The Americans still see Canada as the little brother who will listen to reason and co-operate, whether it's turning down nuclear submarines, keeping an eye on Housewives for Nicaragua, infiltrating left-wing organizations or sifting through the wreckage of the burned-out Soviet embassy. The Soviets regard Canada as a patsy for the U.S.

It's true that CSIS has an extremely — one might almost say unnaturally — close relationship with Canada's great neighbour to the south. The Americans have always taken a great interest in Canadian affairs, which is understandable given the cultural and economic ties between the two nations. However, as friendly as the U.S. is towards Canada, American foreign policy and Canadian foreign policy do not always march hand-in-hand. Both SIRC and the Canadian media have pointed out on numerous occasions that they feel the relationship between Canada's internal intelligence agency and its American counterparts is far too cosy. And indeed, a careful look at CSIS's six-year history would result in the clear impression that when the Americans say "Jump!" CSIS says, "How high?"

In fact, the U.S. may have pulled off the intelligence and espionage coup of all time: it is the perfect mole — so entangled in our lives, so much a part of our culture and economy, that it's easy to forget that the interests of Canada and the U.S. may not always be one and the same. The Americans have infiltrated our security service so completely that not only are they privy to most of our secrets, but in some cases — without even receiving direct orders — CSIS will act almost as a branch of American intelligence. Who would ever question the motives of our friendly uncle to the south, our biggest trading partner and greatest ally? Evidently our security service does not question those motives, and in the game of intelligence, that sort of oversight can be the most dangerous mistake of all.

# HOW DOES CSIS
# MEASURE UP?

**T**HE WORLD IS AT A CROSSROADS. A massive change has been wrought in Eastern Europe. The old post-war era we knew has disintegrated. The Soviet empire has collapsed. Its ideology has been repudiated and its satellites have gone their own way. There is still an Eastern bloc but the Soviets can't count on everybody anymore. The Americans are trying to find themselves. Their politics, also built on having an enemy, is changing as well, and they too must leave behind their war economy and look for a new vision. No one knows where these dizzying changes will lead, nor how changes in economies or the environment will affect our lives. But one thing is certain — espionage and intelligence will always play a part in our future. It will be up to CSIS to produce accurate, up-to-date intelligence on what is happening.

How does CSIS measure up? A current report card on the service's performance would likely say, "Shows some improvement, but still needs to work harder."

Reid Morden claims the service is "more mature" and better than ever: under his centralized management, everybody reports to him. He gives the orders, and his deputy directors execute them. And Morden the bureaucrat is there to ensure that the service doesn't make waves. No noise is good noise, as they say in the public service. Morden's system is silent — there haven't been any fresh scandals lately — but is that simply because CSIS isn't taking risks? Some of the old Mounties and ambitious young intelligence officers believe that's the case, and all Morden is doing is "damage control." And there is some complaining about how much power Morden wields: for instance, he appoints overseas security liaison officers without holding competitions. And when there are competitions, sometimes fourth-place candidates get the jobs. "I wouldn't want CSIS to be a judge at the Olympics," says one CSIS veteran. "Can you imagine the uproar if they gave the gold medal to the fourth-place finisher?"

The organization has a lot of catching up to do — it still doesn't have up-to-date manuals of its own or fully computerized retrieval systems.

Recently, in an ongoing series of games designed to keep personnel on their toes, a game was organized between CSIS staff and International Media Analysis (IMA) Inc., the firm run by CSIS's own former deputy director, Archie Barr. For a month, the two sides collected information on terrorist activities around the world of interest to Canada. The CSIS staff used their traditional methods — human sources, friendly intelligence agencies and clipping services. IMA relied on several thousand international news data banks. At times, IMA was able to find news stories while they were happening, whereas it would take CSIS a week or more to track them down. It was like the proverbial race between a horse and a steam engine: you want the horse to win, but you know the steam engine will. It did: IMA won handily. Unfortunately, that didn't help it win a contract to supply CSIS with information gleaned from its computer network. It might be embarrassing for an intelligence agency spending $200 million a year to have to admit it was buying intelligence from two guys sitting in front of computer terminals. CSIS prefers the old ways.

And there are plenty of other problems. The security clearance backlog is bigger than ever — people are waiting for up to a year. And there are questions about what CSIS does with what it finds. Even if it clears someone for security, the service can still choose to reveal potentially damaging information, such as, "Well, this woman is a prime candidate for security clearance . . .

although we did find out she has a drinking problem." In a case like this, even if CSIS goes on to say that the woman is in counselling for alcoholism and appears to be doing well, the damage has already been done: she may be cleared for security, but she will likely lose any chance for promotion.

Although the service still has a long way to go in hiring minorities, its attitudes to Francophones have improved. The latest batch of graduates are all bilingual; half are Francophone and a quarter speak a third language. And women are better represented; they make up half the class. But even these figures conflict with others: the percentage of Francophone managers actually dropped last year, from twenty-three to eighteen percent, due mainly to early retirement.

And morale continues to be low. One day not long ago, several intelligence officers punched into their terminals the latest American-produced computer model of the modern spy — someone who is highly trained but underpaid, feels no job satisfaction, has little corporate identification, is angered by a real or imagined slight at work . . . and has access to highly classified information.

The officers were horrified when they realized the picture fit them all: graduates of universities and the Academy starting at salaries of only $28,500, stuck in boring jobs, feeling passed over for the best jobs by ex-Mounties, not too attached to their organization and possessing ready access to highly secret information.

Gordon Osbaldeston, who headed the independent task force study of CSIS in 1987, was so worried about morale at CSIS that he recommended that every single employee be sent on a "training course" to learn what CSIS is, the nature of its mandate and the trust placed in it. Whether such a course would affect morale remains to be seen, since CSIS hasn't tried it yet.

More difficult to assess is the priority CSIS should assign to the various functions it must carry out. Its current emphasis on counter-intelligence and counter-terrorism is sound: Canadians are far more likely to be hurt by terrorists and economic or technological spies in the nineties than by the old Commies and left-wing radicals who enjoyed the attention of the counter-sub-version unit.

But, at least in the area of counter-intelligence, the question we must all ask is: "*Who* should we be watching?" Reid Morden thinks he knows. Trained a generation ago at arms talks when the Cold War was at its height, he says that the Soviet espionage threat is still as serious as ever and that we must maintain vigilance — and CSIS's budget. Last year, Morden ended a speech in Quebec City with a quotation from American right-wing thinker William F. Buckley. Only Morden could quote Buckley as an authority on security and intelligence before a Canadian audience and keep a straight face.

And therein lies another problem. Morden is Uncle Sam's favourite nephew. SIRC has repeatedly said that CSIS relies too much on American information and guidance. A security service that confuses American and Canadian foreign policy interests and perceives parliamentary friendship clubs as threats may itself be a threat to Canada's security.

The solution to all these problems is, of course, full public disclosure and debate about what CSIS should be. At the very least, we need a strong watchdog for CSIS. But SIRC has proved to be a failure: it has no teeth, and its part-time non-experts don't have the knowledge or access to the information they would need to act effectively.

Part of the problem is the service's obsession with secrecy. For instance, CSIS has signed more than sixty agreements with foreign police forces and security agencies that allow CSIS to hand over information on Canadians to foreign powers. CSIS refuses to name the countries. But the Sikh community, for instance, believes that information from CSIS has led to torture and death for several Sikh militants back in India.

Some of the agreements allow foreign security services to enter Canada and stage covert operations — a prospect that should disturb Canadians.

There was a glimmer of hope for change at CSIS last summer

when a Commons committee was set up to review the CSIS Act. At first it appeared hard-hitting and aggressive. It even threatened one senior government witness with a subpoena if he didn't start giving straight answers.

But gradually the committee's attitude began to soften. CSIS too began to be less hostile. It invited the MPs to CSIS headquarters, gave them a private little security briefing, trotted out a few tired old military secrets, showed them some fancy electronic hardware . . . and by spring 1990 the MPs and CSIS seemed to be in love. When the committee's report comes out, there will likely be some criticisms and suggestions for changes, but they'll almost certainly be balanced by copious praise.

Committee chairman Blaine Thacker, who had initially been very tough on CSIS, welcomed Reid Morden to a meeting in June with the following words:

"It is clear to us that you took over the service at a time when it was into some difficulties and you have turned it into a first-rate agency overall. While we have several recommendations for you to consider in our report, the fact of the matter is that you have done a very good job. You have given the agency a credibility it did not have or was rapidly losing, and you are to be commended for that."

With critics like this, Morden may not need to worry too much about the Commons committee's final report, due this fall. The rest of us should.

# GLOSSARY

**ASALA** - Secret Army for the Liberation of Armenia. Terrorist group which has claimed responsibility for a series of bombings and the killing of about a dozen Turkish nationals over the past 15 years.

**ASIO** - Australian Security Intelligence Organization. Comprised of a trio of domestic spy agencies.

**ASIS** - Australian Security Intelligence Service. The Australian foreign spy service is one of the latest to join an elite international club.

**CIA** - Central Intelligence Agency. Responsible for foreign espionage and intelligence gathering outside the United States. About 20,000 employees.

**CSE** - Communications Security Establishment. The most secret of all Canadian intelligence-gathering agencies. Using sophisticated high-tech equipment the CSE eavesdrops on foreign embassies and consular offices in Canada and on military communications around the globe. It listens in on all sorts of electronic communications, including telephone, satellite transmission, television, radar, and electro-magnetic emissions from electronic typewriters and computer terminals. Using relays from U.S. communications and spy satellites around the world, the CSE can listen to a Soviet troop commander ordering lunch for his men in the Urals or to two Nigerian sailors on a Panamanian ship in the Atlantic discussing the attractions of the next port, as well as to the faint blips coming from the computer terminal of a business person's secretary in Manchester. The CSE has the capacity to monitor as many as 10,000 transmissions at a time. Officially it answers to the Minister of National Defence, but in practice it answers more frequently to the National Security Agency in Fort Meade, Va., which gets about 98 percent of its work. About 2,000 employees, including 608 unionized civilian employees in 1987.

**CSIS** - Canadian Security Intelligence Service. A mostly domestic service with extensive powers for collecting intelligence on espionage, terrorism and foreign-influenced activities in Canada. It is also responsible for providing immigration, visa, and public service security-clearance screening, as well as providing advice to the government on possible future terrorist and espionage threats. About 2,350 employees.

**DIE** - Departamentul de Informatii Externe (Romanian foreign intelligence service).

Scored a number of impressive intelligence coups in Canada in the seventies.

**DS** - Durzhavna Sigurnost (Bulgarian secret service). The DS has been completely dominated by the Soviet KGB, to the point of having a KGB adviser in each of its five directorates. Famous for doing "black-bag jobs" and other assorted "dirty tricks" for the Soviets. Suspected of being involved in some way with assassination attempt on Pope John Paul II by Turkish fanatic Mehmet Ali Agca in Rome in May 1981. DS is believed to have executed former Bulgarian dissident George Markov in London with a poison-pellet umbrella-gun in 1978. About 30,000 employees in the mid-eighties.

**DGSE** - Direction Generale de la Securite Externe. French external intelligence agency. Formerly called SDCE (Service de Documentation et de Contre-Espionnage Externe).

**DST** - Direction de la Surveillance du Territoire. French domestic security service.

**EII** - Enforcement Information Index. The Canadian immigration officials' equivalent of the Doomsday Book used by American Immigration and Naturalization officials at border entry points. The EII lists the names and descriptions of all known terrorists, crooks and undesirables. The Canadian index, which is on computer, is more sophisticated than the American counterpart, which carries some listings which are 20 years out-of-date.

**FBI** - Federal Bureau of Investigation. Responsible for counter-espionage within the United States. About 23,000 employees.

**GCHQ** - Government Communications Head Quarters. The British equivalent of the CSE or the American NSA. It operates a series of listening posts in Britain and around the world.

**GRU** - Glavnoye Raszvedyvatelnoye Upravleniye (Soviet military intelligence). About 18,000 employees, some in uniform and others undercover, specializing beyond strictly military security and intelligence. Fairly well represented in foreign missions, however. Gouzenko worked for GRU's predecessor.

**KGB** - Komitet Gosudarstvennoy Bezopasnosti (Committee for State Security). Soviet domestic and foreign security and intelligence service. First Chief Directorate conducts spying abroad while the Second Chief Directorate looks after domestic security. The KGB is massive. It also looks after coast guard, immigration security, postal investigations, courtroom security, drug enforcement, firearm controls, tobacco and alcohol smuggling, securities and exchanges frauds, counterfeiting, VIP security, and customs regulations. It has, as well, 300,000 borders guards. In all it has about 1,300,000 employees.

**NSA** - National Security Agency. Monitors telecommunications and electro-magnetic transmissions around the world with help from Canadian CSE and British GCHQ. About 120,000 employees.

**NSID** - National Security Investigation Directorate. A small national security investigation and criminal intelligence unit within the RCMP responsible for investigating national security offences, including security leaks and espionage activities. It is sometimes called by its regional name - NSIS. About 130 employees.

**RCMP** - Royal Canadian Mounted Police. Responsible for enforcement of criminal code, investigation of Official Secrets Act violations, and protective security for VIPs. About 17,500 employees.

**SB** - (Sluzba Bezpieczemstwa). The Polish security service which operates at home and abroad and until recently worked closely with the Soviet intelligence services.

**Securitate** - The dreaded Romanian domestic security and intelligence service, known commonly as the "Secu." It was never officially disbanded after President Nicolae Ceausescu was killed on Dec. 25, 1989. Only 3,575 of 8,400 Securitate officers were fired. The others made peace with new regime. The Securitate had been heavily infiltrated by KGB agents before that. As many as 50 percent of the Securitate agents were already double agents for the Soviets. D5, the Fifth Directorate, was responsible for President Nicolae Ceausescu's personal safety . . . before his death.

**Stasi** - Ministerium fur Staatssicherheit (German Democratic Republic Ministry of State Security). Officially disbanded in Dec. 1989. The East German security service had 85,000 employees and 109,000 human sources. Some six million files were found, many of them in code, on the country's 16 million inhabitants. The best files were taken off to Moscow, West Germany and the United States by fleeing agents.

**STB** - Statni Tajna Bezpecnost. The Czechoslovakian foreign intelligence service, also acted as domestic secret police. Officially disbanded when playwright Vaclav Havel came to power in Dec. 1989.

**Tashnag** - The Armenian Revolutionary Federation. A legitimate political organization whose aim is to keep alive the memory of the Armenian holocaust. Not to be confused with the ASALA.

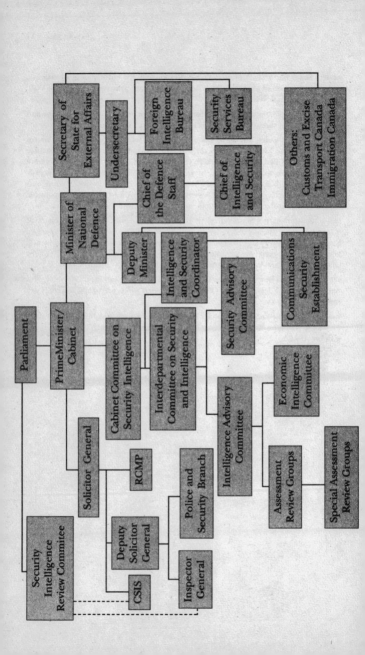

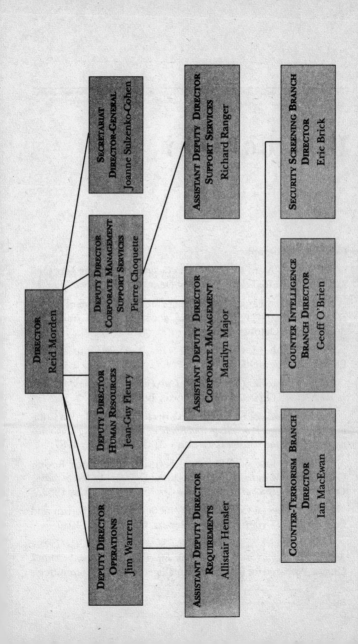

# BIBLIOGRAPHY

## General Bibliography

Borovoy, A. Alan. *When Freedoms Collide: The Case for Our Civil Liberties.* Toronto: Lester & Orpen Dennys, 1988.

Broduer, Jean-Paul. *On Evaluating Threats to the National Security of Canada and to the Civil Rights of Canadians.* Montreal: L'universite de Montreal, October 1985.

Brook-Shepherd, Gordon. *The Storm Birds: Post-War Defectors.* London: Weidenfeld, 1988.

Cameron, Stevie. *Ottawa Inside Out: Power, Prestige and Scandal in the Nation's Capital.* Toronto: Porter Books, 1989.

Canada. House of Commons. Security Intelligence Review Committee. *Minutes of Proceedings and Evidence of the Standing Committee on Justice and the Solicitor General,* no. 31, 17 December 1987.

Canada. House of Commons. Security Intelligence Review Committee. *Minutes of Proceedings and Evidence of the Standing Committee on Justice and the Solicitor General,* no. 3, 30 May 1989.

Canada. Special Committee of the Senate on Terrorism and Public Safety. *Terrorism.* Second Report. Ottawa, June 1989.

Farson, Stuart A. *Countering the Security Threat in the 1980s: McDonald's Legacy and the Need for Effective and Efficient Control.* Ottawa: Prepared for the Security Intelligence Review Committee's

Research Seminar, "Canadian Security Intelligence in the 80s", 11 October 1985.

Fletcher, Joseph F. "Mass and Elite Attitudes about Wiretapping in Canada: Implications for Democratic Theory and Politics." *Public Opinion Quarterly* 53 (Summer 1989): 225-45.

Fletcher, Joseph F. *Wiretappping by the Security Intelligence Service: What Does the Canadian Public Think?* Toronto: University of Toronto and York University, March 1988.

Fraser, Graham. *Playing for Keeps: The Making of the Prime Minister.* Toronto: McClelland & Stewart, 1989.

Kashmeri, Zuhair, and Brian McAndrew. *Soft Target: How the Indian Intelligence Service Penetrated Canada.* Toronto: James Lorimer & Co., 1989.

Kavchak, Andrew. *Canadian National Security and the CSIS Act.* Toronto: Mackenzie Institute, 1989.

Kessler, Ronald. *Moscow Station: How the KGB Penetrated the American Embassy.* New York: Scribner, 1989.

Littleton, James. *Target Nation: Canada and the Western Intelligence Network.* Toronto: Lester and Orpen Dennys, 1986.

Malarek, Victor. *Haven's Gate: Canada's Immigration Fiasco.* Toronto: Macmillan, 1987.

Pacepa, Ion Mihai. *Red Horizons: Chronicles of a Communist Spy Chief.* Washington, D.C.: Regnery Gateway.

Sallot, Jeff. *Nobody Said No.* Toronto: James Lorimer & Co., 1979.

Sawatsky, John. *Men in the Shadows: The RCMP Security Service.* Toronto: Doubleday, 1980, 21-22.

Sibraa, Kerry W. "National Security: Parliamentary Scrutiny of Security and Intelligence Services in Australia." *The Parliamentarian* 68 (July 1987): 120-27.

Vinneau, David. "Confidence was eroded, letter says critics

hurt security, ex-spymaster says." *Toronto Star*, 28 January 1988, sec. A.

Weller, Geoffrey. "Accountability in Canadian Intelligence Services." *International Journal of Intelligence and Counter-Intelligence* 2 (1988): 415-41.

Whitaker, Reg. *Double Standard: The Secret History of Canadian Immigration.* Toronto: Lester & Orpen Dennys, 1987.

## Select Bibliography Chapter 1

Round Trip

"2 Arabs who attacked El Al jet given long jail terms in Greece." *New York Times*, 27 March 1970.

"Bomb trial of 2 Arabs opens in Athens." *New York Times*, 22 March 1970.

Bryden, Joan. "CSIS accused of leaking terrorist's plans." *Citizen*, 25 February 1988, sec. A.

Bryden, Joan. "Spy agency fouled up, terrorist's friend says." *Toronto Star*, 25 February 1988, sec. A.

Cleroux, Richard. "CSIS investigating Israeli link to botched Mohammad flight." *Globe and Mail*, 26 February 1988, sec. N.

Cleroux, Richard. "Rivalry between CSIS, RCMP foiled terrorist's plan to leave." *Globe and Mail*, 27 February 1988, sec. A.

Gibbons, Rick. "PLO spokesman saying Algeria granted Mohammad visa." *Canadian Press Wire*, 24 February 1988.

Hunter, Ian. "Airport file on terrorist 'available.'" *Citizen*, 21 January 1988, sec. A.

"Israel protests as Greece puts off trial of 2 Arabs." *New York Times*, 18 February 1970.

Lussier, Gaetan. Employment and Immigration Canada. *Memorandum to the Minister of State (Immigration).* Ottawa, 18 July 1987. Subject: Mahmud Mohammad Issa Mohammad (sic).

Lussier, Gaetan. Employment and Immigration Canada. *Memorandum to the Minister.* Ottawa, 27 October 1987. Subject: Mahmud Mohammad Issa Mohammad (sic).

Malerek, Victor. "Palestinian lied to immigrate, probe finds claim for refugee status blocks deportation order." *Globe and Mail,* 16 December 1988, sec. A.

Malerek, Victor. "Terrorist got through immigration net." *Globe and Mail,* 18 January 1988, sec. A.

McDonald, Robert. "Greeks pardoned Mohammad official junta statement shows." *Toronto Star,* 28 January 1988, sec. A.

Picton, John. "Unravelling the mystery of Mohammad's flight." *Toronto Star,* 13 March 1988.

Vastel, Michel. "L'affaire Mohammad - La GRC pourchassait la mauvaise personne selon un telex d'Interpol." *Le Devoir,* 17 February 1988.

## Select Bibliography Chapter 2
"I Did Much Worse for the RCMP"

Adams, Ian. "You and Me and the RCMP." *Canadian Dimension* 13 (August-September 1978): 3-8.

Canada. Commission of Inquiry Concerning Certain Activities of the Royal Canadian Mounted Police. *Report.* Ottawa. McDonald Commission. First Report. Security and Information. October 1979. Second Report. Freedom and Security under the Law. 2 vols. August 1981. Third Report. Certain R.C.M.P. Activities and the Question of Governmental Knowledge. August 1981. Supplement to Part IV of the Third Report. (1981?).

Canada. Department of Justice. *The Position of the Attorney General of Canada on Certain Recommendations of the McDonald Commission.* Ottawa, 1983.

Canada. Security Intelligence Review Committee. *Annual Report 1986-87.* Ottawa, 1987.

Canada. Security Intelligence Review Committee. *Closing the Gaps: Official Languages and Staff Relations in the Canadian Security Intelligence Service.* Ottawa, 1987.

Canada. Senate. Special Committee on the Canadian Security Intelligence Service. *Report of the Special Committee of the Senate on the Canadian Security Intelligence Service: Delicate Balance: A Security Intelligence Service in a Democratic Society.* Ottawa, 1983.

Dion, Robert. *Les crimes de la police Montée.* Laval: Éditions coopératives Albert Saint-Martin, 1979.

Farson, Stuart A. *Countering the Security Threat in the 1980s: McDonald's Legacy and the Need for Effective and Efficient Control.* Ottawa: Prepared for the Security Intelligence Review Committee's Research Seminar, Canadian Security Intelligence in the 80's, 11 October 1985.

Fournier, Louis. *F.L.Q.: Histoire d'un mouvement clandestin.* Montréal: Québec/Amerique, 1982.

French, Richard, and Andre Beliveau. *The RCMP and the Management of National Security.* Toronto: Institute for Research on Public Policy, 1979.

Goldbloom, Michael. "CATS on a Warming Tin Roof: The Handyman." *Report* 3 (May 1980): 9-15.

House, Jeff. "The Force Will Be with Us." *Canadian Dimension* (March 1982): 3-5.

Kowch, Steve. "Panthers hid out at FLQ farm: Police file." *Gazette,* 5 November 1977.

Laurendeau, Marc. "La Commission Keable: Une partie serree s'engage." *La Press,* 13 February 1979, sec. A.

Lewis, Robert. "Gumshoe on the Other Foot." *Macleans* 94 (14 September 1981): 34.

Lewis, Robert. "The Gang that Couldn't Spook Straight." *Macleans* 90 (14 November 1977): 21-25.

Littleton, James. *Target Nation: Canada and the Western Intelligence Network.* Toronto: Lester and Orpen Dennys, 1986.

Macdonald, Donald. *Police Powers: McDonald and the Keable Commissions.* Ottawa: Library of Parliament, 1983.

Mandel, Michael. "The Discrediting of the McDonald Commission." *Canadian Forum* 61 (March 1982): 14-17.

Mann, William Edward, and John Alan Lee. *RCMP vs. the People: Inside Canada's Security Intelligence Service.* Don Mills: General Publishing Co., 1979.

Québec. Ministere de la Justice. Commission d'enquête sur des opérations policières en térritoire québecois. *Rapport de la Commission d'enquête sur des opérations policières en térritoire québecois.* Québec, 1981. Keable Commission

Richelson, Jeffrey T. *Foreign Intelligence Organizations.* Cambridge, Mass.: Ballinger Publishing Co., 1988.

Rosen, Philip. *The Canadian Security Intelligence Service.* Ottawa: Library of Parliament, 18 September 1984, reviewed 12 April 1990.

Roy, R. H. *The Security Intellignce Review Committee: The Output.* Victoria: University of Victoria, 30 September 1985.

Sallot, Jeff. *Nobody Said No.* Toronto: James Lorimer & Co., 1979.

Sawatsky, John. "Leak costs Mountie his job." *Vancouver Sun,* 9 December 1976.

Sawatsky, John. *Men in the Shadows: The RCMP Security Service.* Toronto: Doubleday, 1980.

Sawatsky, John. "RCMP victimized their own men." *Vancouver Sun,* 8 December 1976.

Sawatsky, John. "Trail of break-in leads to RCMP coverup." *Vancouver Sun,* 7 December 1976.

Spence, Wishart F. Department of Justice. *Report to the Attorney General of Canada.* Ottawa, 1981.

## Select Bibliography Chapter 3

And Now for Something Completely Different

Bauch, Hubert. "Our new intelligence agency is no Big Brother." *Gazette*, 30 April 1986, sec. A.

Canada. Commission of Inquiry Concerning Certain Activities of the Royal Canadian Mounted Police. *Report.* Ottawa. McDonald Commission. First Report. Security and Information. October 1979. Second Report. Freedom and Security under the Law. 2 vols. August 1981. Third Report. Certain R.C.M.P. Activities and the Question of Governmental Knowledge. August 1981. Supplement to Part IV of the Third Report. (1981?)

Canada. House of Commons. *Minutes of Proceedings and Evidence of the Standing Committee on Justice and the Solicitor General*, no. 21, 3 June 1986. (Ronald Atkey.)

Canada. House of Commons. *Minutes of Proceedings and Evidence of the Standing Committee on Justice and the Solicitor General*, no. 2, 20 November 1986. (Ronald Atkey.)

Canada. Senate. Special Committee on the Canadian Security Intelligence Service. *Report of the Special Committee of The Senate on the Canadian Security Intelligence Service: Delicate Balance: A Security Intelligence Service in a Democratic Society.* Ottawa, 1983.

Canada. Solicitor General Canada. Independent Advisory Team. *People and Process in Transition: Report to the Solicitor General.* Ottawa, 1987. (Osbaldeston Report.)

Farson, Stuart A. *Countering the Security Threat in the 1980s: McDonald's Legacy and the Need for Effective and Efficient Control.* Ottawa: Prepared for the Security Intelligence Review Committee's Research Seminar, Canadian Security Intelligence in the 80's, 11 October 1985.

Farson, Stuart A. "Old Wine, New Bottles and Fancy Labels: The Rediscovery of Organizational Culture in the Control of Intelligence," in *Crimes by the Capitalist State: An Introduction to*

*State Criminality.* Edited by Greg Barak. New York: State University of New York Press, 1989.

Franks, C. E. S. *Parliament and Intelligence and Security Issues.* Ottawa, 1984.

Hay, John. "A Spy Bill's Rites of Passage." *Macleans* 97 (9 July 1984): 12.

Malarek, Victor. "95% of CSIS staff veterans of RCMP, security report says." *Globe and Mail,* 11 July 1985, sec. M.

Rosen, Philip. *The Canadian Security Intelligence Service.* Ottawa: Library of Parliament, 18 September 1984, reviewed 12 April 1990.

Roy, R. H. *The Security Intelligence Review Committee: The Output.* Victoria: University of Victoria, 30 September 1985.

Russell, Peter. "Spy bill: Hot on the right scent." *Toronto Star,* 11 February 1984, sec. B.

Sallot, Jeff. "Security service shedding links with 'Red Squad.'" *Globe and Mail,* 5 December 1987, sec. D.

Sawatsky, John. *Men in the Shadows: The RCMP Security Service.* Toronto: Doubleday, 1980.

Starnes, John. "Who will review the security reviewers? And how?" *Citizen,* 1 October 1986, sec. A.

## Select Bibliography Chaper 4

No Way to Run A Security Service

Auf Der Maur, Nick. "Our new intelligence service seems to be having teething problems." *Gazette,* 5 February 1986, sec. A.

Bindman, Stephen. "CSIS will use lie detectors on recruits despite warning." *Citizen,* 10 June 1988, sec. A.

Canada. House of Commons. *Minutes of Proceedings and Evidence of the Standing Committee on Justice and the Solicitor General,* no. 8, 15 June 1989. (Reid Morden.)

Canada. Security Intelligence Review Committee. *Annual Report 1986-87*. Ottawa, 1987.

Canada. Security Intelligence Review Committee. *Closing the Gaps: Official Languages and Staff Relations in the Canadian Security Intelligence Service*. Ottawa, 1987.

Canada. Senate. House of Commons. *Minutes of Proceedings and Evidence of the Standing Joint Committee of the Senate and of the House of Commons on Official Languages*, no. 17, 29 April 1987. (Thomas D'Arcy Finn.)

Canada. Senate. House of Commons. *Minutes of Proceedings and Evidence of the Standing Joint Committee of the Senate and of the House of Commons on Official Languages*, no. 19, 12 May 1987. (Thomas D'Arcy Finn.)

Girouard, Jean-Denis. "Au Canada il faut espionner en francais." *Journal de Montreal*, 30 April 1987.

*La Grande Encyclopédie Larousse*. 1974 ed., s.v. "Lyautey, Louis Hubert Gonzalve."

Malarek, Victor. "95% of CSIS staff veterans of the RCMP, security report says." *Globe and Mail*, 11 July 1985, sec. M.

Malarek, Victor. "Civilian spy agency clings to RCMP roots, committee head says." *Globe and Mail*, 3 July 1987, sec. A.

Malarek, Victor. "Spy agency trouble could impair security." *Globe and Mail*, 3 July 1986, sec. A.

Martin, Lawrence. "PMO ordered title search of Mulroney's home." *Globe and Mail*, 16 February 1984, sec. P.

Morris, Leslie. "Competition's tough. Psst! Want to be a spy?" *Toronto Sun*, 7 September 1986.

Picton, John. "Security service favors Mounties." *Toronto Star*, 6 April 1986, sec. A.

Rodal, Alti. *Nazi War Criminals in Canada: The Historical and Policy Setting from the 1940s to the Present*. Ottawa: Prepared for the Commission of Inquiry on War Criminals, September 1986.

"Senility robbed Intrepid of reality." *Calgary Herald*, 28 February 1989, sec. A.

Wills, Terrance. "Language problems at spy agency not fault of director, Kelleher says." *Gazette*, 13 June 1987, sec. A.

Wills, Terrance. "Top spy slams language complaints-But CSIS director presents MPs with plan to promote bilingualism." *Gazette*, 13 May 1987, sec. B.


## Select Bibliography Chapter 5

"Greetings from the Polish Embassy"

Canada. House of Commons. *House of Commons Debates: Official Report*, 24 April 1986, 12614-16. (Patrick Boyer).

Gibbons, Rick. "100 agents spy on Canada for Poland, hijacker says." *Toronto Star*, 23 January 1988, sec. A.

Gibbons, Rick. "Life on the inside." *Ottawa Sun*, 13 December 1989.

Gibbons, Rick. "Polish spy network alleged in Canada." *Globe and Mail*, 23 January 1988, sec. A.

Malarek, Victor. "Return of hijacker angers spy agency." *Globe and Mail*, 14 October 1989, sec. A.

Paszkowski, Ryszard. *Immigration and Refugee Board*. 6 June 1990. (Judge John Petryshyn.)

*Paszkowski v. Minister of Immigration*. F.C.A., 9 July 1990. (Judge J. Stone.)


## Select Bibliography Chapter 6

Changing of the Guard

"A Question of Access." *Macleans* 97 (29 October 1984): 16.

Bindman, Stephen. "Spy agency chief quits over false evidence scandal." *Citizen*, 12 September 1987, sec. A.

*Boivon v. the Queen.* F.C.A., 23 August 1989. Statement of Claim, file T-60689.

Canada. House of Commons. *Minutes of Proceedings and Evidence of the Standing Committee on Justice and Legal Affairs,* no. 1, 29 November 1984. (Robert Kaplan.)

Canada. House of Commons. *Minutes of Proceedings and Evidence of the Standing Committee on Justice and the Solicitor General,* no. 21, 3 June 1986. (Ronald Atkey.)

Canada. House of Commons. *Minutes of Proceedings and Evidence of the Special Committee on The Review of the CSIS Act and the Security Offences Act,* no. 2, 31 October 1989. (Pierre Blais.)

Canada. House of Commons. *Minutes of Proceedings and Evidence of the Special Committee on The Review of the CSIS Act and the Security Offences Act,* no 7, 7 December 1989. (Norman Inkster.)

Canada. Security and Intelligence Review Committee. *Annual Report 1985-86.* Ottawa, 1986.

Canada. Security and Intelligence Review Committee. *Annual Report 1986-87.* Ottawa, 1987.

Canada. Solicitor General Canada. Independent Advisory Team. *People and Process in Transition: Report to the Solicitor General.* Ottawa, 1987. (Osbaldeston Report.)

Canadian Association for Security and Intelligence Studies-Association Canadienne pour l'Etude de la Securite et de Renseignement. *Newsletter, no. 14.* Edited by Jean-Paul Brodeur. April 1990.

Cleroux, Richard. "RCMP security team may be rival of CSIS." *Globe and Mail,* 4 July 1989, sec. A.

Cleroux, Richard. "Rivalry between CSIS, RCMP foiled terrorist's plan to leave." *Globe and Mail,* 27 February 1988, sec. A.

Cleroux, Richard. "Role of CSIS informer subject of major probe." *Globe and Mail,* 17 September 1987, sec. A.

Cleroux, Richard. "Spy agency subject of 4 separate probes." *Globe and Mail*, 16 September 1987, sec. A.

Diebel, Linda. "Canada's spy agency is back in shop for refit. Latest CSIS crisis has sunk morale but is inspiring reform." *Gazette*, 19 September 1987, sec. B.

Diebel, Linda. "Spy agency probes too many, fights Mounties for turf: panel." *Gazette*, 30 June 1987, sec. A.

Drolet, Daniel. "CSIS held job competition for labour informer: NDP." *Citizen*, 29 September 1987, sec. A.

Fitterman, Lisa. "Illegal spy service wiretap feared tip of iceberg." *Vancouver Sun*, 15 September 1987, sec. A.

Giguere, Monique. "Boivin réclame un demi million." *Le Soleil*, 24 March 1989, sec. A.

Gray, Charlotte. "Services Rendered." *Saturday Night* 99 (March 1984): 15-17.

Harris, Michael. "RCMP hunt Libyan in air threat." *Globe and Mail*, 17 January 1987, sec. A.

Harris, Michael. "Safe to use planes, Nielsen tells public." *Globe and Mail*, 18 January 1986, sec. A.

Kelleher, James. "Notes for a speech by the Honourable James Kelleher Solicitor General of Canada to the Kiwanis Club of Vancouver - Canada's counter-terrorism program." *News Release*, Vancouver, 5 May 1988.

Kelleher, James. "Notes for a statement by the Honourable James Kelleher Solicitor General of Canada to the news conference on the economic summit security preparations." *News Release*, Toronto, 24 May 1988.

Laver, Ross et al. "The Looking-Glass Trade." *Macleans* 102 (24 July 1989): 12-14.

Macdonald, Neil. "Kelleher admits RCMP infringed on spy agency." *Citizen*, 17 September 1987, sec. A.

Macdonald, Neil. "Spy agency denied access to RCMP computer." *Citizen*, 16 October 1984, sec. A.

Macdonald, Neil. "Spy agency kept Indian minister's visit secret from RCMP." *Citizen*, 15 September 1987, sec. A.

Macdonald, Neil. "Spy agency torn apart by problems." *Citizen*, 14 September 1987, sec. A.

Mackenzie, Hilary, and Deborra Schug. "Spies under Fire." *Macleans* 100 (28 September 1987): 12-14.

Makin, Kirk. "CSIS used false information for bugs, justice lawyer says." *Globe and Mail*, 12 September 1987, sec. A.

Malarek, Victor. "Mounties are trying to thwart agency, some in CSIS feel." *Globe and Mail*, 28 June 1986, sec. A.

McGillivray, Don. "Spy chief's resignation begs a question." *Citizen*, 18 September 1987, sec. A.

Moon, Peter. "Canada's spy agency denied police computer records." *Globe and Mail*, 16 October 1984, sec. P.

Moon, Peter. "CSIS renews bid for access to computer." *Globe and Mail*, 3 October 1987, sec. A.

Noreau, Pierre-Paul. "Même sans mandat, Boivin espionnait la CSL." *Le Soleil*, 30 March 1988.

Paquin, Gilles. "Le SCRS blâme pour ses liens avec Marc Boivin." *La Presse*, 30 March 1988, sec. A.

Sallot, Jeff. "FBI already given data link denied to Ottawa agency." *Globe and Mail*, 17 October 1987, sec. P.

Sallot, Jeff. "Security chief resigns his post under pressure, 3 probes ordered into faulty affidavit." *Globe and Mail*, 12 September 1987, sec. A.

Vienneau, David. "Confidence was eroded, letter says. Critics hurt security ex-spymaster says." *Toronto Star*, 28 January 1988, sec. A.

Vinneau, David. "Ottawa unveils major changes at spy agency." *Toronto Star*, 1 December 1987, sec. A.

Vinneau, David. "Spy agency 'gagged' by Ottawa, official says." *Toronto Star*, 1 October 1987, sec. A.

## Select Bibliography Chapter 7

Of Moles And Men

Beauregard, Pierre. "Le SCRS accusé de favoriser Toronto: Le service de renseignement dégarnit le bureau de Montréal, clamant des fonctionnaires." *La Presse*, 30 June 1988, sec. A.

Beauregard, Pierre. "Pour quelques dollars le transfuge [Yuri Smurov] est laissé sans protection." *La Presse*, 2 July 1988, sec. A.

Canada. House of Commons. *House of Commons Debates: Official Report*, 11 October 1985, 7584-85. (Brian Mulroney).

Canada. House of Commons. *House of Commons Debates: Official Report*, 16 October 1985, 7682. (Erik Nielsen).

Canada. House of Commons. *House of Commons Debates: Official Report*, 17 October 1985, 7724. (John Rodriquez).

Canada. House of Commons. *House of Commons Debates: Official Report*, 14 February 1986, 10841-42. (Ian Waddell).

Canada. House of Commons. *Minutes of Proceedings and Evidence of the Standing Committee on Justice and the Solicitor General*, no. 21, 6 March 1986. (Ronald Atkey.)

"CSIS admits it asked reporter to spy on peers." *Citizen*, 22 September 1988, sec. A.

"CSIS found Soviet secrets in fire debris, TV report says." *Globe and Mail*, 24 June 1987 sec. A.

Dansereau, Suzanne. "[Pour le moment, due moins] Normand Lester n'aura pas à dévoiler ses sources." *Le Droit*, 10 October 1987.

Fagan, Drew. "Deportation of Taiwanese delayed by court action." *Globe and Mail*, 18 February 1984, sec. A.

"Les débris du consulat de l'URSS se révèlent une mine de renseignements." *La Presse*, 25 June 1987, sec. B.

Gauthier, Gilles. "La GRC saisit des documents à Radio-Canada." *La Presse*, 3 August 1988.

"Journalism and spying don't mix." *Gazette*, 22 September 1988, sec. B.

MacDonald, Bruce. "CSIS and the media: Spy vs snoop." *Ottawa Sunday Sun*, 16 October 1988, sec. C.

Malarek, Victor. "Chinese-Canadian leaders angry over deportation of Taiwanese." *Globe and Mail*, 17 February 1986, sec. A.

Malarek, Victor. "Junket linked to deporting of Taiwanese." *Globe and Mail*, 15 February 1986, sec. A.

Malarek, Victor. "Taiwanese ordered to leave Canada." *Globe and Mail*, 12 February 1986, sec. A.

Malarek, Victor. "Taiwanese told to leave, Chang makes Tories uneasy." *Globe and Mail*, 26 February 1986, sec. A.

Malarek, Victor. "Trade official facing deportation flies home on Taiwanese orders." *Globe and Mail*, 3 March 1986, sec. A.

McIntosh, Andrew. "Exports to Canada soaring." *Globe and Mail*, 8 September 1986, sec. B.

"RCMP raid news service office seeking a letter on spy agency." *Montreal Gazette*, 3 August 1988.

"Reporters should snoop but not spy." *Citizen*, 24 September 1988, sec. B.

Schiller, Bill. "Ottawa says Taiwanese official works for intelligence service." *Toronto Star*, 25 February 1986, sec. A.

"Senators, MPs under fire for Taiwan junket." *Globe and Mail*, 11 October 1985, sec. A.

Spears, Tom. "Portrait of the Soviet who defected." *Toronto Star*, 2 July 1988.

Taiwan orders home official to avoid diplomatic dispute." *Citizen*, 3 March 1986, sec. A.

Terrien, Paul. "De Cumberland a Taipei." *Le Droit*, 19 October 1985.

Terrien, Paul. "Les péligrinations de Boudria a Taiwan." *Le Droit*, 22 October 1985.

"TV reporter says spy agency wanted 'scoop' on journalists." *Citizen*, 16 September 1988, sec. C.

## Select Bibliography Chapter 8

Clearing House

Canada. Commission of Inquiry Concerning Certain Activities of the Royal Canadian Mounted Police. *Freedom and Security under the Law*. Second Report. Ottawa, August 1981. Chapter 8 (B), sec. 17.

Canada. House of Commons. *Minutes of Proceedings and Evidence of the Special Committee on The Review of the CSIS Act and the Security Offences Act*, no. 23, 26 March 1990. (Craig Paterson).

Canada. House of Commons. *Minutes of Proceedings and Evidence of the Special Committee on The Review of the CSIS Act and the Security Offences Act*, no. 34, 5 June 1990. (Reid Morden).

Canada. House of Commons. *Minutes of Proceedings and Evidence of the Standing Committee on Labour, Employment and Immigration*. Ninth Report, no. 68, 11 June 1986. Security Clearances, 25.

Canada. Security Intelligence Review Committee. *Annual Report 1986-87*. Ottawa, 1987. El Salvador, 37. Security Clearance, 59.

Canada. Security Intelligence Review Committee. *Annual Report 1987-88*. Ottawa, 1988. Security Clearance, 19.

Canada. Security Intelligence Review Committee. *Annual Report 1988-89*. Ottawa, 1989. Security Clearance, 17.

Canada. Security Intelligence Review Committee. *Immigration*

*Screening Activities of the Canadian Security Intelligence Service.* Ottawa, 1986. (Expurgated Version).

Gigantes, Philippe Deans. "Why Canada needs new spycatching agency." *Gazette*, 5 June 1984.

James, Royson. "Thousands await security clearance; 'Crisis' cited as overburdened agency struggles to clear backlog." *Toronto Star*, 23 March 1988, sec. A.

Koring, Paul. "CSIS backlog leaves air safety suspect." *Globe and Mail*, 3 June 1988, sec. A.

MacQueen, Ken. "The security clearance logjam; An object lesson in contempt for deadlines." *Citizen*, 9 July 1988, sec. B.

Malarek, Victor. *Haven's Gate: Canada's Immigration Fiasco.* Toronto: Macmillan, 1987.

Poirier, Patricia. "Screening delays imperil security, CSIS official says." *Globe and Mail*, 23 May 1987.

Sallot, Jeff. "CSIS to stop taping interviews." *Globe and Mail*, 4 June 1986, sec. A.

Sallot, Jeff. "New policy fails to reduce security requests." *Globe and Mail*, 12 November 1987, sec. A.

Sallot, Jeff. "Security clearance requests jump despite policy to curb screenings." *Globe and Mail*, 12 November 1987, sec. A.

Sawatsky, John. *Men in the Shadows: The RCMP Security Service.* Toronto: Doubleday, 1980, 21-22.

Whitaker, Reg. *Double Standard: The Secret History of Canadian Immigration.* Toronto: Lester & Orpen Dennys, 1987.

Whitaker, Reg. "Witch hunt in the civil service: Ottawa's new security force has taken the role of an Orwellian- style thought police." *This Magazine* 20 (October-November 1986): 24-29.

Wilson-Smith, Anthony. "Uproar of a Firing." *Macleans* 100 (26 January 1987): 16.

## Select Bibliography Chapter 9

What Constitutes A Threat?

Adam, Marcel. "Cette mystérieuse histoire d'espionnage [entre le Canada et l'URSS]." *La Presse*, 30 June 1988, sec. B.

*Boivin v. the Queen*. F.C.A., 23 August 1989. Statement of Claim, file T-60689.

Canada. House of Commons. *House of Commons Debates: Official Report*, 24 April 1986, 12614-16. (Patrick Boyer).

Canada. House of Commons. *House of Commons Debates: Official Report*, 23 January 1986. (Joe Clark).

Canada. House of Commons. *Minutes of Proceedings and Evidence of the Special Committee on The Review of the CSIS Act and Security Offences Act*, no. 13, 8 February 1990. (George Erasmus.)

Canada. House of Commons. *Minutes of Proceedings and Evidence of the Special Committeee on The Review of the CSIS Act and Security Offences Act*, no. 34, 5 June 1990. (Reid Morden.)

Canada. House of Commons. *Minutes of Proceedings and Evidence of the Standing Committee on Justice and the Solicitor General*, no. 29, 10 April 1990. (John Bassett.)

Canada. Security Intelligence Review Committee. *Annual Report 1988-89*. Ottawa, 1989.

Canada. Security Intelligence Review Committee. *Report on the Innu Interview and the Native Extremism Investigation*. SECRET, file no. 2800-10, 28 November 1988.

Canada. Security Intelligence Review Committee. *Complaint by Bhupinder Singh Liddar. Case no. 28*. Vols. 5-6. Hearing before Jean-Jacques Blais. PROTECTED PERSONAL INFORMATION, 3 October 1989.

Cleroux, Richard. "CSIS probed Labrador Innu among other native groups." *Globe and Mail*, 1 June 1989, sec. A.

Cleroux, Richard. "Clark says Chinese spying on their students in Canada." *Globe and Mail,* 17 June 1989, sec. A.

Cleroux, Richard. "Clark to check if Indian diplomats were spies." *Globe and Mail,* 23 June 1989, sec. A.

Cormier, Guy. "Charades: [les expulsions de diplomates entre le Canada et l'URSS]." *La Presse,* 29 June 1988, sec. B.

Cox, Kevin. "Spied for Soviets, jailed 9 years." *Globe and Mail,* 10 March 1989, sec. A.

Feldman, Julien. "Officials slam delay: Firemen not spies." *Montreal Daily News,* 31 March 1988, sec. P.

Gauthier, Marc. "400 Amerindiens sur la colline Parlementaire." *Le Droit,* 15 March 1983.

Goldenthal, Howard et al. "Right Winging It." *This Magazine* 22 (June/July 1988): 14.

"La guerre des espions est terminée." *La Press,* 28 June 1988, sec. B.

"La guerre des expulsions [de diplomates] se poursuit: Moscou évince a son tour un diplomate canadien." *La Presse,* 26 June 1988, sec. A.

Jannard, Maurice. "Fin la 'guerre des espions' entre Ottawa et Moscou." *La Presse,* 28 June 1988, sec. A.

"Joe Clark prépare une nouvelle riposte a l'URSS dans la 'guerre des espions.'" *La Presse,* 27 June 1988, sec. B.

Judd, David. "Tape shows Diefenbaker had column suspended." *Brantford Expositor,* 18 February 1986, sec. B.

Kashmeri, Zuhair, and Brian McAndrew. *Soft Target: How the Indian Intelligence Service Penetrated Canada.* Toronto: James Lorimer & Co., 1989.

MacRae, Penny. "Low flights threaten Innu, weeping chief testifies." *Globe and Mail,* 6 April 1989, sec. A.

Margolis, Eric. "The spies who love us." *Toronto Sun*, 19 October 1989.

Marsden, William. "How Canadian agents tracked computers smuggled to Russia." *Montreal Gazette*, 25 November 1986, sec. A.

Moon, Peter, and Geoffrey York. "Spies at work in many Toronto consulates." *Globe and Mail*, 22 February 1986, sec. A.

Noble, Kimberley. "Stepped up vigilence catching more dealers." *Globe and Mail*, 30 August, 1986, sec. B.

"Ottawa a expulsé huit dimlomates sovietiques." *La Presse*, 22 June 1988, sec. A.

Solomon, Hyman. "Scientific secrets worth guarding." *Financial Post*, 20 July 1987.

Starnes, John. "Canadian Security." *International Perspectives* (September/October 1984): 23-26.

Tardif, Germain. "Diplomates indiens expulsés du Canada pour espionnage." *La Presse*, 29 March 1987, sec. A.

Tison, Marie. "Le Canada réplique et expulse cette fois l'attaché militaire de l'ambassade d'URSS: Moscou annonce de nouvelles represailles." *La Presse*, 25 June 1988, sec. A.

Vinneau, David. "24 countries spy on Canada." *Toronto Star*, 14 October 1989.

**Select Bibliography Chapter 10**

How Does CSIS Measure Up?

Brown, Jim. Untitled wire copy article "Parl-CSIS 0350." *The Canadian Press*, 18 January 1990.

Canada. House of Commons. *Minutes of Proceedings and Evidence of the Special Committee on The Review of the CSIS Act and the Security Offences Act*, no. 20, 13 March 1990. (Brian McAndrew and Zuhair Kashmeri.)

Canada. House of Commons. *Minutes of Proceedings and Evidence of the Special Committee on The Review of the CSIS Act and the Security Offences Act*, no. 28, 25 April 1990. (Gordon Osbaldeston.)

Canada. House of Commons. *Minutes of Proceedings and Evidence of the Special Committee on The Review of the CSIS Act and the Security Offenses Act*, no. 29, 26 April 1990. (Reg Whitaker and Greg Kealey.)

Canada. House of Commons. *Minutes of Proceedings and Evidence of the Special Committee on The Review of the CSIS Act and the Security Offences Act*, no. 30, 10 May 1990. (Andrew Kavchak.)

Canada. House of Commons. *Minutes of Proceedings and Evidence of the Special Committee on The Review of the CSIS Act and the Security Offences Act*, no. 34, 5 June 1990. (Reid Morden.)

Canada. House of Commons. *Minutes of Proceedings and Evidence of the Special Committee on The Review of the CSIS Act and the Security Offences Act*, no. 35, 7 June 1990. (Bernard Marentette.)

Canada. Security Intelligence Review Committeee. *Annual Report 1988-89*. Ottawa, 1989.

Chua-Eoan, Howard G. "New Trench Coats?" *Time*, 23 April 1990, 20.

Hay, John. "CSIS. Clouseau bumbles on." *Citizen*, 25 September 1988.

Makin, Kirk. "Canada imperils refugees ruling says." *Globe and Mail*, 13 March 1990, sec. A.

Martin, Patrick. "Foreign agents free to spy on residents security official says." *Globe and Mail*, 15 January 1985.

Morden, Reid. *Notes for Remarks to Canadian Association for Security Intelligence Studies (CASIS)*. Quebec, 31 May 1989.

Rowe, Trevor. "Open season on the CIA." *Citizen*, 9 July 1990.

Sorensen, Theodore. "Rethinking National Security." *Foreign Affairs* (Summer 1990): 2-18.

# INDEX